GUIDE TO
THE CENSUS

Since 1996, Bloomberg Press has published books for financial professionals on investing, economics, and policy affecting investors. Titles are written by leading practitioners and authorities, and have been translated into more than 20 languages.

The Bloomberg Financial Series provides both core reference knowledge and actionable information for financial professionals. The books are written by experts familiar with the work flows, challenges, and demands of investment professionals who trade the markets, manage money, and analyze investments in their capacity of growing and protecting wealth, hedging risk, and generating revenue.

For a list of available titles, please visit our Web site at www.wiley.com/go/bloombergpress.

GUIDE TO
THE CENSUS

Frank Bass

BLOOMBERG PRESS
An Imprint of
WILEY

Published by John Wiley & Sons, Inc., Hoboken, New Jersey.
Published simultaneously in Canada.

For general information on our other products and services or for technical support, please contact our Customer Care Department within the United States at (800) 762-2974, outside the United States at (317) 572-3993 or fax (317) 572-4002.

Wiley also publishes its books in a variety of electronic formats. Some content that appears in print may not be available in electronic books. For more information about Wiley products, visit our web site at www.wiley.com.

Library of Congress Cataloging-in-Publication Data:

Bass, Frank.
    Guide to the census / Frank Bass.
      p. cm. – (Bloomberg financial series)
    Includes bibliographical references and index.
    ISBN 978-1-118-32801-9 (cloth); ISBN 978-1-118-41989-2 (ebk); ISBN 978-1-118-43395-9 (ebk); ISBN 978-1-118-41660-0 (ebk)
  1. United States–Census.   2. United States–Census–Methodology.   3. United States–Statistical services.   4. United States. Bureau of the Census.   I. Title.
    HA37.U55B373 2013
    317.3–dc23

                              2012041636

Printed in the United States of America

10 9 8 7 6 5 4 3 2 1

This book is dedicated to my family: My wife Lisa, who has been unfailingly supportive and patient during the writing of this book, even during the most stressful of circumstances and largest of animal breakouts; my children, Robin, John and Will, who have invariably lifted my spirits when most needed; my parents, Charles and the late Mary Lucy Bass, whose love and advice have always been incomparable; and my brothers, Richard and B.J., who read almost as much as I did as children, and who have always encouraged me.

Contents

Acknowledgments   xi

Introduction   xiii

PART I: GUIDE TO THE DECENNIAL CENSUS

CHAPTER 1
The Evolution of the Census   3
Who Relies on the Census?   5
Understanding the Current Census   11
Following Census Results   13
Conclusion   14
Notes   15

CHAPTER 2
Understanding Census Geography   17
Narrowing Geographical Scope   18
Working with Standard Geographies   20
Avoiding Geographic Confusion   22
Working with Very Small Geographies   25
Conclusion   28
Notes   28

CHAPTER 3
Understanding Basic Census Counts   29
Determining Political Representation   30
Creating Political Boundaries   31
Understanding the Fundamentals of Redistricting Files   33
Analyzing Age, Gender, and Detailed Race Data   35
Conclusion   37
Notes   38

CHAPTER 4
Analyzing Critical Relationships   **41**
Understanding Household Relationships   42
Digging Deeper into Household Relationships   45
Making Sense of Summary File 2   46
Notes   48

CHAPTER 5
Working with Housing Data   **49**
Grasping the Basics of Housing   50
Understanding Populations within Households   52
Conclusion   54
Notes   55

CHAPTER 6
Analyzing Race and Ethnicity   **57**
Understanding Emerging Groups   58
Analyzing Tribal Affiliations   62
Conclusion   63
Notes   68

PART II: THE AMERICAN COMMUNITY SURVEY

CHAPTER 7
Using the American Community Survey   **71**
Resolving Expensive Data Collection   72
Understanding Potential Weaknesses   74
Modifying Future Surveys   74
Conclusion   76
Notes   77

CHAPTER 8
Making Sense of Housing   **79**
Comparing ACS Housing Data with Decennial Census   80
Assessing Populations with Housing Data   81
Using Ancillary Figures for Insight   84
Conclusion   85
Notes   87

CHAPTER 9
Learning about Education   **89**
Correlating Education and Economic Achievement   90
Discovering Geographic Patterns in Educational Attainment   92

Assessing Strengths and Shortcomings of ACS Education Data   97
Conclusion   99
Notes   102

CHAPTER 10
Speaking the Languages   103
Speaking the Language   104
Conclusion   110
Notes   110

CHAPTER 11
Working with Occupations   111
Understanding Types of Jobs   112
Analyzing Specific Occupations   113
Analyzing Military Service   117
Conclusion   120
Notes   120

CHAPTER 12
Analyzing Transportation Trends   123
Establishing Vehicle Use   124
Determining Commuting Patterns   124
Gauging the Importance of Commuting Patterns   128
Conclusion   131
Notes   131

CHAPTER 13
Assessing Income   133
Understanding Income Variability   134
Measuring Poverty   135
Assessing Income Distribution   139
Conclusion   143
Notes   144

CHAPTER 14
Analyzing Health Data   145
Understanding Types of Health Insurance   146
Parsing Disability Data   146
Understanding Nutrition Data   148
Overlooking an Obvious Health Data Point   150
Conclusion   152
Notes   152

PART III: RESOURCES

APPENDIX A
  Using American FactFinder   157

APPENDIX B
  Using Raw Data Files   171

APPENDIX C
  Glossary of Census Terms   197

APPENDIX D
  Online Resources   221

APPENDIX E
  Mapping Census Data   225

APPENDIX F
  Comparing Census and American Community
  Survey Characteristics   231

About the Website   235

About the Author   237

Index   239

Acknowledgments

I've been privileged to work with a number of people over the years who have provided me with their expertise, knowledge, and patience. I have to begin by thanking the late Freda McVay at Texas Tech University, who shooed an incorrigible introvert out the door of her basic reporting class and told me to come back when I had a good story. Jennifer Allen, formerly of *Columbus Commercial Dispatch*, was the best editor that any cub reporter could have. Jim Tharpe, managing editor at the *Alabama Journal*, guided a team of extremely young reporters to a Pulitzer Prize and taught me more than anyone about the craft of journalism and the possibilities of data. I bow to the entire staff of the late, lamented *Houston Post*, who taught me that you didn't have to drink and be a curmudgeon to have fun in journalism, although it certainly helped. Caleb Solomon, now managing editor at the *Boston Globe*, was kind enough at the *Wall Street Journal* to provide me with computer software, an expense account to roam my native Texas, and a wealth of knowledge about business journalism. I was blessed at the Associated Press to be hired by Bill Ahearn, a visionary who grasped the possibilities of data-oriented reporting even before the organization had thought to acquire personal computers for its writers; supervised by Sandy Johnson, an editor of impeccable judgment and grace under pressure; and managed by John Solomon, whose enthusiasm for big stories and skill in presenting them was (and remains) unparalleled in the business.

One hopes my best work is not behind me, especially if that one is Susan Goldberg, my editor at *Bloomberg News*. In supervising the Washington bureau and our state and municipality team, Susan has proven many times that patience and enthusiasm aren't mutually exclusive character traits. I owe a considerable debt to Mike Riley, editor at *Bloomberg Government*, who hired me for a good job and sheltered me from some not-so-good ones. I'm also fortunate to work frequently for Amanda Bennett, our projects and investigations editor who has probably forgotten about more of her award-winning stories than most newsrooms have earned, and Bob Simison, our in-house "story doctor" who generously serves as a "story trauma surgeon" in my case. Mark McQuillan in Washington and Flynn McRoberts in Chicago have provided me with superb guidance, good humor, and mild obsessive-compulsive editing behaviors that have frequently kept me out of trouble. I may have written this book; Matt Winkler wrote our book on writing books, and I owe him thanks for his vote of confidence in green-lighting this project, as well as apologies for any deviations from the proper use of the mother tongue.

"It takes a village," Paul Overberg, a journalism colleague at *USA Today* and census guru extraordinaire, reassured me a couple of years ago when I e-mailed with a panic-stricken message about an error in my Gini coefficient calculations. I owe a considerable debt to both Paul and Steve Doig, formerly of the Miami Herald and now teaching at Arizona State University, for their patience in showing me the possibilities of the census through Investigative Reporters and Editors workshops and conferences. They've provided assistance throughout the years without making me feel like the village idiot. I've also been lucky enough to benefit from the accumulated wisdom of top-notch researchers and data savants, such as Mark Horvit, former *Post* colleague and executive director of IRE; Jeff Porter at the University of Missouri and the Association for Health Care Journalists; Bill Frey at the Brookings Institution; D'Vera Cohn at the Pew Research Center; Michelle Levander at the University of Southern California's Reporting on Health project; and, I often think, the entire support and public information staffs at U.S. Census Bureau, SAS Institute (with a particular shout-out to Beverly Brown), and the University of Minnesota Population Center. All have been unfailingly gracious in the face of many cringe-inducing questions from the author.

Any and all errors and omissions are mine, and reflect only an occasional lapse of poor judgment on the above people who have helped me through the years.

Introduction

Not everything that can be measured matters, and not everything that matters can be measured.

Albert Einstein

No reasonable person would argue that the Census Bureau's compilation of data is anything other than an extraordinarily helpful addition to our understanding of the United States. Every decade, Americans use the bureau's data to reorganize the representative structure that guides the world's oldest continuous democracy. Every year, Americans take demographic, economic, social, and housing data from the American Community Survey and use it to direct about $450 billion in tax money to specific programs. Schools get built, roads are paved, hungry people are given food, and sick people get healed as a result of accurate, timely data.

The numbers are also used for less-tangible purposes. The figures help us define ourselves. More than 30 years ago, Hispanics didn't exist as part of the traditional decennial census. In 1980, the first time that Latinos were actually counted, there were 14.6 million. More than 50 million Americans described themselves as Hispanics in the 2010 census. There weren't any computer-based occupations in the 1950 census; nine of the 526 detailed occupations listed in the annual American Community Survey include the phrase "computer."

Revolutions are easy. Evolutions take time.

It's important to limit expectations. It's helpful to understand the limits of quantification when it comes to economics, and all other quantitative sciences, for that matter. In a 1968 speech at the University of Kansas, less than three months before he was killed, U.S. Senator Robert F. Kennedy observed that the gross national product, perhaps the single most important economic indicator of the age, suffered a few major shortcomings. The figure, Kennedy said, failed to "allow for the health of our children, the quality of their education or the joy of their play. It does not include the beauty of our poetry or the strength of our marriages, the intelligence of our public debate or the integrity of our public officials. It measures neither our wit nor our courage, neither our wisdom nor our learning, neither our compassion nor our devotion to country, it measures everything in short, except that which makes life worthwhile. And it can tell us everything about America except why we are proud that we are Americans."

Ultimately, the limits to the billions of individual records contained in the decennial census and the annual American Community Survey are set by the user's imagination and creativity. Demographic, social, economic, and housing changes can help tell the story of a single city block or a nation. The data can measure the change over a year, or over a generation. They can be useful or they can be extraneous.

Like any other quantitative exercise, analyzing census data won't yield answers. It will only give you the best questions, and frequently, that's the most difficult part of the exercise.

PART I

Guide to the Decennial Census

CHAPTER 1

The Evolution of the Census

Thomas Jefferson was unhappy.

Two years into his job as the nation's first secretary of state, Jefferson had recently received the 56-page results of the first-ever census, required by the U.S. Constitution. The new government had sent about 650 U.S. marshals door-to-door, spending slightly more than a penny per person to finish the count on August 2, 1790. The number of white men older than 16, white men younger than 16, white females, all other free people, and slaves had fallen short of expectations. Instead of counting more than 4 million Americans, the U.S. marshals in charge of the census came up with 3,982,214 people.

"We know in fact the omissions have been very great," Jefferson wrote to his boss, George Washington.[1]

The nation's first census certainly wasn't perfect. The succeeding 22 censuses haven't been perfect, either. Technically speaking, a census provides a snapshot of every American on a given day, now usually April 1. It's never that simple, though. Some people aren't counted; others are counted multiple times. Some people tell the truth about how much they earn, where they work, and who they are; others lie. It's an imperfect solution in an imperfect world.

Like our form of democracy that originated with Aristotle, the idea of a census had its origins in ancient times. God commanded the Israelites in Exodus to calculate tabernacle upkeep taxes with a census. The oldest existing census records come from China's Han Dynasty in the second century A.D., showing nearly 58 million people.[2] When the constitutional convention began in Philadelphia in 1787, delegates had to decide how best to design the House

3

TABLE 1.1   Ten Largest U.S. Cities, 1790 Census

Rank	City	State	Population
1	New York City	New York State	33,131
2	Philadelphia	Pennsylvania	28,522
3	Boston	Massachusetts	18,320
4	Charleston	South Carolina	16,359
5	Baltimore	Maryland	13,503
6	Northern Liberties Township	Pennsylvania	9,913
7	Salem	Massachusetts	7,921
8	Newport	Rhode Island	6,716
9	Providence	Rhode Island	6,380
10	Marblehead	Massachusetts	5,661
11	District of Southwark	Pennsylvania	5,661

Source: U.S. Census Bureau.

of Representatives, the lower body of the bicameral legislature. There was sharp disagreement over whether states should be awarded House seats based on population, or some combination of population and property. Delegates eventually agreed that a population-based census—with slaves counting as 3/5 of a person—would be the best tool for allocating representatives.

Other than the undercount, the first census held few surprises. New York was the nation's biggest city, with 33,131 people. Philadelphia ranked second, with 28,522, and Boston was the nation's third-largest city, with a population of 18,320. Then, as now, New York remains the largest city in the nation. Philadelphia and Boston, though still large, lost large numbers of their residents during the last half of the twentieth century. Not all cities remain as prominent: Newport, Rhode Island, whose 1790 population of 6,716 as shown in Table 1.1 made it the eighth-largest place in the nation, now has 24,672 residents, which didn't even put it in the top 1,000 largest places in the United States in 2010.

As a predictive model, the first census contained far too little data to be useful, with only six questions:

1. The name of the household head.
2. The number of free white males older than 16.
3. The number of free white males younger than 16.

4. The number of free white females.
5. The number of all other free persons.
6. The number of slaves.[3]

As the nation grew, though, so did the census. Over the next 220 years, it grew from its initial $44,000 budget (about $600,000 in today's dollars) to the nation's largest peacetime mobilization of government workers, costing $13.1 billion.[4] The basic questions dealing with free white males older than 16 became a dizzying array of possibilities, culminating in the ability to determine how many non-Hispanic male children of as many as six races lived in one of roughly 10 million blocks scattered throughout the nation. The census grew invaluable to businesses, as well. In 1810, the census asked its first economic question, breaking down manufactured products in 220 types spread across 25 categories. Nearly two centuries later, economic questions predominated, collecting data ranging from the median household income to the number of waiters and waitresses in any one of thousands of small American towns.

Who Relies on the Census?

Social policy researchers also awoke to the possibilities presented by the census, basing thousands of studies on the data to measure the effectiveness of government programs and to gauge changes sweeping the nation over long periods of time. Government itself became one of the biggest consumers of census-related data. The census was still used by state lawmakers, judges, and commissions to draw congressional and state legislative district boundaries, but it also became useful in directing federal and state spending in fields ranging from school locations to housing for the poor.

The federal government currently bases more than $400 billion in spending on census data,[5] and elected officials consider those funds crucial. In 2010, for example, New York Mayor Michael R. Bloomberg sounded every bit as disappointed as Jefferson (if somewhat less eloquent) after learning that the Census Bureau's estimates were more than 200,000 people short of previous estimates. From a congressional standpoint, the news was bad enough. It meant the state would lose two House seats instead of one. From a financial standpoint, it was worse—the city stood to lose millions in federal aid during the worst economic downturn since the Great Depression. "As they say in Brooklyn," Bloomberg declared, "Fuhgeddaboudit!"[6]

Government spending is also critical for businesses. The federal government spends about $700 billion in direct business contracts annually, buying everything from pencils and pens to nuclear submarines and space station parts. The government's census decisions affect businesses that aren't even doing business directly with Washington. For example, the Small Business Administration sponsors a program to obtain low-cost loans for historically disadvantaged businesses, such as those owned by women or minorities. Companies can take advantage of those loans if they're located in HUB (Historically Underutilized Business) Zones, which are defined by census tracts, small geographic units defined by the Census Bureau that are approximately the size of a neighborhood, usually containing 3,000 to 5,000 people. In 2010, the SBA decided to redefine those areas based on the new census tract boundaries. Thousands of small firms were abruptly located outside of the HUBZones, and many feared they wouldn't be able to survive if they had to pay higher interest rates on loans.[7]

Business wasn't the first priority of the first few censuses, though. Establishing a functioning government and determining the number of able-bodied men took precedence. In 1800, the population was broken out into five age groups, with the top end consisting of people over 45 years old—the elderly, then, because life expectancy in America was roughly 40 years.[8]

The Civil War was still a generation away, but the 1820 census shows an increasing interest in the subjects of race and economics, as well as the first standardized census form used by enumerators who collected information. Besides the expanded age categories for free whites, the 1820 census also collected information on the ages of slaves, and the number of people—slaves included—engaged in commerce, manufacturing, or agriculture. The 1820 census also marked the introduction of another controversial segment of American life, asking for the number of foreign residents.

The expansion of economic questions hadn't run smoothly. The Treasury Department, citing "numerous and very considerable imperfections and omissions," was disappointed with the results, so economic questions weren't asked again until 1840. By 1850, however, the demands of business and government, as well as the new requirement that a record be created for every individual, had led to a massive growth in the number of questions. The census asked for information on everything from "horses, asses, and mules, milch cows, working oxen, other cattle, sheep, and swine" to the quantities produced of dew-rotted hemp and maple sugar.[9] The 1850 census also asked for information about property taxes, average wages for carpenters, number of libraries and churches, and whether or not people in a household were "deaf, dumb, blind, insane, idiotic, pauper or convict."

The 1860 census was the most reliable headcount taken for decades to come. The nation's population growth was heaviest in the northern, free states.

FIGURE 1.1   Center of population, 1790–2010

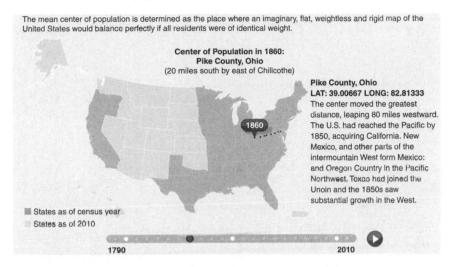

The mean center of population is determined as the place where an imaginary, flat, weightless and rigid map of the United States would balance perfectly if all residents were of identical weight.

Center of Population in 1860:
Pike County, Ohio
(20 miles south by east of Chillcothe)

Pike County, Ohio
LAT: 39.00667 LONG: 82.81333
The center moved the greatest distance, leaping 80 miles westward. The U.S. had reached the Pacific by 1850, acquiring California. New Mexico, and other parts of the intermountain West form Mexico: and Oregon Country In the Pacific Northwest. Texas had joined the Unoin and the 1850s saw substantial growth in the West.

■ States as of census year
  States as of 2010

1790   2010

Source: U.S. Census Bureau, http://2010.census.gov/2010census/data/center-of-population.php.

Minnesota grew from 6,000 people to more than 172,000 over the decade. The North's population grew 41 percent; the South grew only 27 percent. The statistical center of population, shown in Figure 1.1, shifted out of the original 13 colonies for the first time, and also from slave state territory (Virginia) to free (Ohio). The northern growth posed a problem for slave-holding states. And in proof that census conspiracy theories have existed almost as long as the census itself, one southern newspaper editor linked the congressional seats lost in the Deep South to the Underground Railroad, which was responsible for using runaway slaves to bolster the North's population totals.[10]

As a result of the Civil War, the 1870 census broke all nonwhite people into the "colored" category, with tallies for blacks, mulattos, Chinese (including Indians), and Native Americans. The 1870 census also marked the introduction of a machine to compile responses, known as the Seaton Device after its inventor Edward Seaton, the chief clerk and later director of the Census Bureau.[11] By 1890, the census had gone from four basic inquiries (name of household, race, sex, and age) to 13,161 questions. More detailed racial categories had been added to include white, Japanese, Chinese, Negro, mulatto, quadroon, and octoroon. In bulk, it had grown from a 56-page pamphlet to a 25-volume tome with 21,410 pages, and in price, from $44,000 to $11.5 million, or $275 million in current dollars, as Figure 1.2 displays.[12]

FIGURE 1.2 Number of inquiries or details relating to each subject, 1790–1890

Subjects of inquiry.	1790.	1800.	1810.	1820.	1830.	1840.	1850.	1860.	1870.	1880.	1890.
Population	4	4	4	6	7	14	a 22	b 24	23	24	45
Insanity:											
Individuals										14	34
Institutions											54
Feeble-mindedness, etc.										11	31
Deafness:											
Individuals										9	36
Institutions											28
Blindness:											
Individuals										10	35
Institutions											28
Physical disabilities											27
Crime:											
Individuals							4	4	5	19	32
Institutions										139	37
Pauperism							5	5	6	24	42
Benevolence										13	42
Mortality							11	11	11	14	17
Agriculture:											
General schedules						37	46	48	62	108	255
Special schedules										1,572	837
Manufactures:											
General schedules			3	14		6	14	14	18	29	88
Special schedules							c 4	c 4	c 4	705	2,779
Mines and mining						6	(d)	(d)	(d)	1,619	313
Fish and flsheries						5	(d)	(d)	(d)	87	248
Commerce						11					
Education						4	8	8	10	907	76
Insurance										5,779	3,921
Libraries							3	3	3	196	
Real estate mortgages											26
Farms and homes: proprietorship and indebtedness											5
Religious organizations							4	4	5	372	13
Seasons and crops							3	3			
Social statistics of cities										299	222
Trade societies and strikes and lockouts										101	
Transportation										466	1,464
Wages and prices							6	6	6	167	
Wealth, debt, and taxation							8	8	13	105	1,970
Alaska											123
Indians										221	283
Surviving soldiers, etc., and inmates of soldiers' homes											50
Total	**4**	**4**	**7**	**20**	**7**	**82**	**138**	**142**	**156**	**13,010**	**13,161**

Source: Wright & Hunt, "History of the U.S. Census," 87, http://www2.census.gov/prod2/decennial/documents/HisGrow1790-1890/HisGrow03.pdf.

Having spent the better part of three centuries exterminating Native Americans, the federal government decided to begin counting them in 1900. Because it had taken so long to count the results of the 1880 and 1890 censuses, the government dramatically cut back on the number of questions. The new Native questions asked for tribal affiliation, any polygamous relationships, fraction of white ancestry, and whether or not they lived in a teepee or other moveable structure. By 1910, that question was changed to "civilized" or "aboriginal" dwelling.

The 1920 census marked a low-water point for the national headcount. It was obvious that population was shifting to northern, urban areas; the census began asking for the native language of peoples' parents. For the first time in

U.S. history, more people lived in urban than rural places.[13] Yet farming was still important; so important that the U.S. Department of Agriculture was able to successfully petition for the census to begin in January so farmers would have more accurate memories of the previous year's harvest. When the results were released, showing a massive shift in population concentration to cities like New York, Philadelphia, and Boston, rural lawmakers from the South worked to avoid reapportionment, partly by claiming a rural undercount and partly by arguing that the reapportionment process was flawed. Congress finally reached agreement in 1929 that the next apportionment would be based on the results of the 1930 census.

As the Great Depression took hold, Congress was frantic for information that would confirm the apparent depth of the crisis. The initial numbers from the 1930 census were widely considered to underestimate the economic damage; a special employment census was ordered by Congress in January 1931.[14] The numbers confirmed the seriousness of the situation. A second special census was authorized in 1937. The government used the headcount to compare overall results with the results of a sample of 2 percent of American households in a bid to measure the effectiveness of statistical sampling.

The 1930 census also focused on a pair of emerging consumer-oriented issues, asking people if they had a "radio set," which had become more common in the previous decade, and telling the enumerators to cite at least one person in a family household as homemaker. Census Bureau Director Robert L. Austin warned his staff that it might be easier to communicate with each other and to travel, but an enumerator "is quite likely to find, when he gets there that the occupants are out. If it is the time of day when the breadwinners are not at their regular places of work and the housewife, if there is anyone who qualifies as such, is not shopping, and the children, if there are any, are not at school, then they are motoring or have gone to the ball game or the 'movies' or the amusement park."[15]

The current method of reapportionment was created in 1941, when Congress approved legislation that confirmed the number of House seats would remain at 435; before then, the number had been somewhat arbitrarily set by lawmakers. The seats are allocated through the creation of a priority list that measures each state's claim to each seat based on its population, relative to other states.

The census moved into the computer age after the 1950 headcount, using a UNIVAC computer that weighed 16,000 pounds and required 5,000 vacuum tubes.[16] It also counted Americans living abroad for the first time. Most notably, however, the 1950 census marked a milestone that was apparent only more than a half-century later—the peak population of major U.S. cities, including Chicago, Philadelphia, Detroit, Baltimore, Cleveland, St. Louis,

Boston, and Washington, D.C. The creation of the interstate highway system and the postwar Baby Boom began driving people into the suburbs, a geography that the Census Bureau still struggles to measure.

Computers took up more of the workload in 1960. Five-subject questionnaires were mailed to every household in the United States, and enumerators picked them up later for verification. After fine-tuning sampling that had begun in the 1940 census, the government selected about a quarter of households that received a longer-form survey with more detailed questions. By 1970, that number was reduced to 20 percent of households, and the Census Bureau used a master address file that allowed Americans to return their census forms by mail for the first time.

The 1980 census was one of the most controversial of the century. It wasn't any mystery that enumerators missed people. The 1980 headcount missed 1.2 percent of the population, roughly 2.6 million people.[17] About 7.7 percent of blacks were thought to have been undercounted in the 1970 census. Detroit officials sued to require the Census Bureau to submit adjusted, statistically sampled numbers to make up for the shortfall. New York City and several other governments joined the court fight, which was decided in favor of the Census Bureau in 1989.[18]

The census also marked the first appearance of Hispanics on the main population form. The Census Bureau had allowed the use of "Mexican" as a race in 1930 but dropped it. In 1970, the 5 percent sample allowed people to describe themselves as Hispanic or non-Hispanic. The 1980 census showed there were 14.6 million Hispanics in the United States, or 6.4 percent of the total population. Under the census rules, "Hispanic" was treated as an ethnicity; races remained limited to white, black, Native American, Asian/Pacific Islander, and other.

The sampling controversy continued into the 1990 census. Having lost its 1980 case, New York filed suit in 1988 to require the Census Bureau to use statistically adjusted data to hedge against an anticipated undercount. The government agreed to use a small-scale sampling effort and submit the adjusted results to an advisory panel, which would recommend whether to use unadjusted or adjusted numbers in reapportionment. The estimated undercount for blacks was 1.8 percent. The Census Bureau's advisory panel split on the issue of adjusted data. Census Bureau Director Barbara Everitt Bryant came out in favor of the adjusted data; Commerce Secretary Robert Mosbacher vetoed it. New York re-launched its lawsuit, losing before the U.S. Supreme Court in 1996.[19]

The 2000 headcount marked several departures from previous censuses. It was the first that made data publicly available on the Internet, the first where results confirmed explosive growth in the so-called Sunbelt states of the Southwest and West, and the first to count multiracial Americans. Prior to the 2000 census, people who were of mixed race had to choose one or the other. The new approach allowed people to describe their race with as many as six variables. A person could be white, black, Native American, Asian, Pacific Islander, or other—or two, three, four, five, or even all six of the above.

Understanding the Current Census

The most recent census was one of the simplest in a century. Because many of the economic and social indicators from the decennial census were compiled and distributed more than two years after the actual census, much of the information became obsolete immediately. The Census Bureau addressed the problem by launching an annual poll of roughly 3 million households known as the American Community Survey, replacing the decennial long form that had been mailed to 1 of 6 U.S. households in 2000 and creating the basis for Part Two of this guide. The actual census form consisted of 10 basic questions, asking name, sex, race, ethnicity, and relationship and housing status. Even so, it took 565,000 temporary workers added to the government payroll and a budget of $14.7 billion (the Census Bureau returned $1.6 billion after the count) to identify the 308,745,538 people living in the United States on April 1, 2010, and the 10 largest U.S. cities, as shown in Table 1.2[20]

TABLE 1.2 Ten Largest U.S. cities, 2010 Census

Rank	City	State	Population
1	New York City	New York State	8,175,133
2	Los Angeles	California	3,792,621
3	Chicago	Illinois	2,695,598
4	Houston	Texas	2,099,451
5	Philadelphia	Pennsylvania	1,526,006
6	Phoenix	Arizona	1,445,632
7	San Antonio	Texas	1,327,407
8	San Diego	California	1,307,402
9	Dallas	Texas	1,197,816
10	San Jose	California	945,942

Source: U.S. Census Bureau.

The 2010 census also highlighted increasing diversity in the United States. Far from being a sociological item of interest, diversity is a cornerstone of congressional reapportionment. Citing the 1965 Voting Rights Act, the U.S. Supreme Court has generally taken a mixed view of attempts to design race-specific congressional districts. In 1995, the Supreme Court described Georgia's 11th Congressional District, designed to produce a black lawmaker, as a "geographical monstrosity."[21] A Texas creation designed to elect a black lawmaker in Dallas, the 30th Congressional District, shown in Figure 1.3, was "bizarre" in shape, the Supreme Court found in 1996, but not necessarily a violation of the Voting Rights Act.

FIGURE 1.3   Texas' 30th Congressional District

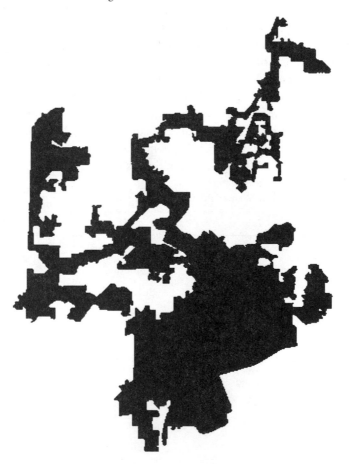

Source: U.S. Supreme Court, *Bush v. Vera*, 517 U.S. 952, June 13, 1996.

Following Census Results

As a practical matter, the first set of census data to be released is the simplest. The first set consists simply of state-by-state population totals that are used to determine the number of House seats and corresponding Electoral College votes that determine the winner of a presidential election. A second set of data, known as the PL94-171 series, is usually released a few states at a time over a two-month period, ending on March 31. The PL94-171 data contain the material that allows reapportionment to occur: It includes population totals by race, ethnicity, and voting age down to very fine levels consisting of areas that can be 500 people or less. A third set of data, known as the Summary File 1 data, includes information about specific ancestry and racial groups, ages, gender, households, relationships, and housing.

The first two census releases, the reapportionment data and redistricting data, act as the sources for political power. The third release, Summary File 1, is far more useful for actual policy. Some of the more than $400 billion steered to individual states and places by the decennial census is based on simple population counts. More often than not, though, it's a combination of variables from the Summary File 1 and other surveys. The location and growth of Americans younger than 5 years old, for example, are used to distribute significant parts of the Education Department's $79.4 billion budget. Likewise, the location of Americans over 65 years old helps the U.S. Department of Health and Human Services decide where to allocate parts of its $909.7 billion budget to support centers and services for the elderly.

Those three releases contain billions of individual records. There are some items, however, that the Census Bureau doesn't capture. Religion is a major omission, and it's not accidental. The government collected data as part of the "Census of Religious Bodies" from 1906–1936. Under a 1976 law, the Census Bureau was specifically prohibited from requiring people to provide information about their religion.[22]

The Census Bureau has asked about telephone service but not whether that telephone service is land- or cell based. It's requested information about home-heating fuel but not alternative energy sources. The Census Bureau has acknowledged it's likely to begin using the Internet more to save money on the decennial census; the 2020 headcount may have an online component similar to Canada's, where households receive a secure password in the mail and use it to fill out their census forms online.[23]

As in previous decades, it's hard to determine how the 2020 census will be different from its predecessor. Like many other federal agencies, the Census Bureau spent much of the year following the 2010 census trying to determine how it could save money. It axed the venerable Statistical Abstract of the United States, a 130-year-old print and online compendium of useful government data, and let go of its Consolidated Federal Funds Report, an annual survey that detailed federal spending on projects ranging from military procurement in Fairbanks, Alaska, to artificial panther insemination in Monroe County, Florida.

Even so, the Census Bureau still has a massive amount of data. Even setting aside the decennial census and its yearly companion, the American Community Survey, the government collects a wide range of data. Its Current Population Survey, a monthly poll of about 60,000 households conducted for the Bureau of Labor Statistics, is considered the most authoritative source for determining median household income, poverty, and health insurance rates at a national level. Recent CPS projects have focused on volunteerism, Internet use, food security, and veteran-related affairs, including the number with service-related disabilities and the effectiveness of programs designed to ease the transition into civilian life.

The Census Bureau also tracks government spending down to an extremely granular degree, compiling the Federal Assistance Awards Data System (FAADS), a quarterly compilation of figures showing the recipient, location, and amount of government grants and assistance. It tracks state and local payrolls, tax receipts, expenditures by category, and school district spending through its Census of Governments. In odd-numbered years, the Census Bureau teams up with the Department of Housing and Urban Development (HUD) to release the American Housing Survey, which relies on responses from 76,000 housing units to provide data ranging from the number of homes in an area to the number of broken toilets by type of home during the past year.[24]

Conclusion

The decennial census, created as a Colonial-era tool to assign congressional seats to each state, has changed dramatically over the last two centuries. The headcount, taken every 10 years, now is used by professionals ranging from urban planners to companies seeking to start or expand businesses. Paradoxically, the census has become easier to use in the last decade. After the 2000 census, the headcount was split into a decennial tally used primarily for voting purposes and an annual American Community Survey that mainly benefits businesses, social scientists, and government planners.

The decennial census is released in three stages, with the most basic level—the population in each state—usually being handed to the president before December 31 in a census year. Subsequent releases detailing the voting age, racial and ethnic composition, and household characteristics of places ranging from street blocks to the entire nation are usually provided on a staggered, state-by-state basis during the next year.

Although the Census Bureau has spent the last several years attempting to curb expenses, it is still the nation's premier data source. Besides population characteristics, the bureau tabulates data on federal grants and awards, state and local government payrolls, and economic indicators.

Notes

1. Carroll D. Wright and William O. Hunt, *The History and Growth of the United States Census* (Government Printing Office, 1900).
2. Sadao Nishijima, *Cambridge History of China*, vol. I, eds. Denis Twitchett and Michael Loewe (Cambridge: Cambridge University Press, 1986).
3. Wright-Hunt, op. cit.
4. U.S. Department of Commerce Office of Inspector General, "2010 Census: Quarterly Report to Congress" (Government Printing Office, January 2011).
5. U.S. Census Bureau, "About Us: How Our Data Are Used," http://www.census. tgov/aboutus/.
6. Michael R. Bloomberg, "Statement of Mayor Michael R. Bloomberg on 2010 Census Undercount," PR-098-11, City of New York, March 27, 2011.
7. Leah Nylen, "U.S. to Slash 4,400 Economic Growth Zones for Small Businesses," *Bloomberg Government*, March 23, 2011.
8. Frank B. Hobbs and Bonnie L. Damon, "65+ in the United States" (U.S. Government Printing Office, April 1996).
9. Wright-Hunt, op. cit.
10. Adam Goodheart, "The Census of Doom," *New York Times*, April 1, 2011.
11. U.S. Census Bureau, "History: Tabulation and Processing," http://www.census. gov/history/www/innovations/technology/tabulation_and_processing.html.
12. U.S. General Accounting Office, "Overview of Historical Census Issues" (U.S. Government Printing Office, May 1998).
13. U.S. Census Bureau, "History: Urban and Rural," http://www.census.gov/ history/www/programs/geography/urban_and_rural_areas.html.
14. U.S. Census Bureau, "History: 1930 Overview," http://www.census.gov/ history/www/through_the_decades/overview/1930.html.
15. David Hendricks and Amy Patterson, "Genealogy Notes: The 1930 Census in Perspective," *Prologue* 34, no. 2 (Summer 2002).
16. U.S. Census Bureau, "History: Technology, Univac I," http://www.census.gov/ history/www/innovations/technology/univac_i.html.
17. U.S. Senate Committee on Governmental Affairs, "Hearing: Undercount and the 1980 Decennial Census" (U.S. Government Printing Office, April 14, 1981).

18. *City of New York v. U.S. Department of Commerce*, 713 F. Supp. 48 (E.D. NY 1989).
19. *Wisconsin v. City of New York et al.*, U.S. Supreme Court, No. 94-1614 (1996).
20. Jennifer D. Williams, "The 2010 Decennial Census: Background and Issues," Congressional Research Service, February 3, 2011.
21. *Abrams et al. v. Johnson et al.*, U.S. Supreme Court, No. 95-142 (1997).
22. Anne Farris Rosen, "A Brief History of Religion and the U.S. Census," The Pew Forum on Religion and Public Life, January 26, 2010.
23. Daniel Castro, Senior Analyst, Information Technology and Innovation Foundation, "Census: Learning Lessons From 2010, Planning for 2020," Hearing Before Senate Homeland Security and Government Affairs Committee, April 6, 2011.
24. U.S. Census Bureau, "American Housing Survey: AHS Main," http://www. census.gov/housing/ahs/.

CHAPTER 2

Understanding Census Geography

Most people learned a basic geographic taxonomy growing up in this country. The United States consists of states, which include counties, which encompass cities, which consist of neighborhoods that are generally broken into zip codes. That's fine, as far as it goes. But the reality of census data is that there are least 20 primary geographies, and dozens of secondary geographies. And people who think that real estate is the only business that's all about location are kidding themselves: In business, everything is all about location.

It's a simple concept, really: Know your audience. It's easy enough to describe your market as being in a state, but hardly efficient. Being able to determine the characteristics of very small areas, such as neighborhoods or even blocks, is much more efficient. A working knowledge of census geography is the market equivalent of targeting spending with a rifle rather than a shotgun.

One of the more important things to know about census geography is that quite a bit of common knowledge is wrong. Zip codes aren't actual spatial geographies; they're postal delivery routes, and they can be quite linear. Not all large collections of people are cities; instead, they're places, municipal subdivisions, consolidated cities, or census-designated places. Even commonly understood boundaries don't follow the same rules when it comes to census geography. Neighborhoods are a prime example; subdivisions seldom, if ever, correspond directly to census tracts. Proper use of census data requires a solid understanding of geographical advantages and disadvantages.

This chapter explains the broad range of geographies that can be used for analyses, ranging from states that encompass thousands of square miles and hundreds of thousands of people to city blocks that contain several hundred people. It also provides a foundation for understanding benefits and potential pitfalls in analyzing census data from decade to decade.

Narrowing Geographical Scope

For most business applications, a solid understanding of fewer than 10 geographies included in Figure 2.1 will provide a solid foundation for analyzing demographic patterns and changes. The size of useful areas include states,

FIGURE 2.1   Taxonomy of Census Geography

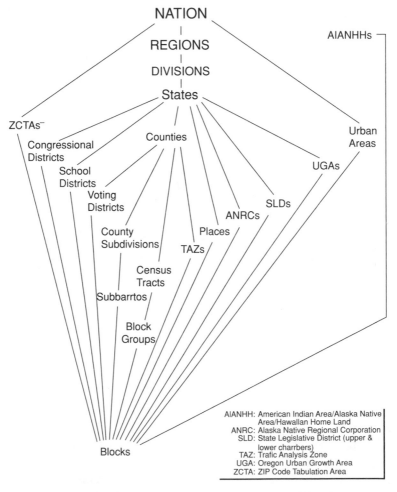

Source: 2010 Census Summary File 1 Technical Documentation, 2–6, http://www.census.gov/prod/cen2010/doc/sf1.pdf.

which can contain anywhere from the 37,253,956 people in California to the 563,626 people in Wyoming, to blocks, which contain an average of 28 people.

Analyzing data is much easier at high levels because there aren't as many. There are 50 states and 11 million census blocks, for example. States, however, aren't often homogenous enough for business purposes. The southern and northern parts of New York are an excellent example of areas in one state that have more in common with areas in neighboring states than with each other. The biggest advantage of states is that the sheer size of their populations means that sample data will be reasonably accurate and provided often. State-level data is the first part of any decennial census and is part of every release in the annual American Community Survey.

State-level data also is useful for looking at broad trends over a period of time. A late-century shift in population to the Sunbelt, for example, was determined by finding changing population patterns, with states like Arizona, California, and Nevada gaining population at the expense of Ohio, Michigan, and Pennsylvania. State-level census data also has been useful in examining population shifts for racial and ethnic groups, as well. Over the last three decades, there's been a substantial shift in the Hispanic population from the border states of the Southwest to the lower Midwest that was first observed in state-level populations.

Larger areas can also be used for analysis and marketing. The White House Office of Management and Budget defines places smaller than states but larger than counties as "core-based statistical areas," or CBSAs.[1] The areas consist of metropolitan or micropolitan areas, which are economically and socially integrated. A micropolitan area usually has a core urban area with 10,000 people or more. A metropolitan area, such as one in the examples shown in Figure 2.2, has a core urban area with 50,000 or more. The city of Fredericksburg, Texas, for example, had 10,530 people in 2010; the micro area contained 24,837. Arlington County, Virginia, was home to 208,000 people in 2010; the Washington-Arlington-Alexandria metropolitan area in Virginia, Maryland, District of Columbia, and West Virginia, included 5.6 million people.

The disadvantage of using metro or even micro areas to guide strategy lies with the diversity of many of these places. Gwinnett County, Georgia, was 20.1 percent Hispanic in 2010, and Pickens County, Georgia was 2.8 percent Hispanic. Both areas are part of the Atlanta-Sandy Springs-Marietta metropolitan area, which has 5.3 million people and is 10.4 percent Hispanic. A metro or micro area may have advantages for reaching a large number of people. It's not always terribly useful for reaching a large number of homogenous people.

FIGURE 2.2   Georgia: Metro Areas, Counties, and Central Cities

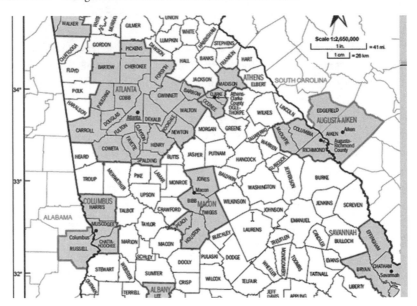

Source: U.S. Census Bureau, http://www.census.gov/geo/www/mapGallery/stma99.pdf.

Congressional districts have the advantage of being fairly large geographical areas that are constrained by state boundaries. There are 435 districts, and boundaries are changed after every decennial census. To complicate matters, states can gain or lose congressional districts based on population growth over the preceding decade. The average congressional district has about 700,000 people. As a final disincentive to using congressional districts for anything other than political purposes, the districts are created by government panels, legislatures, or courts with the primary goal of ensuring equal political representation. Because redrawing boundaries is primarily a political exercise, these boundaries often not only fail to reflect geographic reality, such as the example shown in Figure 2.3, they also fail to reflect demographic reality. Finally, states don't redraw their districts all at once. It often takes many years before legislative, judicial, and executive agreement results in redrawn congressional districts.

Working with Standard Geographies

Technically speaking, the nation's 42,000 zip codes aren't spatial geographies; they're delivery routes that were designed to improve the efficiency of the

FIGURE 2.3 North Carolina's 12th Congressional District

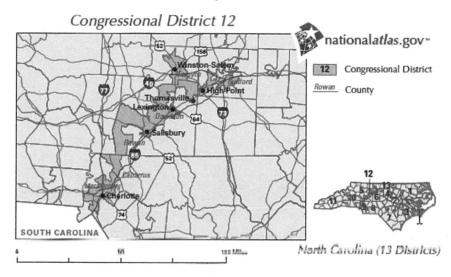

Source: nationalatlas.gov.

U.S. Postal Service, and the shape they take can be linear or polygonal. They still can be useful for demographic research, simply because they're one of the smallest geographies that are familiar to residents. Most people, for example, don't know their congressional district. They do, however, know their own zip code.

The Census Bureau began developing zip code tabulation areas (ZCTAs), such as the downtown New York City examples shown in Figure 2.4, in the 1990s by putting together blocks where mailing addresses were in a given zip code. This is helpful but not foolproof, because many zip codes with a small number of addresses don't have ZCTAs, and many zip codes have been changed while ZCTAs have remained the same. In 2010, the Census Bureau eliminated three-digit ZCTAs and decided against assigning codes to national parks, large water bodies, and densely populated large areas.[2]

For business-planning purposes, the nation's 3,100-plus counties are much more granular boundaries of economic activity than states or metropolitan areas. As people have migrated from inner cities to suburbs, county-level data has displayed growth beyond core urban areas. Every year for the last several decades, census estimates have shown the fastest-growing counties are suburbs. Between 2000 and 2009, the Census Bureau estimated that Kendall County, Illinois, a suburb of Chicago, grew 92.1 percent to lead the

FIGURE 2.4   Lower Manhattan Zip Code Tabulation Areas (ZCTAs), 2000 Census

2.8 miles across

Source: American FactFinder.

nation, as shown in Table 2.1. Some of the nation's most rapid population growth was also recorded in counties surrounding Atlanta, Dallas, Denver, and Washington, D.C.

Avoiding Geographic Confusion

Problems using county-level data tend to be isolated to certain states. Changes between the 2000 and 2010 decennial censuses have left Alaska with a patchwork of 30 different boroughs and census areas that range in size from the 291,826 people in Anchorage Municipality to the 662 counted in Yakutat City and Borough. Virginia has 95 counties; those don't include the 39 independent cities, responsible for all but three in the nation (Baltimore, St. Louis, and Carson City, Nevada). In the Washington, D.C., suburbs, for example, the independent cities of Fairfax and Falls Church are located within Fairfax County. Alexandria, another independent city, borders Arlington and Fairfax counties. Although it's an independent unit of 139,966 people, parts of the two counties are commonly referred to as "Alexandria."

Another common problem with counties lies in different iterations of the American Community Survey. The three stages of the survey—one-, three-, and five-year estimates—only include certain levels of geographies for each

TABLE 2.1   Fastest-growing U.S. Counties, 2000–2009

Rank	Geographic Area	Population Estimates		Change, 2000 to 2009	
		July 1, 2009	April 1, 2000 Estimates Base	Number	Percent
1	Kendall County, IL	104,821	54,563	50,258	92.1
2	Pinal County, AZ	340,962	179,720	161,242	89.7
3	Rockwall County, TX	81,391	43,079	38,312	88.9
4	Flagler County, FL	91,622	49,832	41,790	83.9
5	Loudoun County, VA	301,171	169,599	131,572	77.6
6	Forsyth County, GA	174,520	98,367	76,153	77.4
7	Lincoln County, SD	41,218	24,147	17,071	70.7
8	Paulding County, GA	136,655	81,613	55,042	67.4
9	Williamson County, TX	410,686	249,979	160,707	64.3
10	Douglas County, CO	288,225	175,766	112,459	64.0
11	Henry County, GA	195,370	119,338	76,032	63.7
12	Newton County, GA	99,944	62,001	37,943	61.2
13	Collin County, TX	791,631	491,772	299,859	61.0
14	Union County, NC	198,645	123,777	74,868	60.5
15	Hays County, TX	155,545	97,582	57,963	59.4
16	Fort Bend County, TX	556,870	354,452	202,418	57.1
17	Osceola County, FL	270,618	172,493	98,125	56.9
18	Franklin County, WA	77,355	49,347	28,008	56.8
19	Barrow County, GA	72,158	46,144	26,014	56.4
20	Delaware County, OH	168,708	109,992	58,716	53.4

Source: U.S. Census Bureau, 2000 Census SF1 and intercensal estimates.

stage. The one-year estimates include geographies for all places with more than 65,000 people, which would only include 805 counties in 2010. The three-year survey results include places with more than 20,000 people. Again, that would only include 1,838, or a little more than half. Only the five-year survey results include all counties.

Because most suburbs are located in places and towns, these smaller geographies represent high-reward potential for businesses that are trying to understand the composition and change within given areas. Quite frequently, statistics about a given place don't represent useful information about that place. For example, the median household income of Houston, Texas, was $42,355 in 2010, according to single-year estimates from the American Community Survey, far less than the national figure of $50,046. That figure would include numbers for places like Missouri City, where the median household income is $72,010, or The Woodlands, where it's $91,378.

The biggest issue with analyzing data from a place, however, is a matter of definition. The Census Bureau defines a place as one that's been "established to provide governmental functions for a concentration of people as opposed to a minor civil division, which generally is created to provide services or administer an area without regard, necessarily, to population."[3] As a practical matter, this doesn't shed very much light on the problem. It's possibly more helpful to be aware that an area can be a city, place, town, or village within a minor civil division (also frequently known as a county subdivision), or it can be a freestanding entity with no connection to a county subdivision.

There are 29 states that recognize minor civil divisions: Arkansas, Connecticut, Illinois, Indiana, Iowa, Kansas, Louisiana, Maine, Maryland, Massachusetts, Michigan, Minnesota, Mississippi, Missouri, Nebraska, New Hampshire, New Jersey, New York, North Carolina, North Dakota, Ohio, Pennsylvania, Rhode Island, South Dakota, Tennessee, Vermont, Virginia, West Virginia and Wisconsin. In nine states—Maine, Massachusetts, New Hampshire, New Jersey, North Dakota, Pennsylvania, Rhode Island, South Dakota, and Wisconsin—a place is always independent of a county subdivision. In the other 20 states, it's possible for a place to be part of a county subdivision.

Some places and county subdivisions even have the same name, but different population totals, so it's best to know your geographic area well before drawing conclusions. Take Ohio, for example. It's got 1,604 county subdivisions that include towns, townships, and cities. It's got another 1,204 places. In general, large cities such as Akron tend to have the same population totals for both place and county subdivision tallies. Not all places are that neat, though. The city of Athens had 20,832 people, according to the 2010 census. The township of Athens, one of 14 townships in Athens County, had 30,473. Athens Township in Harrison County had 505 people. This requires knowing the difference between Harrison County and Athens County (about 120 miles) and understanding which parts of Athens, the city, are contained within Athens, the township.

It's also worth knowing about census-designated places, or CDPs, which are unincorporated places usually adjacent to an incorporated place or visible boundary. Census-designated places don't have municipal governments or any legal status. They're quite common; nationwide, there were 41,526 county subdivisions and 34,333 places in 2010. Census-designated places made up 9,721 places across the nation.

The Census Bureau lists five cities as "consolidated cities," including Butte-Silver Bow, Montana; Athens-Clarke County, Georgia; Augusta-Richmond County, Georgia; Columbus, Georgia; Indianapolis, Indiana; Milford, Connecticut; and Nashville-Davidson, Tennessee. A city becomes a consolidated city when the government functions for a place and county subdivision merge.[4]

Working with Very Small Geographies

For granular planning, businesses are best served by census tracts, a relatively new geography. Prior to 1990, some counties were assigned block numbering areas and others were given census tracts. Beginning in 2000, all numbering areas were replaced by 65,443 tracts. There were 73,057 tracts in 2010, most designed by local governments to be demographically, economically, and socially homogenous. As a general rule, census tracts have about 4,000 people. They can range in size from 1,200 to 8,000. Counties and places with fewer than 1,500 people are usually part of a single census tract.

The best way to think of a census tract is to consider it a neighborhood approximation. A tract will almost never coincide with neighborhood boundaries established by a developer, government, or population. Because of their sizes and homogeneity, they can be effective substitutes for a neighborhood or subdivision. They're also small enough to be combined to create useful geographies while retaining enough data to provide useful information. An example of an area's tracts is shown in Figure 2.5.

It's important to remember where census tracts fit in the overall taxonomy of a decennial census. Tracts can cross place and town boundaries, although they usually remain within those boundaries. They have to be contained wholly within a county.

One of the few disadvantages to using census tracts for planning and marketing purposes is that they're not completely static boundaries. Census tracts change every 10 years, usually being combined because of population declines or split because of population growth. The Census Bureau maintains a "crosswalk" file that allows users to compare tract characteristics across more than one decade. The file requires some technical expertise to manipulate the data.[5]

FIGURE 2.5   Lower Manhattan Tracts, 2000 Census

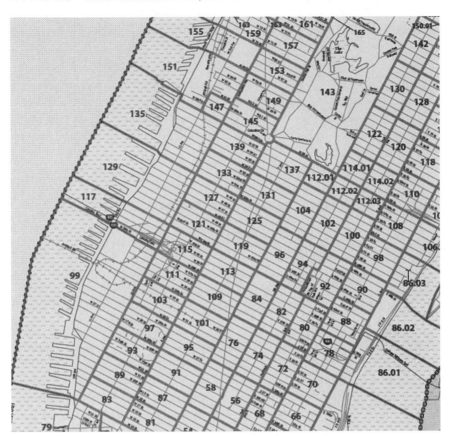

Source: U.S. Census Bureau, http://www2.census.gov/geo/maps/dc10map/tract/st36_ny/ c36061_new_york/DC10CT_C36061_002.pdf.

Census blocks can be both the best and worst of geographies. The block is essentially the atom of the census. There are 11,078,297 census blocks in the United States, up from 8,205,582 in 2000, and they're used as the foundation of every geography, from a tract to the entire nation. About 2 million are unpopulated.[6]

One of the beauties of the census block for analysis is the rule that any census block has to include visible boundaries, such as a road, stream, or even utility line. This rule provides users with some semblance of rational justification when creating unique geographies.

In most populated areas, a block is just that: one square block. The average block contains somewhere between 30 and 40 people. This is extraordinarily

FIGURE 2.6   Lower Manhattan Blocks, 2000 Census

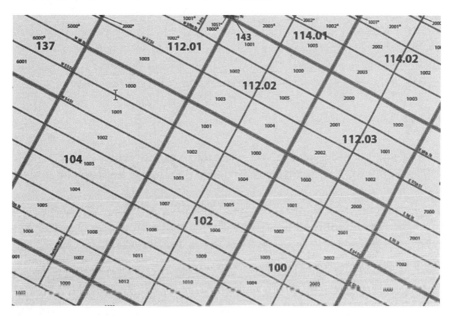

Source: U.S. Census Bureau, http://www2.census.gov/geo/maps/dc10map/GUBlock/st36_ny/county/c36061_new_york/DC10BLK_C36061_010.pdf.

useful, because you can create virtually any geography using your own des-ignated blocks to isolate an area or a collection of people. A good example of a block collection is shown in Figure 2.6, showing several of thousands of New York City blocks.

That's the tremendous upside of using census blocks. There are a few downsides. The biggest problem is simply that data is limited because of privacy protections at the block level. The Census Bureau is prohibited from releasing information that could identify any one person, which is much more likely to occur at very small geographies, even in the decennial census. It's possible for users to determine the number of Hispanics in a block. It's not possible to obtain the number of Mexicans, or the number of 24-year-olds, or the number of Hispanic 24-year-olds within a block. In some cases, users may have to resort to tract-level calculations.

Like tracts, census block boundaries can change every 10 years. They've been used since 1990. The Census Bureau makes a series of block relationship files available for users. The relationship between blocks over decades can be a one-to-one relationship, where the blocks remain the same; a one-to-many relationship, where a 2000 block is split into one or more 2010 blocks; a many-to-one relationship, where more than one 2000 blocks are consolidated into a 2010 block; or a many-to-many relationship, where different parts of 2000 blocks are allocated across more than one 2010 block. It helps considerably for users to have a solid understanding of relational database manipulation before attempting to compare blocks across one or more decades.[7]

Conclusion

Selecting proper geographies is crucial to effective use of census data. There are millions of possibilities, ranging from one of 50 states to more than 8 million individual census blocks.

People analyzing census data should take care to define a geographic area properly. A commonly understood zip code, for example, may not always follow the boundaries created by the Census Bureau. Places can be located within a county subdivision of the same name. And boundaries can and do often change from decade to decade, most frequently at place, tract, and block levels.

The most granular analyses generally can be done at tract and block levels. A tract is analogous to a neighborhood. A block can be just that—a square block containing only a few hundred people. Though blocks are generally so small as to defy consistent patterns, they're the de facto atom of the census. Their small size makes them very flexible in creating custom geographies that adhere more closely to user needs.

Notes

1. Office of Management and Budget, "2010 Standards for Delineating Metropolitan and Micropolitan Statistical Areas," *Federal Register* 75, no. 123 (June 2010).
2. U.S. Census Bureau, "Zip Code Tabulation Areas," http://www.census.gov/geo/ZCTA/zcta.html.
3. U.S. Census Bureau, "Geographic Terms and Concepts," http://www.census.gov/geo/www/2010census/gtc/gtc_place.html.
4. Ibid.
5. University of Michigan Population Studies Center, "Census Tract Crosswalks," http://www.psc.isr.umich.edu/dis/data/resource/detail/1457.
6. U.S. Census Bureau, "2010 National Geographic Tallies," http://www.census.gov/geo/www/2010census/geo_tallies/national_geo_tallies.html.
7. U.S. Census Bureau, "2010 Census Block Relationship Files," http://www.census.gov/geo/www/2010census/rel_blk.html.

CHAPTER 3

Understanding Basic Census Counts

The most important thing to remember about the decennial census is simple: It's a snapshot. In some places, not everyone is counted; in others, some people are counted more than once. People are born, and people die. People move from place to place, and sometimes they move to places where census enumerators can't or won't go. Even with the billions spent by the Census Bureau, the headcount is a very imperfect process and is likely to remain that way for many years.

First and foremost, the census is a political process. It was created to ensure that all Americans (or at least, free, white Americans) had an equal voice in the nation's government. An extremely long and bloody war had been fought for independence, primarily because of Great Britain's refusal to allow its colonies to govern themselves. From the start, the decennial census was created as a tool to allocate representation on an equitable basis.

In an ideal world, the census would have created congressional districts of equal size. Again, though, it's an imperfect process; people are born and die, they move to different places, and populations change, sometimes dramatically, over a decade. The total population of some states is much smaller than the average population in a congressional district of other states; because the Constitution doesn't allow for states to go without representation or have congressional districts that cross state lines, this can be problematic. Theoretically, Congress could increase the number of seats to allow more representatives for a smaller number of Americans. The current number, 435, hasn't been changed since 1929.

The procedure for reapportionment is fairly straightforward. The Census Bureau delivers the state-by-state population counts to the president before the end of the year in which the decennial census is taken. The president certifies them as accurate, and then sends the counts to Congress. At that point, it's too late to challenge the results. In 2011, for example, New York City officials claimed the bureau missed as many as 225,000 residents during the 2010 census.[1] Even so, the apportionment results—which would have resulted in New York's losing one congressional seat instead of two—had been certified, so New York lost two seats.

Determining Political Representation

The number of congressional seats for each state is currently determined by a method known as "the Hill," which is described as an equal proportions method. It's been used since 1941. The total population is divided by 435 to determine the best population for each congressional district. As many seats as possible are assigned to each state, based on their share of the national population. The remainder for each state is then assigned a priority value, based on this formula:

$$PV = P/[(n(n - 1)]^{1/2}$$

where PV is the state's priority value, P is the state's population, and n is the state's n-th congressional seat. For example, the Congressional Research Service used the following example to obtain the priority value of Oregon's sixth congressional seat:

$$PV_{OR6} = 3,848,606/[6(6 - 1)]^{1/2}$$
$$= 3,848,606/[30]^{1/2}$$
$$= 3,848,606/5.477225575$$
$$= 702,656.11$$

The formula returned a priority value of 702,656—well below the 645,931 priority value that North Carolina got for its 13th congressional seat, which was the 435th (and last) seat assigned after the decennial census.[2]

This method seems to work fairly well, although it's periodically protested. The formula was overturned by an appeals court in 1991 when Montana argued that it didn't "achieve the greatest possible equality." Montana, with a population slightly larger than 900,000, protested that it should have more political influence in Congress than a state like Wyoming, with fewer than 500,000 people. The Supreme Court agreed with the common sense nature of Montana's argument that districts should be roughly the same size within each state but decided that Congress had properly used its authority to divide the nation into appropriately sized congressional districts.[3]

Other options have been considered. On the face of it, the simplest method would seem to be dividing the national population by 435 to create an appropriately sized congressional district, and then using fractions (rounding up or down) to allocate the remaining seats for each state. The problem here, of course, is that the numbers wouldn't always add up to 435. Using this method in 1991 would have resulted in a 438-seat House of Representatives; in 2001, there would have been 433 congressional seats.

Alexander Hamilton, the nation's first treasury secretary, was an advocate of the "fractional representation" method. Instead of rounding, the remainders of each state's unrepresented population would be ranked by size, and congressional seats would be allocated based on their ranking. Congress passed a bill using this method in 1792; after consulting with Thomas Jefferson, George Washington exercised the first-ever presidential veto. Washington told Congress that the legislation didn't create a proportion for each state's allocation of lawmakers, and that it also exceeded the limit of one congressman for every 30,000 people in eight states.[4]

Despite Washington's disapproval, the Hamilton method was adopted after the 1850 census and used until 1901. It began falling out of favor after the 1880 census, partially because of the "Alabama Paradox."[5] The state had eight seats out of a 299-seat Congress; the addition of one seat in the House of Representatives, however, reduced its number to seven. The Webster method was used in the 1910 and 1930 census (there wasn't a reapportionment in 1920 because rural lawmakers, fearful of losing power, derailed the process until 1929). It simply used the arithmetic mean to round at the midpoint of the remainder. If a state's remainder was above .5, it got an extra seat; if it was below .5, it kept its proportionate number of seats.[6]

The controversies surrounding reapportionment may seem a bit extreme. Consider, though, the stakes that are involved. The federal government currently spends more than $1 trillion on grants and contracts, many of which are distributed according to location and/or political connections. The loss or gain of a congressional seat can influence political careers, and those political careers can influence private fortunes.

Creating Political Boundaries

Reapportionment also is the first step in a lengthy, extremely political process known as redistricting, or the creation of new boundaries for political geographies, such as congressional and state legislative districts. The Brennan Center at the New York University School of Law described the importance of the redistricting process:

> Our representatives in local, state, and federal government set the rules by which we live. In ways large and small, they affect the taxes we pay, the food we eat, the air we breathe, the ways in which we make each other safer and more secure. Periodically, we hold elections to make sure that these representatives continue to listen to us.[7]

All of our legislators in state government, many of our legislators in local government, and most of our legislators in Congress are elected from districts, which divide a state and its voters into geographical territories. In most of these districts, all of the voters are ultimately represented by the candidate who wins the most votes in the district. The way that voters are grouped into districts therefore has an enormous influence on who our representatives are, and what policies they fight for. For example, a district composed mostly of farmers is likely to elect a representative who will fight for farmers' interests, but a district composed mostly of city dwellers may elect a representative with different priorities. Similarly, districts drawn with large populations of the same race, or ethnicity, or language, or political party are more likely to elect representatives with the same characteristics.

Think of redistricting as a seemingly endless series of reapportionment exercises, done on a state, legislative district, county, city, and school district level. The congressional redistricting efforts by states, which usually coincide with the decennial census, tend to get the most attention because of their political nature. Arguments over the size, shape, and scope of districts are hardly new. The word "gerrymander," for example, came into use after Massachusetts Governor Elbridge Gerry signed off on an 1811 plan that ensured his party's continued domination of the state Senate. The narrow size of some outlying districts led artists to dub the plan a "Gerry-mander." The plan resulted in a reelection defeat, but he was chosen as vice president to James Madison and served until his death in 1814.

Three dozen states assign redistricting duties to legislative committees, which often leads to gerrymandered districts, where a majority party draws districts designed to keep its members in office. Seven states—Arizona, California, Hawaii, Idaho, Minnesota, New Jersey, and Washington—have created independent bodies to draw congressional district boundaries to remove as much political influence from the exercise as possible. Three states (Florida, Iowa, and Maine) also have independent redistricting commissions

whose work must be approved by the state legislature. Seven other states—
Alaska, Delaware, Montana, North Dakota, South Dakota, Vermont, and
Wyoming—only have one at-large congressional seat because of their small
populations, so a formal redistricting effort isn't necessary.[8]

How political can redistricting become? A political deadlock in Texas in
2001 led to a judicial panel resolving the matter, and Democrats maintained
a 17-15 majority in Congress. In 2002, Republicans won control of the Texas
Legislature for the first time in 130 years. They launched a 2003 effort to
redraw congressional boundaries. Because Texas Democrats didn't have the
votes or the legal ability to stop the mid-decade redistricting, 52 fled to Okla-
homa and refused to return until Governor Rick Perry agreed that the issue
wouldn't be brought up during a regular legislative session. Perry then called
a special session. Eleven Democrats fled to Albuquerque, New Mexico, but
returned, and Republicans were able to push their plan through, resulting in
the election of 21 Republicans and 11 Democrats. A challenge was eventually
heard by the U.S. Supreme Court, which generally held that a mid-decade
redistricting plan was constitutional, although it ruled that one of the state's
new districts violated the Voting Rights Act. Sixteen states are required to seek
Justice Department approval before changing voting district boundaries.[9]

(Even an independent panel can't escape politics. In Arizona, for example,
Republican Governor Jan Brewer accused the chair of the state redistricting
panel of being overly partisan and secretive. The Arizona Senate voted in
November 2011 to impeach Colleen Mathis, the chair. Mathis, a registered
independent, sued and was reinstated in time to swing a 2-2 partisan deadlock
in favor of a Democratic plan.)[10]

Redistricting can have unanticipated results, to put it mildly. In 2000,
a Democratic primary challenger to incumbent Illinois Congressman Bobby
Rush won more than 30 percent of the vote, setting the stage for a potential
rematch in 2002. Illinois lawmakers, who have traditionally been deferential
to incumbents, obligingly redrew Rush's district to exclude the challenger's
house by a matter of one block. Rush ran unopposed in 2002 and 2004,
winning more than 80 percent of the vote. His 2000 Democratic challenger,
Barack Obama, had to find other opportunities.[11]

Understanding the Fundamentals of Redistricting Files

The Census Bureau delivers its reapportionment file to Congress and the
White House in December of a year in which the decennial census is conducted. The series of files that govern redistricting, known as the PL94-171

data, are delivered to state officials the following spring. They're generally released in clusters of three to four states every week. The first element of redistricting files contains two age groups: Older than 18 and younger than 18. This part of the redistricting file tells officials how many eligible voters live in their states, counties, cities, towns, tracts, and blocks.

The second key element of the redistricting files divides the nation into racial and ethnic groups by age. This is often a source of much confusion, because the Census Bureau defines race and ethnicity differently from most Americans. The Census Bureau has six basic racial groups:

1. White
2. Black
3. Native American
4. Asian
5. Pacific Islander
6. Other

and includes every permutation of multiracial categories possible. Beginning with the 2000 census, the government gave citizens the option to pick one or more racial groups. Using the redistricting files, it's possible to tell how many white people who are eligible to vote live in a block—or how many people who are multiracial across all six categories and are younger than 18 live in a block. Multiracial Americans currently make up about 3 percent of the population; most check both the black and white racial categories on their census form.

The second subset, ethnicity, is defined differently from popular understanding. Most Americans might think of their ethnicity as an ancestral characteristic, such as German or Polish or Irish or English. The Census Bureau defines ethnicity as one of two categories: Hispanic, or non-Hispanic. The ethnic categories are mixed with the racial categories, allowing researchers to determine the number of white non-Hispanics within a given area, or the number of Hispanic people who claim to be multiracial within an area.

A glaring weakness in the Census Bureau's current scheme is its inability to allow people of mixed ethnicity to describe themselves as such. The son of a black mother and white father, for example, can describe himself as a multiracial American. A child of a Hispanic mother and non-Hispanic father, however, doesn't currently have that option. It's an especially inconvenient omission, given that Hispanics are one of the fastest growing segments of the nation's population, and intermarriage is common.

A less-noted problem is the issue of self-identification. In 2000, for example, Census Bureau officials were concerned about the potential for a "Dances with Wolves" effect, where millions of Americans with Native ancestry would claim both white or black and Native ancestry (the percentage of Native Americans stayed more or less steady at 0.9 percent of the population). Likewise, the inclusion of Hispanics as an ethnic group, but not a racial group, tends to overstate the number of "Other" races in the decennial census.

Given the number of permutations involving racial and ethnic groups in any one area, it's sometimes best to resort to statistical tools to gauge the composition of a geographical area. The diversity index, developed for *USA Today* in 1991 by Phil Meyer and Shawn McIntosh, applied simple probability theory to determining the homogeneity or diversity of census geographies. The index measures the likelihood that two people selected at random will be of the same race, using the following formula:

$$\text{Diversity} = 1 - [(W^2 + B^2 + \text{AmIndI}^2 + A^2 + \text{PI}^2)*(H^2 + \text{Non} - H^2)]$$

where W is the percentage of the white population, B is the percentage of blacks, AmIndI is the percentage of Natives, A is the percentage of Asians, PI is the percentage of Pacific Islanders, H is the percentage of Hispanics, and Non-H is the percentage of non-Hispanics.[12]

The diversity index will approach zero as a geographic area becomes more homogenous; a diverse area will have an index closer to one. The value of a diversity index should be intuitive for market researchers. More care will need to be taken in trying to reach customers in a diverse area than a heterogeneous place.

Analyzing Age, Gender, and Detailed Race Data

Most businesses could be excused for thinking that the census can only be used for political gain on a congressional level. True, the redistricting files will determine how hundreds of billions of federal tax dollars are spent. For simple market research, though, the Summary File 1 (SF1) release can be pure gold. The SF1 file, which includes all geographies down to a block level, is generally released about a month after the PL94-171 series is released. Like the redistricting files, the SF1 data is usually released on a staggered basis, about three or four states per week, over a four-month period.

The SF1 release expands on the PL94-171 series by adding gender totals, as well as individual ages for the major racial and ethnic groups, from people whose age ranges from less than 1 year old to 99 years old. The release also includes age breakdowns for people between 100 and 104 years old; 105 and 109 years old; and older than 110. The age data can be especially useful to businesses targeting specific demographics. An automobile insurance company, for example, might focus more heavily on certain areas within New England and Appalachia, because people in those areas tend to be older; companies focusing on young children and their parents might want to direct their efforts to places in Utah and Nevada, which are much younger states. The Census Bureau also releases median ages for major racial and ethnic groups by all geographic areas, providing even more information about the demographic makeup of a place.

The other major population-related benefit of the SF1 series is its breakdown of the population by individual groups. Anyone who's ever paid any attention to the Hispanic market, one of the nation's fastest-growing groups, knows that it's not a monolithic, one-size-fits-all group. The distance between people from Patagonia and Coahuila is measured in more than miles. Fortunately, the Census Bureau breaks the Hispanic population down into separate components in the SF1 release:[13]

Mexican	Salvadoran	Peruvian
Puerto Rican	Other Central	Uruguayan
Cuban	American	Venezuelan
Dominican	Argentinean	Other South
Costa Rican	Bolivian	American
Guatemalan	Chilean	Spaniard
Honduran	Colombian	Spanish
Nicaraguan	Ecuadorian	Spanish-American
Panamanian	Paraguayan	All Other Hispanic

The Asian population, the fastest-growing racial group in the nation over the first decade of the twenty-first century, is also broken down into separate components. Again, selling goods and services to Chinese can be a quite different proposition from selling them to Japanese or Vietnamese:[14]

Asian Indian	Indonesian	Sri Lankan
Bangladeshi	Japanese	Taiwanese
Cambodian	Korean	Thai
Chinese	Laotian	Vietnamese
Filipino	Malaysian	Other Asian
Hmong	Pakistani	

More than three dozen federally recognized Native tribes are broken out into fine detail:[15]

Apache	Iroquois	Seminole
Blackfeet	Kiowa	Shoshone
Cherokee	Latin American	Sioux
Cheyenne	Natives	Tohono
Chickasaw	Lumbee	O'odham
Chippewa	Menominee	Ute
Choctaw	Navajo	Yakama
Colville	Osage	Yaqui
Comanche	Ottawa	Yuman
Cree	Paiute	Other tribes
Creek	Pima	Alaska Athabascan
Crow	Potawatomi	Aleut
Delaware	Pueblo	Eskimo
Houma	Puget Sound Salish	Tlingit-Haida

The SF1 series doesn't go into too much detail for each of these groups; it's possible to get the number of people by gender, median age, and individual age for the major racial or ethnic groups from the SF1 file. For a higher degree of detail, the Summary File 2 (SF2) series, usually released about six months after the SF1 series, is useful. The SF2 series provides detailed age and gender data for all of the groups listed above. In other words, the SF1 data tells you how many Koreans are in a given area; the SF2 file tells you how many Korean women over the age of 85 are in that same area.

An advantage of the PL94-171, SF1, and SF2 files is their comprehensive nature. These figures involve an actual headcount. Because an actual headcount involves hiring thousands of enumerators and spending billions of dollars, these data only come out once every decade. Even so, they're much more reliable than intercensal population estimates released annually by the Census Bureau.

Conclusion

The primary function of the decennial census is political. It allocates proportional representation among states, although there's frequently been disagreement about the best means of doing so. Once the number of representatives has been allocated to a given area, people can begin the task of creating district boundaries for their representatives.

The primary census redistricting file is known as the PL94-171 series and is usually released about one year after a decennial census is taken. It contains counts for the number of people within all geographies; their race and ethnicity; and whether they're old enough to vote.

A second decennial census file is generally released about three months after the PL94-171 files. This file, known as the Summary 1 File, contains all the PL94-171 data, plus information about age, sex, household status, housing arrangements, family relationships, and detailed race and ethnicity figures.

The PL94-171 redistricting file, for example, provides people with the number of Hispanics in a given geographical area. The SF1 data represents a deeper slice of that information, providing the origin of Hispanics and various characteristics for groups ranging from Argentinians to Venezuelans. The SF1 release also includes more detailed data for Native American, Asian, and Pacific Islander groups.

Notes

1. Timothy R. Homan and Esme Deprez, "Errors Bedevil Census Bureau in Drawing U.S. Portrait," *Bloomberg News*, October 3, 2011.
2. Royce Crocker, "House Apportionment 2010: States Gaining, Losing, and on the Margin," Congressional Research Service, January 13, 2011.
3. *Department of Commerce v. Montana*, 503 U.S. 442 (1992).
4. George Washington, "Veto Message to Congress," April 5, 1792, via "The Papers of George Washington Project," University of Virginia, http://gwpapers.virginia.edu/documents/presidential/veto.html.
5. Royce Crocker, "The House of Representatives Apportionment Formula: An Analysis of Proposals for Change and Their Impact on States," Congressional Research Service, January 1, 2011.
6. Ibid.
7. Justin Levitt, "A Citizen's Guide to Redistricting, 2010 Edition," New York University School of Law Brennan Justice Center, November 29, 2010.
8. Peter S. Wattson, "How to Draw Redistricting Plans That Will Stand Up in Court," National Conference of State Legislators, National Redistricting Seminar, Washington, D.C., January 22, 2011, http://www.ncsl.org/documents/legismgt/How_To_Draw_Maps.pdf.
9. U.S. Department of Justice, "Redistricting Information," http://www.justice.gov/crt/about/vot/redistricting.php.
10. Amanda J. Crawford, "Arizona's High Court Overturns Brewer's Firing of Redistricting Panel Head," *Bloomberg News*, November 18, 2011.

11. Micah Altman and Michael P. McDonald, "Pulling Back the Curtain on Redistricting," Brookings Institution for the *Washington Post*, July 9, 2010.
12. Phil Meyer and Paul Overberg, "Updating the *USA Today* Diversity Index," January 2001, http://www.unc.edu/~pmeyer/carstat/tools.html.
13. U.S. Census Bureau, "Summary File 1, 2010 Census of Population and Housing, Technical Documentation," July 2010.
14. Ibid.
15. Ibid.

CHAPTER 4

Analyzing Critical Relationships

The census might best be thought of as a collection of data about more than 300 million Americans. But like census geography, relationships among those Americans tend to be hierarchical, and subject to a wide number of variations. The individual is the building block of census data, but households are a close second. Household data is generally introduced in the Summary File 1 (SF1) release, which is distributed state by state, on a piecemeal basis, in the summer after the decennial census. As it stands right now, the SF1 release is a halfway point for the decennial headcount, falling between the PL94-171, or redistricting, release in the spring, and the Summary File 2 release in the following year.

The traditional American view of a household is a bit different from the Census Bureau's definition. Most of us would probably consider a household to consist of a family unit, something like Ward, June, Wally, and the Beaver, or a husband, wife, and 2.3 children. The Census Bureau takes a much broader look at households:

"A household includes all of the people who occupy a housing unit."[1]

The definition begs several questions. What if only one person lives in a home? That's a household. What if two unrelated people share a household? That's a household, too. What if the home is subdivided into apartments and occupied by five families? Those are five households. And what exactly is a housing unit? The Census Bureau defines a housing unit as "a house, an apartment, a mobile home, a group of rooms, or a single room occupied (or if vacant, intended for occupancy) as separate living quarters. Separate living quarters are those in which the occupants live separately from any other people in the building and that have direct access from the outside of the building or through a common hall."

The vast majority of Americans live in households. People in prisons, however, can hardly be said to be living in households. College dormitories and nursing homes also wouldn't fall into the household category. The Census Bureau lumps these Americans into a "group quarters" category, and subdivides the category into institutionalized and noninstitutionalized populations. The institutional category includes prisons and halfway houses, nursing homes, long-term hospitals and juvenile detention centers. The non-institutional category includes group homes, college dormitories, military barracks, homeless and domestic violence shelters, maritime lodging, and even living quarters for victims of natural disasters.

So we have a working definition of households, housing units, and group quarters. What are the advantages of looking at household characteristics? After all, we know we can look at just about any variable on an individual basis. The advantages of household data lie in their structure—we don't have to assume that everyone is living by themselves or in a nuclear family—and the level of detail that allows us to include certain segments as an integral part of research, whether it's targeted at married families with children, multigenerational households, or single people.

The example of median household income is instructive. Unless otherwise specified, per-capita income is usually measured by the Census Bureau for the population 16 years and older. This includes a lot of high school students, who frequently don't have a full-time job; stay-at-home parents; elderly people living on a fixed income; and people who are unemployed for a short or significant period of time. All of these factors work to decrease the per-capita income. Median household income, on the other hand, narrows the focus more by consolidating individuals into more comparable units.

Understanding Household Relationships

As with race, ethnicity, and geography, there's a specific taxonomy associated with households. There are two primary types of households: family households and nonrelative households. Family households, for census purposes, consist simply of people who are related by birth, marriage, or adoption. Nonrelative households are all others.

Whether or not the household is family or nonrelative, there's only one householder within a household. The householder can be any individual living within a household. In a single-person household, the person living there is the householder. In a family household, it's usually a spouse or other relative, such as a grandparent. The Census Bureau allows for wide flexibility in defining the types of family members. Generally speaking, a family household can consist of a householder and spouse, as well as own children, adopted children, stepchildren, and other relatives, including grandchildren, siblings, parents, and in-laws. Nonrelative households can include roommates, boarders, unmarried partners, and foster children.[2]

There are three final breakdowns for family households. The most traditional involves married-couple households, with a husband and wife. A substantial number of family households include a female householder with her own children and no spouse present, as well as a growing number of households that consist of a male householder with his own children and no spouse present.

Ultimately, the taxonomy looks like this:

Total population:
    Total population, in households:
        Total population in family households:
            Male householders
            Female householders
            Spouses
            Children:
                Natural or adopted children
                Stepchildren
            Grandchildren
            Siblings
            Parents
            Other relatives
            Nonrelatives
        Total population in nonfamily households:
            Male householders, living alone
            Male householders, not living alone
            Female householders, living alone
            Female householders, not living alone
            Nonrelatives
        Group quarters population:
            Institutionalized population
            Noninstitutionalized population

A pair of relatively new variables has been introduced over the past two censuses. In 2000, the Census Bureau began keeping track of unmarried partnered householders, both of different and same sex. The new data was widely seen as a way of measuring the size of the gay and lesbian population. The 2010 Census marked the first time that the government attempted to track the number and age of children living with grandparents. The ages are broken down into children younger than 3 years old; 4 and 5 years old; 6 to 11 years old; and 12 to 17 years old.

Household growth generally tracks, but doesn't always follow, population gains. During the first decade of the new century, for example, household growth outpaced the 9.7 percent population growth by nearly a full percentage point. There were 116.7 million households, up 10.6 percent from the 105.5 million households that existed in 2000. Almost exactly two-thirds of 2010 households were family households; the figure was down slightly from the 68 percent recorded in the 2000 census.

The number of households reflected an important trend: Fewer people were getting married during the decade, as the number of married-couple households increased to 56.6 million households as shown in Figure 4.1, only a 3.9 percent increase from 54.5 million in 2000.

FIGURE 4.1   Married-couple households, 2010

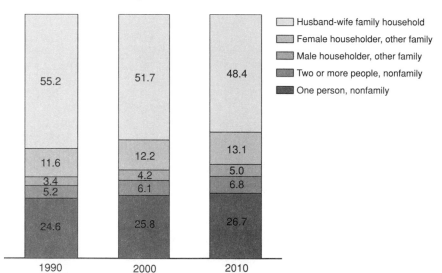

Source: U.S. Census Bureau, Census 2010 Summary File 1; Census 2000 Summary File 1; Census of Population, Summary Population and Housing Characteristics, United States (1990 CPH-1-1), http://www.census.gov/prod/cen2010/briefs/c2010br-14.pdf.

Digging Deeper into Household Relationships

Household size data is also available to some degree of detail. Between 2000 and 2010, the average number of people per household fell to 2.58, down very slightly from the 2.59 reported in the 2000 census. A more relevant piece of data might be the number of differently sized households within given geographical areas. The Census Bureau collects the number of one-, two-, three-, four-, five-, six-, and seven or more-person households within each geography. It also keeps track of the number of householders for the following age ranges:

15 to 24 years old
25 to 34 years old
35 to 44 years old
45 to 54 years old
55 to 59 years old
60 to 64 years old
65 to 74 years old
75 to 84 years old
85 years and older

In addition to householder characteristics, the Census Bureau keeps tabs on children of householders, breaking the population younger than 18 into the following groups for related and unrelated minors:

Under 3 years
3 and 4 years
5 years
6 to 11 years
12 and 13 years
14 years
15 to 17 years

The child population is counted in other ways. The Census Bureau accounts for own, related, and nonrelated children living in married-couple, single-mother, and single-father households, breaking them down into five separate age groups (under 3 years, 3 and 4 years, 5 years, 6 to 11 years, and 12 to 17 years). This data can be useful for everyone from school board members trying to decide where to locate a new school to people looking for a good place to start a day-care center, driver's education school, or pediatrician's office.

The other end of the spectrum is represented by data on the population over 60, 65, and 75 years old. It includes the elderly population living in a household with a spouse, parent, or other relative. The single elderly populations are broken down into males and females who live alone.

The Census Bureau takes nearly all of these variables in the Summary File 1 release and adds another layer of complexity, making them available for the following races: White, black, Native American, Asian, Pacific Islander, other, multiracial, Hispanic, and white non-Hispanic. These data may or may not be available down to a block level; many tables, such as the number of nonrelatives by types of households by race, are only available to a tract level because of privacy concerns. The data can also be limited by the "Rule of 100," an informal policy that protects privacy by suppressing or reallocating population group results where there are fewer than 100 of any given race or ethnicity, or any other amount that would jeopardize the privacy of Americans.[3]

Making Sense of Summary File 2

That's not the end of it, by any stretch, though. The Summary File 2 release usually comes out about nine months after the SF1 data is finished, and tallies the SF1 data for each of 331 population groups, including the total population and 74 race groups, ranging from Americans who are white to Americans of varying multiracial categories. It includes SF1 data iterated for 78 Native categories, reflecting 60 tribal groupings, from Athabascan to Yup'ik:[4]

Alaskan Athabascan	Lumbee
Aleut	Menominee
Apache	Mexican American Indian
Arapaho	Navajo
Assiniboine Sioux	Osage
Blackfeet	Ottawa
Canadian and French American Indian	Paiute
Central American Indian	Pima
Cherokee	Potawatomi
Cheyenne	Pueblo
Chickasaw	Puget Sound Salish
Chippewa	Seminole
Choctaw	Shawnee
Colville	Shoshone
Comanche	Sioux

Cree	South American Indian
Creek	Spanish American
Crow	Indian
Delaware	Tlingit-Haida
Eastern Tribes	Tohono O'odham
Eskimo	Tsimshian
Hopi	Ute
Houma	Yakama
Iñupiat	Yaqui
Iroquois	Yuman
Kiowa	Yup'ik

The SF2 release includes SF1 data for 51 Hispanic or Latino groups, the nation's second-fastest growing racial or ethnic population during the 2000s, including:[5]

Mexican	Salvadoran
Puerto Rican	South American
Cuban	Argentinian
Other Hispanic or	Bolivian
Latino	Chilean
Dominican	Colombian
Central American	Ecuadorian
Costa Rican	Paraguayan
Guatemalan	Peruvian
Honduran	Uruguayan
Nicaraguan	Venezuelan
Panamanian	Spaniard

Another 43 Pacific Islander categories are cited, including:[6]

Polynesian	Kosraean
Native Hawaiian	Mariana Islander
Samoan	Marshallese
Tahitian	Palauan
Tokelauan	Pohnpeian
Tongan	Saipanese
Micronesian	Yapese
Carolinian	Melanesian
Chuukese	Fijian
Guamanian or Chamorro	Papua New
I-Kiribati	Guinean

Finally, the Census Bureau provides information on 47 Asian categories, including the following groups:[7]

Asian Indian	Korean
Bangladeshi	Laotian
Bhutanese	Malaysian
Burmese	Mongolian
Cambodian	Nepalese
Chinese	Okinawan
Taiwanese	Pakistani
Filipino	Singaporean
Hmong	Sri Lankan
Indonesian	Thai
Japanese	Vietnamese

The breakdowns may seem esoteric, even excessive. Still, there's tremendous value in being able to go beyond the fallacy of monolithic populations. The differences between Hispanic groups often lie even deeper than the differences between people in the United State and Great Britain ("two countries separated by a common language," as the quip attributed to George Bernard Shaw went). Argentinian cuisine can be quite different from Dominican food. The groups don't always get along, either; in 2008, for example, Ecuador, Colombia, and Venezuela almost went to war after Colombian troops chased guerillas into Ecuador, killing more than 20 people. A lot of attention is paid to the fast-growing Asian and Hispanic population, but it's important to keep in mind that they are about as monolithic in their cultures, tastes, consumer patterns, and occupations as, say, the white population.

Notes

1. U.S. Census Bureau, "Summary File 1, 2010 Census of Population and Housing, Technical Documentation," July 2010.
2. Ibid.
3. Asoka Ramanayake and Laura Zayatz, "Balancing Disclosure Risk with Data Quality," U.S. Census Bureau Statistical Research Division, February 22, 2010.
4. U.S. Census Bureau, "2010 Census Summary File 2, 2010 Census of Population and Housing, Technical Documentation," 2011.
5. Ibid.
6. Ibid.
7. Ibid.

CHAPTER 5

Working with Housing Data

The importance of having good data about American housing should be obvious; if you don't believe me, go back to 2008 when a speculative housing bubble came close to causing the entire global economy to collapse, resulting in the worst economic downturn in two generations. In the twenty-first century, housing has become about more than simple shelter; it's an integral part of the economy that influences how the consumers whose expenditures account for two-thirds of the U.S. economy actually spend money. It isn't just about the real estate market; people build a home, which affects the construction and manufacturing industries. They take out a mortgage, which affects the finance and insurance industry. They buy furniture and appliances (durable goods), paper towels (nondurable goods), and food for the refrigerator (agriculture). No wonder the collapse of the housing market wreaked such havoc on the U.S. economy, as readers can see from homeownership rates in Figure 5.1.

The Census Bureau presents most decennial housing data in the Summary File 1 (SF1) collection, which is normally released in the spring after a census year, with releases being made on a state-by-state basis staggered over a few months, all the way down to the block level. The Census Bureau defines housing units as a dwelling that "may be a house, an apartment, a mobile home, a group of rooms, or a single room that is occupied (or, if vacant, is intended for occupancy) as separate living quarters."[1] The reference to "separate living quarters" is key; it means people live separately from other households within the building and have direct access to the unit either from outside the building or through a common hall.

FIGURE 5.1   Homeownership rates, 2010

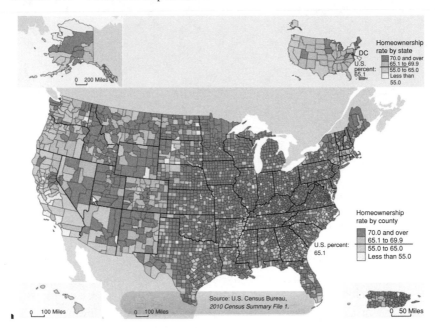

Source: U.S. Census Bureau, 2010 Census Summary File 1, http://www.census.gov/prod/cen2010/briefs/c2010br-07.pdf.

The decennial tally also allows for a few nontraditional dwellings: Boats, recreational vehicles, vans, and tents are considered housing units if they're occupied. Vacant mobile homes are counted as housing units if they're located on a site where they'll be occupied.

Grasping the Basics of Housing

Housing units can be occupied or unoccupied. An occupied housing unit is usually defined as a place where people normally live. It can consist of one or more households, and can be anything from a single-family home to a hotel room where someone has a permanent residence. An unoccupied unit is a housing unit where no one is living permanently and includes vacation homes to varying degrees as shown in Table 5.1. The Census Bureau takes pains to note that boats, recreational vehicles, tents, "caves and similar shelter that no one is using as a usual residence are **not** considered living quarters and

TABLE 5.1 Ten States with the Highest Percentage of Seasonal, Recreational, or Occasional-use homes, 2010

Area	Total housing units	For seasonal, recreational, or occasional use	Percentage
United States	131,704,730	4,649,298	3.5%
Maine	721,830	118,310	16.4%
Vermont	322,539	50,198	15.6%
New Hampshire	614,754	63,910	10.4%
Alaska	306,967	27,901	9.1%
Delaware	405,885	35,939	8.9%
Montana	482,825	38,510	8.0%
Wisconsin	2,624,358	193,046	7.4%
Florida	8,989,580	657,070	7.3%
Arizona	2,844,526	184,327	6.5%
Idaho	667,796	41,660	6.2%

Source: U.S. Census Bureau, 2010 Census Summary File 1, http://www.census.gov/prod/cen2010/briefs/c2010br-07.pdf.

therefore are not enumerated at all."[2] There are six basic types of unoccupied or vacant housing:

1. For rent
2. For sale
3. Rented, not occupied
4. Sold, not occupied
5. Seasonal or recreational
6. Housing for migrant workers

The number of housing units within a given area can be useful. It's more useful, though, to know the density of housing within the area. If you're selling consumer goods, for example, it's always best to be close to as many people as possible. If you're manufacturing something, you might want to be as far from other people as possible. Housing density can also be a nice economic indicator. An area where density is increasing is a prime location for additional housing, and all that it entails.

(Calculating density from census figures isn't as straightforward as it could be. The Census Bureau measures area in square meters. This means you have to divide the area by 1,000,000 to get square kilometers [10,000 * 10,000], then divide by 2.589988 to convert that figure into square miles.)[3]

Knowing who owns housing in an area is as valuable as knowing how much housing is in an area. The Census Bureau uses a phrase called "tenure," which simply translates to ownership. Occupied housing is either owned or rented. With very few exceptions—mostly in very wealthy vacation towns—people in owner-occupied housing will have higher incomes than people in renter-occupied housing.

The Census Bureau took its collection of housing-related data two steps further in 2010, primarily as a result of the housing market collapse in the middle of the decade. It began introducing housing data earlier in the process, with the number of housing units, occupied housing units, and vacant housing units counted in the PL94-171 redistricting release. The Census Bureau also began counting the number of households where the property was owned without mortgage.

Understanding Populations within Households

Once housing counts are tallied, the Census Bureau begins iterations of different housing characteristics, including the race and age of the householder by tenure, such as the number of housing units owned by black people or the number of housing units rented by Asian people between the ages of 25 and 34 years old. Family characteristics within housing tenures are also explored.

> Total occupied housing units:
>> Owner-occupied:
>>> Family households:
>>>> Husband-wife family:
>>>>> Householder 15 to 34 years old
>>>>> Householder 35 to 64 years old
>>>>> Householder 65 years and older
>>>> Other family:
>>>>> Male householder, no wife present
>>>>>> Householder 15 to 34 years old
>>>>>> Householder 35 to 64 years old
>>>>>> Householder 65 years and older

Female householder, no husband present
Householder 15 to 34 years old
Householder 35 to 64 years old
Householder 65 years and older
Nonfamily households:
Male householder:
Living alone:
Householder 15 to 34 years old
Householder 35 to 64 years old
Householder 65 years and older
Not living alone:
Householder 15 to 34 years old
Householder 35 to 64 years old
Householder 65 years and older
Female householder:
Living alone:
Householder 15 to 34 years old
Householder 35 to 64 years old
Householder 65 years and older
Not living alone:
Householder 15 to 34 years old
Householder 35 to 64 years old
Householder 65 years and older

Census housing data also tracks children by household:

Total housing units:
Owner-occupied:
With own children under 18 years:
Under 6 years only
Under 6 years and 6 to 17 years old
6 to 17 years old only
No own children under 18 years old
Renter-occupied:
With own children under 18 years:
Under 6 years only
Under 6 years and 6 to 17 years old
6 to 17 years old only
No own children under 18 years old

Group quarters are closely related to housing units; both fall under the category of "living quarters," according to the Census Bureau. But where people in housing units are frequently related, residents of group quarters seldom have any family relationship. The Census Bureau defines group quarters as:

> ... places where people live or stay in a group living arrangement, which are owned or managed by an entity or organization providing housing and/or services for the residents. This is not a typical household-type living arrangement. These services may include custodial or medical care as well as other types of assistance, and residency is commonly restricted to those receiving these services. People living in group quarters are usually not related to each other.[4]

The most common types of group quarters include jails, nursing homes, dormitories, and military bases. It's important to account for group quarters when examining characteristics of certain geographic areas. During the 2000 census, for example, a hapless television reporter presented a special exclusive on where the most single men could be found within the viewership area. The numbers were accurate, but single women likely weren't knocking each other over to get to the county that housed a maximum-security prison full of single men.

Conclusion

Housing is a crucial element of the U.S. economy, accounting for as much as $1 in every $5 worth of goods and services produced, according to the National Association of Home Builders. The housing bubble of the early 2000s and its subsequent collapse underscored the importance of the industry to the overall U.S. economy.

The Census Bureau has begun including very basic elements about housing in its redistricting file, such as the number of housing units, occupied and vacant. The vast majority of housing data in the decennial census is presented in the subsequent Summary File 1 data, generally released more than a year after the census is taken. The SF1 file includes information about the number of houses that are rented, owned, used for vacations, or being sold.

The SF1 data also include valuable information about housing arrangements for different households, whether they're traditional married-couple with children households, or single people living alone. These household types are further broken down by race and ethnic group, and frequently by age, so it's possible to determine the number of Asian senior citizens living alone in rental homes.

The Census Bureau also tracks the population living in group quarters, which can be anything from a college dormitory or nursing home to a prison or homeless shelter.

Notes

1. U.S. Census Bureau, "2010 Census Summary File 1, 2010 Census of Population and Housing, Technical Documentation," July 2011.
2. Ibid.
3. Ibid.
4. Ibid.

CHAPTER 6

Analyzing Race and Ethnicity

It's an understatement to say that America has never been comfortable dealing with race. Every 10 years, that level of discomfort is ratcheted up a bit as the Census Bureau struggles to calculate the number of people of each race in a nation of more than 300 million. It should be a simple task, complicated only by the growing diversity of the nation. It is far from simple.

By and large, race matters, unless you are white (and even then, occasionally). Since the first Europeans arrived in Jamestown, Virginia, in the seventeenth century with black slaves and met Native Americans, questions about race have been a near-constant feature of American life. The Census Bureau hasn't always facilitated the discussion; Natives weren't counted as Americans until 1900; Asians were required to check off a "Chinese" box until 1870; and even in 2010, people who have an Anglo mother and Hispanic father aren't allowed to describe themselves as being of mixed ethnicity. In the Census Bureau's eyes, either you're Hispanic or you're non-Hispanic.

For all the attention paid to the American melting pot, the nation remains predominantly white, almost overwhelmingly so. In 2010, there were 196.7 million non-Hispanic, white Americans, or 63.7 percent. Whites were described by the Census Bureau as Americans "having origins in any of the original peoples of Europe, the Middle East, or North Africa. It includes people who indicate their race as 'white' or report entries such as Irish, German, Italian, Lebanese, Arab, Moroccan, or Caucasian."

True enough, the percentage of Americans who describe themselves as white, non-Hispanic has fallen by one third over the past 220 years. The number of whites, however, is still nearly four times as many as the nation's 50.5 million Hispanics and outpaces the nation's 37.7 million black

FIGURE 6.1   Percent Change in Black or African-American Population: 2000–2010

Source: U.S. Census Bureau, (http://www.census.gov/prod/cen2010/briefs/c2010br-06.pdf).
Note: Countries with a black or African American population of at least 1,000 are included
in the maps. For more information on confidentiality protection, nonsampling error, and
definitions, see www.census.gov/prod/cen2010/doc/pl94-171.pdf.

Americans, the nation's second-largest racial group, by a 5-to-1 margin. For
Census Bureau purposes, blacks are simply described as "a person having origins in any of the black racial groups of Africa." Their ranks have grown, as
shown in Figure 6.1.

White and black, then, is a simple concept for decennial census purposes.
But what about other groups?

Understanding Emerging Groups

Hispanics are currently one of the nation's fastest-growing groups. Between
2000 and 2010, their numbers increased 43 percent, barely surpassed by the
43.3 percent growth over the decade that was registered by Asians. Besides
being one of the nation's fastest-growing groups, Hispanics are also one of the
nation's newest groups, according to the Census Bureau. Hispanics were only
counted in a full decennial census after 1980, when they first had the option
of describing themselves as being "of Spanish origin."[1]

One of the most frequent and vexing issues about the Hispanic population during census years has been the potential for an undercount

because of the illegal residency status of an estimated 9.1 million Hispanics, according to the Department of Homeland Security 2011 figures.[2] Even with significant outreach programs, the government feared in 2010 that a slew of anti-immigration laws in states such as Arizona and Alabama would dissuade Hispanics from cooperating with the Census Bureau, causing some states to lose federal funding, and in some places like New York, a congressional seat. The Census Bureau has long argued that it doesn't release data about individual citizenship to anyone until 72 years after a decennial headcount, but many immigrants (and a large share of the native-born population) don't trust the government. Indeed, in 2000, the bureau estimated it missed counting as many as 3.5 million Hispanics who may have been in the country illegally.[3]

The introduction of "Hispanic" as one of two possible ethnicities (the other being "non-Hispanic") helped improve the counting for the Latino population. It didn't do much to reduce confusion about the difference between race and ethnicity. Every decade, there are millions of people who describe themselves as being "Other" race, instead of white, black, Native, Asian, or Pacific Islander. It's likely that a substantial number of those are Hispanic. In 2010, 21.7 million Americans, or about 1 in every 16, described themselves as "Some other race."

The Census Bureau has tried to clarify the issue, moving the "Ethnicity" question on the census form before the "Race" question in 2000 and releasing instructions in 2010 that emphasized people must include both an ethnicity and a race. More than 60 percent, or 31.8 million of Hispanics in the United States, are of Mexican origin, so they've traditionally chosen "white" as their race. Black Hispanics are much more likely to hail from the Caribbean or parts of South America.

After people of Mexican origin, the greatest number of Hispanic Americans, about 4.6 million, claims Puerto Rican origins, shown in Figure 6.2. The third-largest amount are the 3 million who claim "other Hispanic or Latino" origins, which can include Tejano, Spanish Native, or Caribbean, other than Dominican or Cuban. It's reasonable to assume that based on the lexicon, the third category, which also covers people who describe themselves as Californio and Nuevo Mexicano, represent Americans who have been in the country for some period of time, perhaps generations.

The Census Bureau has an extensive breakdown within the different Hispanic origin categories that captures most potential groups. For example, the "Spaniard" origin includes people who claim Andalusian, Asturian, Castillian, Catalonian, Balearic Islanders, Gallego, Valencian, Canarian, or Spanish Basque origins. The South American category includes people who identify Argentinian, Bolivian, Chilean, Colombian, Ecuadorian, Paraguayan, Peruvian, Uruguayan, Venezuelan, South American Indian, and Criollo origins.

FIGURE 6.2   Hispanic or Latino Population: Origin by Type, 2010

Origin and type	2000 Number	2000 Percent of total	2010 Number	2010 Percent of total	Change, 2000 to 2010 Number	Change, 2000 to 2010 Percent
HISPANIC OR LATINO ORIGIN						
Total	281,421,906	100.0	306,745,538	100.0	27,323,632	9.7
Hispanic or latino	35,305,818	12.5	50,477,594	16.3	15,171,776	43.0
Not Hispanic or latino	246,116,068	87.5	258,267,944	83.7	12,151,856	4.9
HISPANIC OR LATINO BY TYPE						
Total	35,305,818	100.0	50,477,594	100.0	15,171,776	43.0
Mexican	20,640,711	58.5	31,798,258	63.0	11,157,547	54.1
Puerto Rican	3,406,178	9.6	4,623,716	9.2	1,217,538	35.7
Cuban	1,241,685	3.5	1,785,547	3.5	543,862	43.8
Other Hispanic or Latino	10,017,244	28.4	12,270,073	24.3	2,252,829	22.5
Dominican (Dominican Republic)	764,945	2.2	1,414,703	2.8	649,758	84.9
Central American (excludes Mexican)	1,686,937	4.8	3,998,280	7.9	2,311,343	137.0
Costa Rican	68,588	0.2	126,418	0.3	57,830	84.3
Guatemalan	372,487	1.1	1,044,209	2.1	671,722	180.3
Honduran	217,569	0.6	633,401	1.3	415,832	191.1
Nicaraguan	177,684	0.5	348,202	0.7	170,518	96.0
Panamanian	91,723	0.3	165,456	0.3	73,733	80.4
Salvadoran	655,165	1.9	1,648,968	3.3	993,803	151.7
Other Central American	103,721	0.3	31,626	0.1	−72,095	−69.5
South American	1,353,562	3.8	2,769,434	5.5	1,415,872	104.6
Argentinian	100,864	0.3	224,952	0.4	124,088	123.0
Bolivian	42,068	0.1	99,210	0.2	57,142	135.8
Chilean	68,849	0.2	126,810	0.3	57,961	84.2
Colombian	470,684	1.3	906,734	1.8	438,050	93.1
Ecuadorian	260,559	0.7	564,631	1.1	304,072	116.7
Paragvayan	8,769	–	20,023	–	11,254	128.3
Poruvian	233,926	0.7	531,358	1.1	297,432	127.1
Uruguayan	18,804	0.1	56,884	0.1	38,080	202.5
Venezuelan	91,507	0.3	215,023	0.4	123,516	135.0
Other South American	57,532	0.2	21,809	–	−35,723	−62.1
Spaniard	100,135	0.3	635,253	1.3	535,118	534.4
All other Hispanic or Latino	6,111,685	17.3	3,452,403	6.8	−2,659,262	−43.5

Source: Census Bureau, http://www.census.gov/prod/cen2010/briefs/c2010br-04.pdf.

Asian Americans, who originate from the world's largest and most populous continent, were the fastest-growing racial and ethnic group during the first decade of the millennium. Their ranks grew 43.3 percent, slightly faster than Hispanics, and growth patterns are displayed in Figure 6.3. Even though Asians make up nearly 60 percent of the global population, their large numbers are a relatively new development in American demographics. Asian Americans numbered about 16.3 million in 2010, roughly 5.6 percent of the total population. As relative newcomers, the history of Asians in the decennial census is much less complicated than that of Hispanics, or nearly any other racial or ancestral group. Asians first appeared in the 1860 census, when people living in California were allowed to describe themselves as "Chinese" if they were Asian; the answer was expanded to other states a decade later, as well as a "Japanese" category for California. Beginning in 1910, the Census Bureau collected data on Asian subcategories from the "Other" racial category; in 1990, it began presenting racial data for Asians, together with Pacific Islanders, before separating Asians into a more unique category in 2000.

The lack of American experience with substantial numbers of people of Asian origin may be a factor in the simplification of Asian categories. The

FIGURE 6.3 Asian as a Percentage of County Population: 2010

Source: U.S. Census Bureau, *2010 Census Redistricting Data (Public Law 94-171) Summary File*, Table P1.

Census Bureau's code list for the different Asian origins is considerably less complex than those for Hispanics or Native Americans. It includes categories for Asian Indians, Bangladeshis, Bhutanese, Burmese, Cambodian, Tai-wanese, Filipino, Hmong, Indonesian, Japanese, Korean, Laotian, Malaysian, Okinawan, Pakistani, Sri Lankan, Thai, Vietnamese, and other Asian. It also includes less-frequently used codes for Asiatic, Mongolian, Oriental, Whello, Yello, Indo-Chinese, Iwo Jiman, Maldivian, Nepalese, and Singaporean origins.

As with many Census Bureau categories, what's omitted is almost as interesting as what's included. In the case of Asians, it's worth wondering if and when people from the Middle East will be included in the Asian category rather than the current "white" group, as well as people originally from the independent republics created by the 1989 collapse of the Soviet Union, including Kazakhstan, Tajikistan, Uzbekistan, Armenia, Azerbaijan, Turkmenistan, and Kyrgyzstan. And certainly the presence of American troops in Iraq and Afghanistan for the better part of a decade should result in a greater awareness of other categories of Americans who are geographically part of Asia while being tallied with a predominantly European population.

Analyzing Tribal Affiliations

Native Americans have posed considerably more complex challenges for the Census Bureau. They were virtually ignored by the Census Bureau for much of the first century of the country's existence, with no nationwide count until 1890. A special form was created for the 1900 census to inquire if people who described themselves as Natives lived in a fixed or moveable structure (i.e., a teepee or tent) and if they were in a polygamous relationship (illegal in most U.S. jurisdictions). Attempts to count Natives through the next century were hampered by poor efforts on reservations; state-sanctioned racism, such as Virginia's decision to describe all non-white people as "colored" on birth certificates until 1975, making it impossible for generations of Natives to prove their tribal identity; and the federal government's periodic refusal to recognize individual tribes for fear they might launch gambling operations that are sanctioned and sponsored by 43 state governments, as well as the District of Columbia and Puerto Rico.

The National Congress of American Indians cites 565 federally recognized tribes, with 229 in Alaska alone.[4] The Census Bureau reported there were 5.2 million Natives in the United States in 2010, a 26.7 percent increase from the 2000 population. Nearly four of every five Natives now live outside a reservation, as shown in Figure 6.4; the Census Bureau reported in 2010 that

FIGURE 6.4 Native American as Percentage of County Population: 2010

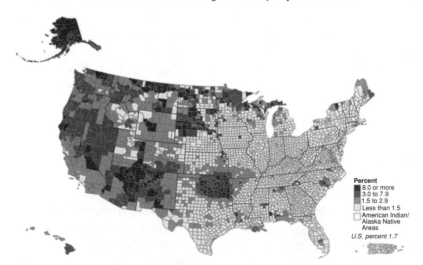

Source: U.S. Census Bureau, *2010 Census Redistricting Data (Public Law 94-171) Summary File*, Table P1, http://www.census.gov/prod/cen2010/briefs/c2010br-10.pdf.

111,749 Natives live in New York—more than any reservation land outside the Navajo Nation in New Mexico, Arizona, and Utah, where 169,321 Natives were reported to live.

As with the Asian and Hispanic groups, the Summary File 2 dataset, released about a year after the first redistricting data are unveiled, is the best source for information on specific Native tribes. The Census Bureau compiles population, housing, relationship, age, and gender data for 114 Native groups, including 60 tribes. More so than with most racial or ethnic groups, extreme caution is advised when attempting to compare results for the Native population across decades. In 2010, for example, the Census Bureau took all "Eskimo" tribal groupings from the 2000 headcount except the Yup'ik and aggregated them into the Inupiat group. The Tlingit-Haida category absorbed several Alaskan tribes that were listed as "Other specified Alaska Native tribes" in the 2000 census.

The Native Hawaiian and Pacific Islander category has had a slightly less convoluted history, given Hawaii's relatively recent ascension to statehood in 1959. One year later, Hawaiians were allowed to describe themselves as "Hawaiian" or "part Hawaiian" for the 1960 census; that question was extended to all states in 1970.

Guamanians and Samoans were added to the Pacific Islander mix in 1980, and a separate "Other Asian or Pacific Islander" category made its debut in 1990. Pacific Islanders were split from the Asian population in 2000, as shown in Table 6.1. By 2010, the Census Bureau was tracking 22 Native Hawaiian and Pacific Islander groups.

Conclusion

Race and ethnicity have been fluid concepts since the first census. Native Americans, for example, weren't counted as Americans until the 1900 census, and significant undercounts have existed in the Hispanic and black populations, even as late as the 2010 census.

The current census racial and ethnic classification scheme establishes seven major racial groups: white, black, Native American, Asian, Pacific Islander, other, and multiracial. These racial groups may be of one ethnicity, Hispanic or non-Hispanic. Despite all these permutations, it's important to recognize that the United States remains a predominantly white, non-Hispanic nation that's not likely to switch to minority status until deep into the twenty-first century.

The Census Bureau maintains especially thorough records for Hispanic and Asian populations, the nation's two fastest-growing significant minority

TABLE 6.1 Native Hawaiian and other Pacific Islander population by detailed group: 2000

Area	1990			2000					
	Total population	Native Hawaiian and other Pacific Islander population		Total Population	Native Hawaiian and other Pacific Islander alone population		Native Hawaiian and other Pacific Islander alone or in combination population		Native Hawaiian and other Pacific Islander in combination population only as a percentage of Native Hawaiian and other Pacific Islander alone or in combination
		Number	Percentage of total population		Number	Percentage of total population	Number	Percentage of total population	
United States	248,709,873	365,024	0.1	281,421,906	398,835	0.1	874,414	0.3	54.4
Region									
Northeast	50,809,229	10,510	–	53,594,378	20,880	–	63,907	0.1	67.3
Midwest	59,668,632	12,666	–	64,392,776	22,492	–	55,364	0.1	59.4
South	85,445,930	28,069	–	100,236,820	51,217	0.1	117,947	0.1	56.6
West	52,786,082	313,779	0.6	63,197,932	304,246	0.5	637,196	1.0	52.3
State									
Alabama	4,040,587	709	–	4,447,100	1,409	–	3,169	0.1	55.5
Alaska	550,043	1,914	0.3	626,932	3,309	0.5	5,515	0.9	40.0
Arizona	3,665,228	3,507	0.1	5,130,632	6,733	0.1	13,415	0.3	49.8
Arkansas	2,350,725	405	–	2,673,400	1,668	0.1	3,129	0.1	46.7
California	29,760,021	110,599	0.4	33,871,648	116,961	0.3	221,458	0.7	47.2

Colorado	3,294,394	2,740	0.1	4,301,261	4,621	0.1	10,153	0.2	54.5
Connecticut	3,287,116	620	–	3,405,565	1,366	–	4,076	0.1	66.5
Delaware	666,168	169	–	783,600	285	–	671	0.1	57.8
District of Columbia	606,900	291	–	572,059	348	0.1	785	0.1	55.7
Florida	12,937,926	4,446	–	15,982,373	8,625	0.1	23,998	0.2	64.1
Georgia	6,478,216	2,017	–	8,186,453	4,245	0.1	9,689	0.1	56.2
Hawaii	1,108,229	162,269	14.6	1,211,537	113,539	9.4	282,667	23.3	59.8
Idaho	1,006,749	873	0.1	1,293,953	1,303	0.1	2,847	0.2	54.1
Illinois	11,430,602	2,742	–	12,419,293	4,613	–	11,848	0.1	61.1
Indiana	5,544,159	957	–	6,080,485	2,005	–	4,367	0.1	54.1
Iowa	2,776,755	435	–	2,926,324	1,009	–	2,196	0.1	54.1
Kansas	2,477,574	1,042	–	2,688,418	1,313	–	3,117	0.1	57.9
Kentucky	3,685,296	829	–	4,041,769	1,460	–	3,162	0.1	53.8
Louisiana	4,219,973	926	–	4,468,976	1,240	–	3,237	0.1	61.7
Maine	1,227,928	233	–	1,274,923	382	–	792	0.1	51.8
Maryland	4,781,468	1,571	–	5,296,486	2,303	–	6,179	0.1	62.7
Massachusetts	6,016,425	1,255	–	6,349,057	2,489	–	8,704	0.1	71.4
Michigan	9,295,297	1,482	–	9,938,444	2,692	–	7,276	0.1	63.0
Minnesota	4,375,099	934	–	4,919,479	1,979	–	5,867	0.1	66.3

(*Continued*)

TABLE 6.1 (*Continued*)

Area	1990 Total population	Native Hawaiian and other Pacific Islander population Number	Percentage of total population	2000 Total Population	Native Hawaiian and other Pacific Islander alone population Number	Percentage of total population	Native Hawaiian and other Pacific Islander alone or in combination population Number	Percentage of total population	Native Hawaiian and other Pacific Islander in combination population only as a percentage of Native Hawaiian and other Pacific Islander alone or in combination
Mississippi	2,573,216	337	–	2,844,658	667	–	1,901	0.1	64.9
Missouri	5,117,073	2,006	–	5,595,211	3,178	0.1	6,635	0.1	52.1
Montana	799,065	301	–	902,195	470	0.1	1,077	0.1	56.4
Nebraska	1,578,385	477	–	1,711,263	836	–	1,733	0.1	51.8
Nevada	1,201,833	2,895	0.2	1,998,257	8,426	0.4	16,234	0.8	48.1
New Hampshire	1,109,252	222	–	1,235,786	371	–	777	0.1	52.3
New Jersey	7,730,188	1,682	–	8,414,350	3,329	–	10,065	0.1	66.9
New Mexico	1,515,069	761	0.1	1,819,046	1,503	0.1	3,069	0.2	51.0
New York	17,990,455	4,457	–	18,976,457	8,818	–	28,612	0.2	69.2
North Carolina	6,628,637	2,196	–	8,049,313	3,983	–	8,574	0.1	53.5
North Dakota	638,800	145	–	642,200	230	–	475	0.1	51.6
Ohio	10,847,115	1,456	–	11,353,140	2,749	–	6,984	0.1	60.6

Oklahoma	3,145,585	1,561	–	3,450,654	2,372	0.1	5,123	0.1	53.7
Oregon	2,842,321	5,037	0.2	3,421,399	7,976	0.2	16,019	0.5	50.2
Pennsylvania	11,881,643	1,654	–	12,281,054	3,417	–	8,790	0.1	61.1
Rhode Island	1,003,464	305	–	1,048,319	567	0.1	1,783	0.2	68.2
South Carolina	3,486,703	983	–	4,012,012	1,628	–	3,778	0.1	56.9
South Dakota	696,004	185	–	754,844	261	–	556	0.1	53.1
Tennessee	4,877,185	895	–	5,689,283	2,205	–	4,587	0.1	51.9
Texas	16,986,510	7,541	–	20,851,820	14,434	0.1	29,094	0.1	50.4
Utah	1,722,850	7,675	0.4	2,233,169	15,145	0.7	21,367	1.0	29.1
Vermont	562,758	81	–	608,827	141	–	308	0.1	54.2
Virginia	6,187,358	3,017	–	7,078,515	3,946	0.1	9,984	0.1	60.5
Washington	4,866,692	15,040	0.3	5,894,121	23,953	0.4	42,761	0.7	44.0
West Virginia	1,793,477	176	–	1,808,344	400	–	887	–	54.9
Wisconsin	4,891,769	801	–	5,363,675	1,630	–	4,310	0.1	62.2
Wyoming	453,588	168	–	493,782	302	0.1	614	0.1	50.8
Puerto Rico	3,522,037	(X)	(X)	3,808,610	1,093	–	2,894	0.1	62.2

For information on confidentiality protection, nonsampling error, and definitions, see www.census.gov/prod/cen2000/doc/sf1.pdf. – Percentage rounds to 0.0. X Not applicable.
Source: U.S. Census Bureau, Census 2000 Summary File 1; 1990 Census of Population, General Population Characteristics: United States (1990 CP-1).

groups. Members of both groups can describe their heritage to a specific degree, ranging from Uruguayan to Okinawan.

Because of changing attitudes about race, it's often difficult to compare changes in different racial and ethnic populations over a lengthy period of time. Native American tribal affiliations are a particularly difficult issue, because smaller tribes are often absorbed into larger ones and often simply vanish because of intermarriage and a heritage of bureaucratic abuse and neglect.

Notes

1. Roland Chilton and Gordon F. Sutton, "Classification by Race and Spanish Origin in the 1980 Census and Its Impact on White and Nonwhite Rates," *The American Statistician* 40, no. 3 (August 1986).
2. Michael Hoefer, Nancy Rytina, and Bryan Baker, "Estimates of the Unauthorized Immigrant Population Residing in the United States: January 2011," U.S. Department of Homeland Security, March 2012.
3. U.S. Census Bureau, "Technical Assessment of A.C.E. Revision II," March 12, 2003.
4. National Congress of American Indians, "Annual Report 2010–2011: Toward a New Era," 2011.

PART II

The American Community Survey

CHAPTER 7

Using the American Community Survey

For more than two centuries, the decennial census suffered from a fatal flaw for businesses: The data collected every decade was released months after the official census was taken and then only useful for one or two years. The 2000 census, for example, was taken on April 1; state population numbers used to determine reapportionment were released nearly nine months later. The redistricting data showing basic population from 2000 was still being released a year after the census. Age, gender, housing, and household relationship data were released in summer 2001, and the most complete data, showing economic, social, and demographic characteristics came out in summer 2002, two years after the census was taken. In many places, the data were obsolete almost before they were released. Between April 2000 and August 2002, for example, the United States went from being a prosperous country at peace to a recession-battered country at war.

This isn't just about general trends. A business hoping to expand in Dallas, Texas in 2010 would have been able to determine that the median household in the city made $37,628 in 2000. The business could have used 2000 census Summary File 3 data to break that figure down into neighborhood-sized tracts to figure out the best neighborhood for a new location. That number wouldn't have remained static in the intervening decade, though. It would have taken another two years to get updated information from the 2010 census, by which time actual median household income had grown to $41,682, or 10.8 percent over the decade, less than half as much as the national median household income growth.

There were substitutions, of course. A smart business could cobble together a rough approximation of growth and income patterns by looking at property tax records, building permits, and other public records, but that would take time. Businesses also could (and did) spend large amounts of money on proprietary, third-party data that would provide information about how much people in a certain area spend, and where they spent it. Again, though, this took time and was expensive, as well.

Resolving Expensive Data Collection

The phenomenon of stale data after the 2000 census wasn't the first time that events or the passage of time had overtaken the relevance of the data. In the early 1980s, the Census Bureau recognized the need for more frequent data. Congress authorized funds for a mid-decade survey in 1985, but never appropriated money to pay for it. The biggest barrier was cost: The Summary File 3 data was a gold mine for businesses, but it relied on a survey of one in every six U.S. households that was routinely described by the Census Bureau as the largest peacetime mobilization of federal employees in history. The bureau could certainly pare the number of households surveyed from 15 million to 10 million to about 3 million, but those numbers wouldn't be accurate for many places with fewer than 50,000 people, meaning that nothing would be available for hundreds of U.S. counties, thousands of cities, and even more neighborhood-sized tracts.

Leslie Kish, a Hungarian-American statistician best known for his development of a grid that helps researchers identify members of a household to be interviewed, is given credit for breaking through the dilemma. Kish's idea relied on continuous surveying, with varying degrees of specificity over time.[1] One year of survey results, for example, could certainly cover all states and larger counties. Three years could provide valuable insights into most small and mid-sized places. Five years of data could be used to cover just about all geographic levels down to a tract level with minimal margins of error. To minimize costs, the survey would rely heavily on mailings to gather initial figures; households that didn't respond would be contacted by telephone, with personal visits as a last resort. The rolling survey idea, which gained traction in 1992, aimed to replace the long-form decennial census data that was based on a sample of roughly one in every six American households. The Census Bureau tested the American Community Survey in three dozen counties shown in Figure 7.1 between 1999 and 2001, using the decennial census to measure the accuracy of the survey.

FIGURE 7.1   Test, C2SS, and 2005 Expansion Counties: American Community Survey, 1996 to Present

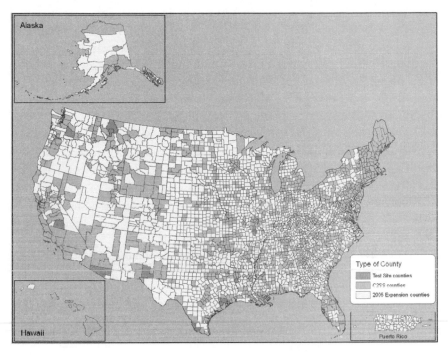

Source: U.S. Census Bureau, http://www.census.gov/history/pdf/ACSHistory.pdf, pages 2–7.

Full implementation of the American Community Survey began in 2005, building up to an annual survey of approximately 3 million U.S. households. Single-year estimates for places with more than 65,000 people were initially released, with a limited series of variables. This was helpful, but not as useful as tract-level data, which generally contains between 3,000 and 8,000 people. Three-year estimates for places with 20,000 or more people were released in 2007, and five-year estimates, making all data available down to the block group level, came out in 2009. The five-year ACS data essentially duplicated the Summary File 3 release, providing data about age, gender, occupation, income, housing, health insurance, marital status, educational attainment, commuting patterns, ancestry, language, home ownership, and housing characteristics. As a general rule, single-year estimates have been released in September; three-year estimates have followed in October; and the five-year estimates have been made available in December.

Understanding Potential Weaknesses

The five-year ACS figures mark an enormous improvement over decennial long-form data. Even so, the figures are subject to different weaknesses. It's not as thorough as the long-form survey; even the five-year ACS data are based on 15 million household surveys, or about 250,000 surveys per month, while the SF3 data from the 2000 census were built upon roughly 20 million households. John Blodgett, a University of Missouri demographer, observes that the survey's accuracy will wane over time because Congress has authorized only a set number of surveys annually, rather than a percentage of households. As the number of households increase, a static number of surveys means a smaller percentage of U.S. households will be reflected in the ACS figures, and the margins of error in the sampling will be greater.[2]

There's also been uncertainty about the inclusion of zip code tabulation areas (ZCTAs) in the American Community Survey. A U.S. Postal Service zip code doesn't represent a spatial geography; it's simply a postal delivery route. Even so, many people associate zip codes with certain neighborhoods or places. The 2000 census contained ZCTAs, which approximated the areas included in an actual zip code, covering the entire country; the 2010 census omitted ZCTAs that were in sparsely populated land areas or water bodies. The current plan calls for ZCTAs to be available in the 2007-2011 estimates.[3]

Congress tinkered further with the American Community Survey by considering making participation voluntary, similar to the decennial census. The Census Bureau considered the idea and tested it, finding that it would add roughly $60 million annually to the cost of the survey. Lawmakers backed off the idea until 2012, when the House of Representatives voted to make the ACS voluntary, then killed funding for it over the protests of researchers, business organizations, and the Census Bureau.[4] As of this writing, funding remained intact in the U.S. Senate.

Blodgett notes that the American Community Survey won't hit its stride until 2015, when nonoverlapping five-year data sets will be available. In other words, researchers will be able to compare the 2005–2009 ACS figures with the 2010–2014 data. While margins of error will still exist, they'll be more predictable and smaller as the Census Bureau obtains more data, following the schedule outlined in Table 7.1.

Modifying Future Surveys

Like the decennial census, too, the American Community Survey will be a work in progress. Since its inception, the Census Bureau has added questions

TABLE 7.1   Data Products Release Schedule

Data product	Population threshold	Year of data release							
		2006	2007	2008	2009	2010	2011	2012	2013
1-year estimates	65,000+	2005	2006	2007	2008	2009	2010	2011	2012
3-year estimates	20,000+			2005–2007	2006–2008	2007–2009	2008–2010	2009–2011	2010–2012
5-year estimates	All areas*					2005–2009	2006–2010	2007–2011	2008–2012

*All legal, administrative, and statistical geographic areas down to the tract and block group level.
Source: U.S. Census Bureau Link: http://www.census.gov/acs/www/Downloads/survey_methodology/acs_design_methodology_ch14.pdf, pages 14–17.

that weren't available from the 2000 Summary File 3 dataset. A major addition has been the presence of a question that began in 2008 to answer how many Americans don't have health insurance. The ACS differs from the Current Population Survey, the other prominent tool used to measure health insurance coverage that relies on a monthly survey of 60,000 households to provide coverage data for large areas, by asking if people have been uninsured at any point in the last year; the Current Population Survey provides a generally lower estimate by asking if people were uninsured during the entire previous year.[5]

The American Community Survey also collected new data about marital status that wasn't initially available, counting the number of single, married, separated, divorced, and widowed people, and asking the number of times that married people had tied the knot. The question, which first appeared in the 2007 ACS single-year estimates, helps community planners develop services for displaced homemakers and children who may need special services.

The worst economic downturn since the Great Depression added urgency to another question about government assistance. As of 2012, roughly one of every seven Americans needed government help to buy food; the ACS began measuring the ranks of people participating in the Supplemental Nutrition Assistance Program (SNAP, formerly known as the Food Stamp Program) to determine where people who needed help were located, and if they had access to grocery stores or farmer's markets.

The Census Bureau dropped one question between 2000 and the 2010 American Community Survey, deciding to refrain from asking if veterans had fewer than two years of military service. The question was removed because veterans traditionally weren't eligible for many benefits if they served less than two years, but so many exceptions had been created as a result of wars in Iraq and Afghanistan that the Veterans Affairs Department didn't consider the figures to be reliable any more. The veterans agency, however, prevailed upon the Census Bureau to include a new 2010 question about service-connected disability ratings.[6]

In 2010, the census began planning for a pair of new questions, including one that would ask for the place of birth of parents, a nod to the foreign origins of many of the nation's fastest-growing groups, Asian- and Hispanic-Americans.[7] The Census Bureau is also testing a question to gauge Internet access, providing valuable detail about disparities in online access.[8] Given that the Census Bureau is considering a multimodal decennial census in 2020 to save money, it seems wise to find the answers before the next tally takes place.

Conclusion

The American Community Survey, launched in 2006, represents a potential solution to the inevitable obsolescence of figures from the decennial census. Before the ACS, key information about housing, income, occupations, and living conditions were obtained from a once-every-decade survey known as the Summary File 3 data. The data was usually released about 18 months after the decennial census and become outdated very quickly.

Because it would be prohibitively expensive to survey as many households as the SF3 file (approximately 20 million in 2000), the ACS uses rolling surveys and adjusts the release of results by size. Three ACS surveys are released annually: a single-year survey that's the most current and covers all places with more than 65,000 people; a three-year survey that covers geographic areas with more than 20,000 people; and a five-year survey that includes all geographic areas larger than a census tract.

The ACS is far from perfect. Because Congress only authorized a set number of households to be surveyed, its usefulness may wane as the population grows. It's also been the subject of ill-informed attacks about privacy and usefulness; a Republican-controlled House of Representatives voted in 2012 to kill the survey, even after traditional GOP allies in business pleaded against its elimination. The U.S. Senate didn't vote on the issue, so the ACS continued to function.

One of the key advantages of the ACS is that its year-to-year nature allows for flexibility with questions and tinkering. Wars in Iraq and Afghanistan spurred the Census Bureau to accept a request from veterans' groups and ask questions about service-connected disabilities. The growing numbers of Asian and Hispanic immigrants have persuaded bureau officials to include a question about the place of parental birth. And curiosity about the possibilities of an online decennial census component appear to be leading up to a new ACS question that would measure the prevalence of online access for different segments of the population.

Notes

1. U.S. Census Bureau, "Design and Methodology: American Community Survey," April 2009.
2. John Blodgett, "The American Community Survey vs. the Decennial Census Long Form: Are We Better Off Than We Were a Decade Ago?" Missouri Census Data Center, June 2009, http://mcdc2.missouri.edu/pub/data/acs/acsVScensus.shtml.
3. U.S. Census Bureau, "A Compass for Understanding and Using American Community Survey Data: What the Business Community Needs to Know," October 2008.
4. Matthew Philips, "Killing the American Community Survey Blinds Business," *Bloomberg Businessweek*, May 10, 2012.
5. State Health Access Data Assistance Center, "Comparing Federal Government Surveys That Count the Uninsured," Robert Wood Johnson Foundation, September 2010.
6. Kelly Ann Holder, "Evaluation of New Content on the 2008 American Community Survey: Service-Connected Disability Status and Ratings," U.S. Census Bureau, August 2009.
7. Larsen, Luke J., Grieco, Elizabeth M., and de la Cruz, Patricia, "2010 ACS Content Test Evaluation Report Covering Parental Place of Birth," U.S. Census Bureau, January 31, 2012.
8. U.S. Department of Commerce, "Exploring the Digital Nation: Computer and Internet Use at Home," November 2011.

CHAPTER 8

Making Sense of Housing

For the early part of the twenty-first century, the $15 trillion U.S. economy revolved around housing. The finance, insurance, and real estate, or FIRE, sector made up barely 10 percent of the national economy in 1947. By 2007, its share had doubled, and about $1 of every $5 spent or produced in the United States involved housing or finance.[1] Mortgage loans drove the bulk of the finance and insurance industry, from simple, fixed-rate 30-year loans to complex tranches of subprime mortgages that were packaged and sold to investors around the planet. The real estate boom of the earliest years pulled the nation out of a recession complicated by an Internet bust and terror attacks on New York and Washington, with explosive growth in the Southwest and California over the decade shown in Figure 8.1. Consumers bought furniture and other durable goods for their homes, as well as cars (and sport utility vehicles) to go from their homes to work, and back again, and food from restaurants and groceries that popped up at increasingly great distances from cities. The explosive growth in housing in places like Phoenix and Las Vegas drove government spending on new schools, highways, health care, and other public services. Larger houses and bigger cars meant increasing consumption of oil, taken to such an extreme that traditional food sources were distilled into gasoline to help fuel the housing bubble.

At the same time, the real estate boom set the table for a near-catastrophic economic meltdown in fall 2008. Because so many industries were so dependent on a never-ending, constantly expanding real estate bubble, the collapse of Lehman Brothers investment bank in October sent the stock market into a tailspin. The lack of confidence in the economy dried up credit for consumers and businesses, and the economy began grinding to a halt. Eventually, the

FIGURE 8.1   Housing Unit Change, 2000–2010

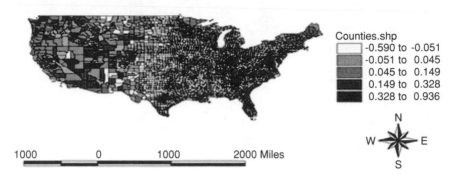

Source: U.S. Census Bureau, 2006–2010 American Community Survey.

government would both covertly and overtly put taxpayers on the hook for staggering amounts of money to restore confidence in the nation's financial system and pass a stimulus bill valued at more than $800 billion to curb unemployment, which flirted with real levels not seen since the Great Depression.

Real unemployment soared well into the double digits. Millions lost homes. Small businesses, the primary provider of jobs in the nation, shut down. More than one in seven Americans needed government aid to put food on the table, and even more were left without reliable health insurance. Traditionally stable employers such as hospitals, schools, and other government agencies shed employees, and record numbers of young people returned to live with their parents, unable to find jobs. The National Bureau of Economic Research claimed the worst economic downturn since the Great Depression lasted 18 months; millions of Americans were still feeling the pain from the near-collapse more than four years after Lehman.

Comparing ACS Housing Data with Decennial Census

A researcher relying only on decennial census data to deconstruct the housing collapse would have noticed two things. First, the researcher would have seen explosive growth in the number of housing units during the decade. Then, it would appear that housing values helped drive the economy. Between 2000 and 2010, the median value of a U.S. home soared to $188,400, up 68 percent from $111,800—hardly the story of an economic collapse shown in Figure 8.2.[2] A closer look, however, would have revealed a 3 percent drop in those prices between 2007 and 2010. Given the tendency of homeowners to inflate the estimated value of their homes and the far-from-perfect nature

FIGURE 8.2 Median Value Changes, 2000–2010

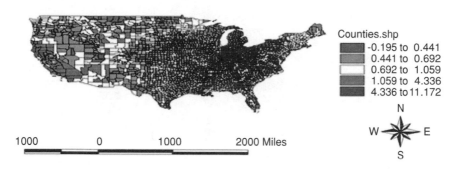

Counties.shp
-0.195 to 0.441
0.441 to 0.692
0.692 to 1.059
1.059 to 4.336
4.336 to 11.172

N
W — E
S

1000   0   1000   2000 Miles

Source: U.S. Census Bureau, 2006–2010 American Community Survey.

of real estate appraisal, it's likely that a smart researcher could have understood a small portion of the calamity that has continued to reverberate throughout the U.S. economy.

Even given the economic struggles taking place in the young century, businesses needed information about the housing market. As the United States struggled to escape the recession in 2011, the Federal Reserve Board estimated the value of the nation's residential real estate market at roughly $16 trillion, or more than twice the amount of outstanding corporate debt.

The American Community Survey was a slowly developing concept during the first decade of the 2000s. And as it's been shown by the slight drop in real estate values during the recession, many of its questions are in need of refinement. Yet its value won't just be eventually measured in timeliness; the ACS also asks detailed questions that aren't available in the decennial census' Summary File 1 release, which is limited to about a dozen homeownership questions. Because of the size of the housing economy, these annual figures remain one of the most important barometers of economic well-being across the country for simple economic reasons. Homeowners tend to be more affluent than renters; a decline in homeownership is a potential indicator of a neighborhood in economic trouble. Conversely, an increase in the number of housing units in a neighborhood can serve as an indicator of economic improvement, and a large percentage of homeowners can indicate a healthy economy as shown in Figure 8.3.

Assessing Populations with Housing Data

A closely related housing barometer is the status of the homes. The American Community Survey establishes if the homes are occupied by owners or renters,

FIGURE 8.3   Ownership change, 2000–2010

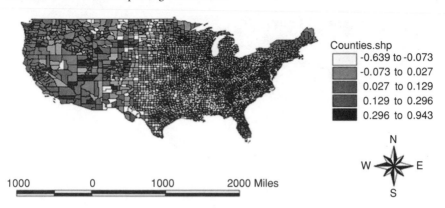

Source: U.S. Census Bureau, 2006–2010 American Community Survey.

as well as whether vacant homes are meant to be occupied by owners or renters. This is particularly useful information at census tract levels that can be mined from the five-year ACS releases and helps researchers gauge the economic strength of a given area.

Questions involving monthly housing costs are another important canary-in-the-coal-mine question asked as part of the survey. The Census Bureau asks a series of questions shown in Figure 8.4 that are designed to provide a complete picture of an area's housing market, beginning with the type of housing units available. A housing unit can be defined as a single-family home; apartment or condominium; mobile home; or even a recreational vehicle or boat.

The ACS asks the age of the house. In the 2012 survey, it allowed households to set the age of the unit in decade-long intervals, back to 1940. The age of housing has been a useful indicator for government programs that have provided funding for public safety issues ranging from removing lead paint from homes to protect children to weatherizing older homes to maximize energy efficiency. Besides being helpful for government programs, knowing the age of housing stock in an area can be a gold mine for nearly any contractor, hardware provider, or financial institution looking to expand. Older homes need a lot more work than new homes, and depending on the neighborhood, their value can fluctuate rapidly, creating mini-booms and busts that are independent of the larger economy.

A newer question in the ACS deals with property acreage; if the housing unit is located on more than one acre, the Census Bureau asks for the sales

FIGURE 8.4 American Community Survey housing questions, 2010

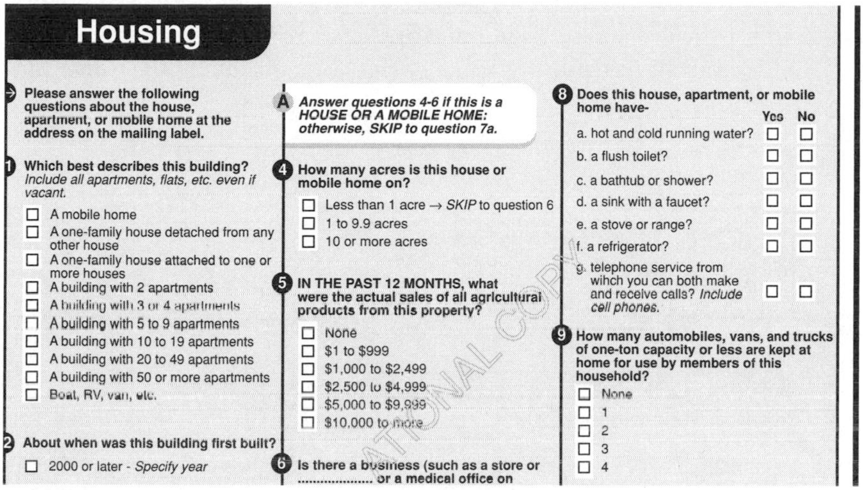

Housing

➔ **Please answer the following questions about the house, apartment, or mobile home at the address on the mailing label.**

1 **Which best describes this building?** *Include all apartments, flats, etc. even if vacant.*
- ☐ A mobile home
- ☐ A one-family house detached from any other house
- ☐ A one-family house attached to one or more houses
- ☐ A building with 2 apartments
- ☐ A building with 3 or 4 apartments
- ☐ A building with 5 to 9 apartments
- ☐ A building with 10 to 19 apartments
- ☐ A building with 20 to 49 apartments
- ☐ A building with 50 or more apartments
- ☐ Boat, RV, van, etc.

2 **About when was this building first built?**
- ☐ 2000 or later - *Specify year*

A *Answer questions 4-6 if this is a HOUSE OR A MOBILE HOME: otherwise, SKIP to question 7a.*

4 **How many acres is this house or mobile home on?**
- ☐ Less than 1 acre → *SKIP* to question 6
- ☐ 1 to 9.9 acres
- ☐ 10 or more acres

5 **IN THE PAST 12 MONTHS, what were the actual sales of all agricultural products from this property?**
- ☐ None
- ☐ $1 to $999
- ☐ $1,000 to $2,499
- ☐ $2,500 to $4,999
- ☐ $5,000 to $9,999
- ☐ $10,000 to more

6 **Is there a business (such as a store or .... or a medical office on**

8 **Does this house, apartment, or mobile home have-**

	Yes	No
a. hot and cold running water?	☐	☐
b. a flush toilet?	☐	☐
c. a bathtub or shower?	☐	☐
d. a sink with a faucet?	☐	☐
e. a stove or range?	☐	☐
f. a refrigerator?	☐	☐
g. telephone service from wihch you can both make and receive calls? *Include cell phones.*	☐	☐

9 **How many automobiles, vans, and trucks of one-ton capacity or less are kept at home for use by members of this household?**
- ☐ None
- ☐ 1
- ☐ 2
- ☐ 3
- ☐ 4

Source: U.S. Census Bureau, http://www.census.gov/acs/www/Downloads/questionnaires/2011/Quest11.pdf.

total of agricultural products. Given the propensity for the real estate industry to overbuild in the early part of the century, with "McMansions" springing up on large lots in subdivisions like mushrooms after heavy summer rains, fewer properties on more than an acre are working farms. The question can help identify farms, though, which is valuable information for any agricultural business. Agriculture only provides a little more than 1 percent of U.S. GDP; it still provides 100 percent of its food. The Census Bureau also provides annual information about farms that's not readily available from the U.S. Department of Agriculture, which only collects widespread farm information every five years.[3]

The ACS housing section also asks if businesses are attached to housing units; the number of rooms, excluding bathrooms, halls, and unfinished basements, within a home; the number of bedrooms; and whether the home has full plumbing and kitchen facilities, as well as telephone service. (In a nod to the wireless realities of the twenty-first century, cell phones count as telephone service.) The inclusion of questions about the availability of running water and flush toilets may seem at first blush to be a remnant of 1960s Appalachian antipoverty programs. There's still good reason to ask, and the "complete plumbing facilities" question has traditionally yielded a result that can be surprising to people living in the Lower 48: Alaska always has the lowest rate of completely plumbed homes, primarily because its cold temperatures make it difficult for owners to have individual wells and septic tanks, or for small towns to build municipal sewage and water systems.

The Census Bureau asks the value of the home, breaking the values into increments:

Less than $50,000
$50,000 to $99,999
$100,000 to $149,999
$150,000 to $199,999
$200,000 to $299,999
$300,000 to $499,999
$500,000 to $999,999
$1,000,000 or more

The median value is also included in the ACS housing section. It's good information to have, although there are a number of caveats. One of the biggest issues with the ACS housing value questions is that they rely heavily on the person being surveyed to provide accurate information. In many cases, home owners either don't actually know the value of their home or, post–housing market collapse, haven't acknowledged the amount of lost value in their largest investment. Even with controls to ensure that housing values aren't skewed by a few incorrect answers, the median home value should be taken with a grain of salt.

Using Ancillary Figures for Insight

Other questions included in the housing section cross the line between real estate and other industries, asking how many vehicles are available for each household, ranging from none to six or more, and surveying households for their primary source of heating fuel. The vast majority of U.S. homes heat with municipal gas, although it's interesting to note that wood is a primary source of fuel for many areas of the Rocky Mountains and New England. The ACS expands on this question by asking the monthly cost of home heating fuel, as well as the monthly cost of electricity and gas.

A series of questions about monthly housing costs can be valuable for businesses, especially when combined with income data. The Census Bureau asks if the home is rented, mortgaged, or owned free and clear. As a general rule, homes that are owned without mortgages are in older neighborhoods, which are useful data for businesses that focus on an older clientele, such as health care. If the home is rented, the ACS asks for monthly rent. Homeowners are asked to provide their monthly mortgage amounts, as well as the costs of property taxes and hazard insurance. The Census Bureau also asks if the homeowner has a second mortgage or equity loan on a housing unit. The existence of multiple second mortgages and home equity loans was a particular problem during the housing bubble of the 2000s, with tens of thousands of new homeowners amassing debt by taking out second mortgages on homes that had skyrocketed in value during the boom. The heavily mortgaged homeowners found it impossible to maintain payments when the housing bubble collapsed; it was financially advantageous to walk away from the properties, leading to a glut of abandoned homes that depressed property values across the nation.

One of the most valuable pieces of housing-related information for businesses comes from a table that the Census Bureau generates using a combination of income and mortgage or rent plus other housing costs. The table displays the percentage of income devoted to housing costs within a geographic area, such as the Texas example in Figure 8.3. The data are broken into quintiles, ranging from less than 20 percent to more than 35 percent. The data are also broken out by income levels, so it's possible to determine how many people who earn more than $100,000 are spending between 30 and 35 percent of their income on housing. This is an especially useful bit of data for businesses looking for neighborhoods or areas where people may have more disposable income than the average American. It can also help determine neighborhoods where homeowners may be financially overextended as a result of housing costs; traditionally, the costs of housing shouldn't run more than a third of household income. The ACS also includes another potential barometer, calculating the ratio of home values to household income. The bottom range of the ratio is two or less; the top end is four, meaning that someone's house is worth four times their annual income.

Conclusion

Given the size of the housing market in the U.S. economy, annual figures provided by the American Community Survey are a crucial piece of intelligence for anyone seeking to do business in the country. At its peak during the first decade of the new millennium, the housing industry and related businesses made up one-fifth of the nation's gross domestic product. Even after the collapse of the market in 2008, housing plays a key role in the economy.

FIGURE 8.5 Median Selected Monthly Owner Costs as Percentage of Income in Texas: 2010

| B25092 | MEDIAN SELECTED MONTHLY OWNER COSTS AS A PERCENTAGE OF HOUSEHOLD IN THE PAST 12 MONTHS
Universe: Owner-occupied housing units
2006-2010 American Community Survey 5-Year Estimates |

Thematic Map of Estimate; Median selected monthly owner costs as a percentage of household income in the past 12 months-- - Housing units with a mortgage

Geography by: County

> Supporting documentation on code lists, subject definitions, data accuracy, and statistical testing can be found on the american community survey website in the Data and Documentation section.
>
> Sample size and data quality measures (Including coverage rates, allocation rates, and response rates) can be found on the American Communitty survey website in the Methodology section.
>
> Although the American Community survey (ACS) produces population, demographic and housing unit estimates, for 2010, the 2010 Census provides the offical counts of the population and housing units for the nation, states, counties, cities and towns. For 2005 to 2009, the Population Estimates Program provides Intercensal estimates of the population for the nation, states, and counties.

Legend:
Data Classes
☐ 14.5–17.7
☐ 17.9–20.3
☐ 20.4–22.4
■ 22.5–25.2
■ 25.6–31.9
Boundaries
    State
    'to County
Features
    Major Road
    Street
    Stream/Waterbody
Items in grey text are not visbal at this zoom level

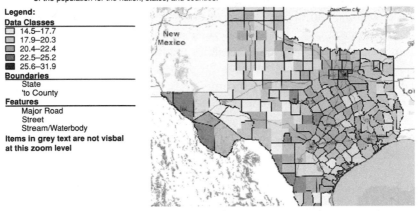

Data are based on a sample and are subject to sampling variabilty. The degree of uncertainty for an estimate arising from sampling variability is represented through the use of a margin of error. The value shown here is the 90 percent margin of error. The margin of error can be interpreted roughly as providing a 90 percent probabilty that the interval defined by the estimate minus the margin of error and the estimate plus the margin of error (the lower and upper confidence bounds) contains the true value. In addition to sampling variability, the ACS estimates are subject to nonsampling error (for a discussion of nonsampling varlability, see Accuracy of the Data). the effect of nonsampling error is not represented in these tables.

Source: U.S. Census Bureau, American Community Survey.

General housing data can serve as a proxy for the economic affluence and well-being of a community. People who own homes usually have more money than renters, who have more money than people living in mobile homes, who often have more money than those living in group quarters, and so on. The housing stock present in an area can also provide clues about the needs of any given geographical region. The ACS includes questions about age of housing units, acreage, and facilities, such as kitchen and plumbing availability.

Housing value is also extensively discussed in the survey. Although the owner-provided estimates of housing value tend to be overstated, the Census Bureau provides a wide variety of possible ranges, reducing the probability of excessive inflation. The ACS asks questions about mortgage status, home equity loans, and monthly ownership costs as a percentage of income.

A number of tangential housing issues are also raised, such as the type of home heat used, as well as the average costs of electricity and other utilities. People analyzing the annual survey data may also rely on other data, such as the number of vehicles owned, estimated property taxes, and ownership by income quintile to assess business opportunities within an area.

Notes

1. Global Macro Monitor, "America's FIRE Economy," http://macromon.wordpress.com/2011/02/03/americas-fire-economy/.
2. Frank Bass, based on calculations from 2000 Summary File 3 Census of Population and Housing, 2006–2010 American Community Survey.
3. U.S. Department of Agriculture, "2007 Census of Agriculture," February 2009.

CHAPTER 9

Learning about Education

Americans' love affair with education began with the founding of Harvard College in 1636. Millions of people have viewed the nation's schools as the ticket to a better life, or at least a better career. The importance of education was promoted heavily in the early 1980s, when manufacturing jobs that didn't require a college degree began disappearing, the victim of technology, a greater focus on corporate profits, and the shift to a service-based economy. The costs of a four-year college education soared from roughly $10,000 for tuition, room, and board to $40,000 or more at public universities. Even in the middle of a recession, students were willing to borrow tens of thousands of dollars to afford undergraduate and graduate school.

Education wasn't always so important when the United States was primarily an agrarian society, or even when it began moving into manufacturing. The first reference to education came in the 1840 census, when the government simply asked if people were illiterate (more than 1 in 5 responses, which didn't include Natives or slaves, came from Americans who couldn't read and write).[1] The Census Bureau began collecting data about educational attainment in 1940, when only 5 percent of the nation's population had college degrees as shown in Figure 9.1. By 2010, the number was approaching 30 percent. A college degree was viewed as the sine qua non for a comfortable middle-class existence, as high-wage jobs that had once been available to young people without a college degree were disappearing rapidly.

The expansion of education has caused a correlating increase in federal, state, and local activity. Chances are good that schools in your area are funded primarily by local taxes, with substantial help from the federal government. The federal government sets aside roughly $1 of every $25 in federal tax

FIGURE 9.1 Percentage of the Population 25 years and Over Who Have Completed High
School or College: Selected Years 1940–2009

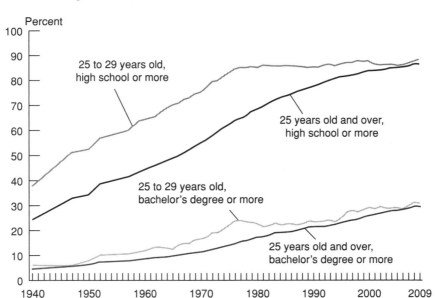

Source: U.S. Census Bureau, http://www.census.gov/prod/2012pubs/p20-566.pdf, page 3.

dollars for education, including school meals, programs for disadvantaged
children, Pell grants, and subsidized loans. All told, the United States now
spends about $500 billion annually on public schools alone. More than 90
percent is split fairly evenly between state and local governments.[2]

Correlating Education and Economic Achievement

This data is useful for governments that need to plan the best places for
schools, the best services for children, and the best return on investments in
loans and grants. It can also be extremely useful for businesses looking for
neighborhoods with large numbers of children, or areas where a significant
percentage of the population has college degrees, or places where parents are
likely to spend money on educating their children. Education can be a proxy
for a number of economic variables because it has strong correlations to wealth
and income. In a 2012 report, the Census Bureau reported that earnings for a
college graduate were 77 percent higher than earnings for someone who had
only a high school diploma. Earnings for people with advanced degrees were

TABLE 9.1 Greatest Earnings Gaps between High School Dropouts and College Graduates, 2009

Geography	Population older than 25	Median earnings	No high school diploma, median earnings	College degree, median earnings
San Jose-Sunnyvale-Santa Clara, CA Metro Area	1,195,158	$50,339	$21,863	$70,054
Lexington Park, MD Micro Area	64,802	$50,761	$27,037	$69,227
Bridgeport-Stamford-Norwalk, CT Metro Area	607,347	$47,598	$21,911	$65,680
Washington-Arlington-Alexandria, DC VA MD-WV Metro Area	3,602,253	$51,154	$22,883	$62,701
San Francisco-Oakland-Fremont, CA Metro Area	2,959,736	$46,637	$21,013	$60,583
Trenton-Ewing, NJ Metro Area	241,243	$44,563	$20,358	$59,989
Oxnard-Thousand Oaks-Ventura, CA Metro Area	516,739	$40,978	$19,562	$58,718
Los Alamos, NM Micro Area	12,830	$60,113	$11,250	$58,569
Poughkeepsie-Newburgh-Middletown, NY Metro Area	428,812	$42,463	$21,555	$56,472
Culpeper, VA Micro Area	30,319	$38,371	$21,475	$56,472
Vallejo-Fairfield, CA Metro Area	266,344	$41,804	$20,105	$56,277

Source: U.S. Census Bureau, American Community Survey.

31 percent higher than workers with an undergraduate degree and greater in places shown in Table 9.1.[3]

The American Community Survey has two primary questions involving education. Those two questions, however, serve as a floodgate of information about the social, economic, and demographic makeup of a place. One question involves enrollment; the other asks about attainment, or the level of education achieved.

The first question asks if anyone in the household has attended school in the last three months, and offers two options: public school or public college, and private school or private college and home school. For each person who has attended school, the levels of enrollment are specified; preschool, kindergarten, individual elementary and/or secondary grade, college undergraduate, and graduate school are the available options.

This question has obvious benefits for policy makers and businesses alike. A rapid growth in the number of third graders, for example, might require a new middle or high school. An increase in the number of high school students might influence the location of a youth-oriented business, such as a fast-food restaurant or clothing store. An increasing number of college students might represent an opportunity for apartment construction.

Discovering Geographic Patterns in Educational Attainment

Although the national focus has been rather relentless on the subject of college education, it's worth noting that a substantial number of children do leave school before graduation, often to the detriment of their potential earnings and local economies. A 2010 study by the Alliance for Excellent Education, a Washington-based advocacy group, found that 1.3 million children fail to graduate from high school every year; that's about 7,000 dropouts every school day. More than half of the dropouts are nonwhite or Hispanic, according to the alliance.[4] Enrollment figures within the ACS can raise red flags about local, state, or regional educational systems. A high number of children of school age relative to population, for example, may indicate a higher-than-ordinary number of students who have dropped out of school. A 1993 study by the Census Bureau showed a stark regional pattern summarized in Figure 9.2:[5]

The Census Bureau avoids the potential problem of proportional populations of very small children by limiting the enrollment universe to people over the age of 3, because most toddlers won't be in preschool. The ACS school enrollment figures also are broken out into male and female students, both by private and public schools, as shown in Table 9.2.

School enrollment is only one part of the education equation; it offers a universe of children who will hopefully reach higher levels of academic accomplishment. The end game in the education story is attainment, or how much education people obtain. One of the little-recognized flaws in many surveys of higher education attainment has been the presumption that people who respond that they've spent four years in college have undergraduate degrees. This isn't always the case, and a growing number of college students

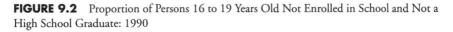

FIGURE 9.2   Proportion of Persons 16 to 19 Years Old Not Enrolled in School and Not a High School Graduate: 1990

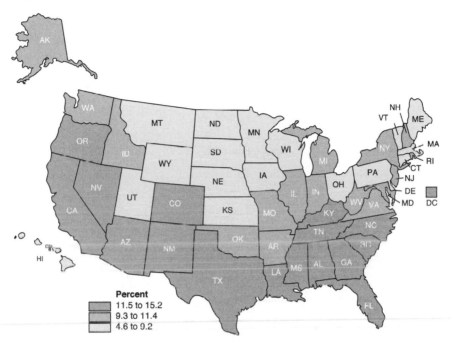

Source: U.S. Census Bureau link, http://www.census.gov/apsd/wepeople/we-11.pdf, page 6.

are spending longer than four years to earn their undergraduate degrees. The ACS resolves part of that issue by segmenting the universe of educational attainment in many tables to the population over 25 years old. Extreme caution should be used in determining the universe of the population when measuring educational attainment, because a good portion of adults—that is, people older than 18—haven't even started college yet, much less completed an undergraduate degree.

The Census Bureau sets out a reasonable grouping for the educational attainment category, with the following categories:

No schooling completed
Nursery or preschool
Kindergarten
Grades 1–11 (individual grades)
Grade 12 (no diploma)
High school graduate

TABLE 9.2   Enrollment by Sex, Grade, and Type of School, 2010

Population	Enrolled in school:	Grade level:	Type school:	291,985,651
Male:				**143,278,658**
Male:	Enrolled in school:			39,877,311
Male:	Enrolled in school:	Enrolled in nursery school, preschool:		2,540,944
Male:	Enrolled in school:	Enrolled in nursery school, preschool:	Public school	1,406,714
Male:	Enrolled in school:	Enrolled in nursery school, preschool:	Private school	1,134,230
Male:	Enrolled in school:	Enrolled in kindergarten:		2,111,194
Male:	Enrolled in school:	Enrolled in kindergarten:	Public school	1,839,133
Male:	Enrolled in school:	Enrolled in kindergarten:	Private school	272,061
Male:	Enrolled in school:	Enrolled in grade 1 to grade 4:		8,251,244
Male:	Enrolled in school:	Enrolled in grade 1 to grade 4:	Public school	7,376,903
Male:	Enrolled in school:	Enrolled in grade 1 to grade 4:	Private school	874,341
Male:	Enrolled in school:	Enrolled in grade 5 to grade 8:		8,471,803
Male:	Enrolled in school:	Enrolled in grade 5 to grade 8:	Public school	7,599,028
Male:	Enrolled in school:	Enrolled in grade 5 to grade 8:	Private school	872,775
Male:	Enrolled in school:	Enrolled in grade 9 to grade 12:		9,004,575
Male:	Enrolled in school:	Enrolled in grade 9 to grade 12:	Public school	8,154,105
Male:	Enrolled in school:	Enrolled in grade 9 to grade 12:	Private school	850,470

(Continued)

Population	Enrolled in school:	Grade level:	Type school:	291,985,651
Male:	Enrolled in school:	Enrolled in college undergraduate years:		7,903,841
Male:	Enrolled in school:	Enrolled in college undergraduate years:	Public school	6,123,271
Male:	Enrolled in school:	Enrolled in college undergraduate years:	Private school	1,780,570
Male:	Enrolled in school:	Enrolled in graduate or professional school:		1,593,710
Male:	Enrolled in school:	Enrolled in graduate or professional school:	Public school	916,120
Male:	Enrolled in school:	Enrolled in graduate or professional school:	Private school	677,590
Male:	Not enrolled in school			103,401,347
Female:				**148,706,993**
Female:	Enrolled in school:			41,061,691
Female:	Enrolled in school:	Enrolled in nursery school, preschool:		2,383,201
Female:	Enrolled in school:	Enrolled in nursery school, preschool:	Public school	1,287,811
Female:	Enrolled in school:	Enrolled in nursery school, preschool:	Private school	1,095,390
Female:	Enrolled in school:	Enrolled in kindergarten:		2,002,655
Female:	Enrolled in school:	Enrolled in kindergarten:	Public school	1,727,451
Female:	Enrolled in school:	Enrolled in kindergarten:	Private school	275,204
Female:	Enrolled in school:	Enrolled in grade 1 to grade 4:		7,840,480
Female:	Enrolled in school:	Enrolled in grade 1 to grade 4:	Public school	6,971,951
Female:	Enrolled in school:	Enrolled in grade 1 to grade 4:	Private school	868,529

(Continued)

TABLE 9.2   (*Continued*)

Population	Enrolled in school:	Grade level:	Type school:	291,985,651
Female:	Enrolled in school:	Enrolled in grade 5 to grade 8:		8,015,281
Female:	Enrolled in school:	Enrolled in grade 5 to grade 8:	Public school	7,148,204
Female:	Enrolled in school:	Enrolled in grade 5 to grade 8:	Private school	867,077
Female:	Enrolled in school:	Enrolled in grade 9 to grade 12:		8,527,606
Female:	Enrolled in school:	Enrolled in grade 9 to grade 12:	Public school	7,709,574
Female:	Enrolled in school:	Enrolled in grade 9 to grade 12:	Private school	818,032
Female:	Enrolled in school:	Enrolled in college undergraduate years:		10,037,928
Female:	Enrolled in school:	Enrolled in college undergraduate years:	Public school	7,705,169
Female:	Enrolled in school:	Enrolled in college undergraduate years:	Private school	2,332,759
Female:	Enrolled in school:	Enrolled in graduate or professional school:		2,254,540
Female:	Enrolled in school:	Enrolled in graduate or professional school:	Public school	1,348,393
Female:	Enrolled in school:	Enrolled in graduate or professional school:	Private school	906,147
Female:	Not enrolled in school			107,645,302

Source: U.S. Census Bureau, American Community Survey, 2006–2010.

General equivalency degree
Less than one year of college
More than one year of college, no degree
Associate's degree
Bachelor's degree
Master's degree
Professional degree (such as law or medicine)
Doctoral degree

FIGURE 9.3   Percentage of the Population 25 Years and Over Who have Completed a Bachelor's Degree or More: 2005–2009

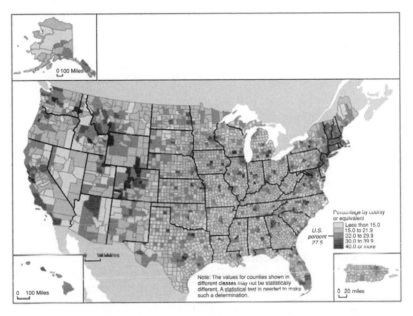

Source: U.S. Census Bureau link, http://www.census.gov/prod/2012pubs/p20-566.pdf, page 8.

As a general rule, it's very difficult to tease out much more than the basic grade levels on American FactFinder without delving into microdata. Even so, the general groupings—less than twelfth grade, twelfth grade but no diploma, high school graduate, associate's degree, bachelor's, and graduate or professional degree—are adequate for most research.

Obviously, geographic patterns can help businesses determine the educational composition of potential customers or workers. A map shows extreme regional concentrations of people with bachelor's or master's degrees, usually clustered around state capitals and major university towns. As always, care should be taken to consider both the numeric and percentage figures involved in measuring educational attainment, because small counties, including many shown in Figure 9.3, may have a sizeable percentage of high school or college graduates without a large actual number of high school or college graduates.

Assessing Strengths and Shortcomings of ACS Education Data

The ACS, unfortunately, doesn't completely specify the type of higher education degrees obtained by undergraduate and graduate students, although it now includes a field of study question for a first bachelor's degree. The question was included after years of lobbying by organizations that included the National Science Foundation.[6] The written answer helps define parameters, although there are also other venues for the data, such as the National Center for Education Statistics' Integrated Postsecondary Education Data System (IPEDS) if the responses prove unwieldy or inaccurate.

Even without detailed data on fields of study, the Census Bureau has sliced the educational attainment data into more than two dozen tables. The key tables, which are generally the broadest measures of gauging educational accomplishment, break out attainment by gender and race and/or ethnicity. The series allows geographic comparisons for white, non-Hispanic, Hispanic, black, Asian, Native, Pacific Islander, other, and multiracial Americans over 25 years old.

The American Community Survey also attempts to measure the politically sensitive issue of native-born American educational levels. The Census Bureau reports general educational attainment numbers for the total population; people born in their state of residence; people born in a state other than their residence; Americans born outside the country; and the foreign-born population. The latter category is currently the source of much controversy, given the concern about the perceived failure of the U.S. educational system to generate more scientists, mathematicians, and engineers, particularly at the postgraduate level. Assessing the relative worth of educational credentials in the United States and other countries, however, is a task far beyond the scope of the annual survey.

The Census Bureau provides educational attainment figures for a number of special populations, including veterans and women. The issue of education for mothers is another sensitive subject, both politically and economically. The ACS includes data showing educational attainment for women between the ages of 15 and 50 who have had a child born in the most recent year. The figures break the female childbearing population down further, specifying marital status (married or single, including divorced or widowed). For example, an American FactFinder-generated map shown in Figure 9.4 of single, divorced, or widowed mothers with advanced degrees and newborn babies shows there are some regional patterns.

Tables showing median earnings by education are among the most useful elements in the educational attainment series for policy makers and businesses. From a policy standpoint, this information helps determine where job training and educational assistance funds should be directed. From a business standpoint, the data can represent real dangers or opportunities. Businesses relying on low-skilled labor, for example, might want to locate someplace

FIGURE 9.4   Women Who Had a Birth in the Past 12 months: Unmarried (Never Married, Widowed, and Divorced), Graduate or Professional Degree, by State

Source: U.S. Census Bureau, American Community Survey, 2006–2010.

where there's a surplus of underpaid high school graduates. Companies that need well-educated workers might want to consider entering a market where there are already lots of well-paid people with college graduate degrees. Geographic variation tends to be substantial, as shown in Table 9.3.

Conclusion

Educational attainment in the United States correlates highly to economic status. People with advanced degrees earn more than those who fail to complete high school by tens of thousands of dollars annually. This correlation can prove extremely useful for people trying to start, maintain, or expand businesses within a given geographic area.

The ACS also includes data that can assist employers in finding concentrations of appropriately educated workers. After years of lobbying by the National Science Foundation, the Census Bureau has begun asking the field of college major. The Census Bureau also provides useful data about the politically sensitive issue of educational attainment among native- and foreign-born Americans.

TABLE 9.3   Median Earnings by Education, 2010

State	Total population 25 years and over	Less than high school graduate	High school graduate (includes equivalency)	Some college or associate's degree	Bachelor's degree	Graduate or professional degree
Alabama	30,895	17,983	25,316	30,633	44,842	54,292
Alaska	39,694	20,317	31,391	39,174	49,219	64,913
Arizona	34,112	19,968	27,252	33,970	47,454	59,528
Arkansas	28,175	18,826	23,986	28,277	41,485	53,206
California	37,162	19,219	29,040	37,453	54,186	75,544
Colorado	36,696	20,162	29,256	34,480	46,891	60,848
Connecticut	43,324	22,635	32,961	40,326	57,222	73,963
Delaware	37,648	21,350	30,610	36,841	50,002	65,094
District of Columbia	48,881	20,793	29,884	37,607	57,386	80,683
Florida	31,427	18,701	25,583	31,730	43,212	56,747
Georgia	33,285	18,822	26,586	32,436	48,807	61,224
Hawaii	36,048	21,543	29,494	35,132	44,766	60,382
Idaho	29,721	19,461	25,221	28,042	40,201	55,804
Illinois	36,868	20,800	28,271	34,790	50,603	65,145
Indiana	32,303	20,074	27,431	32,167	44,235	57,767
Iowa	32,068	20,134	26,888	31,360	42,115	54,684
Kansas	32,744	20,580	26,155	31,019	43,671	54,727
Kentucky	30,615	17,771	25,600	30,725	42,458	51,646
Louisiana	31,553	18,453	26,360	31,127	43,965	53,740
Maine	31,282	20,314	25,884	30,773	40,254	51,624
Maryland	44,405	22,743	32,701	42,062	56,272	76,400
Massachusetts	42,322	22,348	32,096	38,138	53,381	67,553
Michigan	33,403	18,007	25,862	31,952	47,924	66,034
Minnesota	37,183	20,479	29,006	35,270	48,759	63,035
Mississippi	28,413	17,728	24,067	28,619	40,054	50,923

(Continued)

State	Total population 25 years and over	Less than high school graduate	High school graduate (includes equivalency)	Some college or associate's degree	Bachelor's degree	Graduate or professional degree
Missouri	31,773	18,620	26,045	31,370	42,716	53,491
Montana	28,125	17,651	24,093	26,588	35,133	47,088
Nebraska	31,722	21,463	25,950	30,576	41,794	53,751
Nevada	34,546	24,282	30,639	36,303	45,598	61,699
New Hampshire	38,735	25,294	31,299	36,526	48,370	62,551
New Jersey	44,085	22,061	32,546	41,124	58,392	80,895
New Mexico	30,154	16,841	24,658	29,720	42,203	53,693
New York	38,347	20,020	29,259	36,286	51,933	66,329
North Carolina	31,350	17,927	25,668	30,914	43,914	56,461
North Dakota	31,525	18,416	25,904	30,561	38,667	52,230
Ohio	33,021	18,727	27,078	32,177	46,608	60,809
Oklahoma	30,393	18,544	24,749	30,032	40,897	51,499
Oregon	31,808	19,248	26,210	31,002	42,783	54,506
Pennsylvania	34,670	20,484	27,665	33,815	47,289	63,230
Rhode Island	37,450	22,249	30,273	35,708	50,212	65,726
South Carolina	30,860	18,116	25,600	31,057	42,192	52,373
South Dakota	30,049	19,355	25,271	29,122	36,891	49,501
Tennessee	30,754	18,105	25,293	31,136	43,423	54,189
Texas	32,413	18,064	26,102	33,016	49,462	62,261
Utah	33,554	21,026	27,752	31,595	42,407	61,876
Vermont	32,571	20,605	27,275	31,684	39,855	51,010
Virginia	39,409	21,001	29,064	36,137	53,522	75,613
Washington	37,830	20,481	30,498	35,839	51,102	63,216
West Virginia	29,053	17,689	24,868	28,597	40,128	50,354
Wisconsin	34,080	20,493	28,392	33,081	45,248	58,634
Wyoming	33,734	20,353	30,108	31,871	43,306	54,353
Puerto Rico	17,011	10,505	13,555	16,826	25,658	36,708

Source: U.S. Census Bureau, American Community Survey, 2006–2010.

The Census Bureau provides a series of educational attainment tables for special populations as well, including racial and ethnic groups; veterans; single mothers; and senior citizens.

Notes

1. U.S. Census Bureau, "History: 1840 Overview," http://www.census.gov/history/www/through_the_decades/overview/1840.html.
2. U.S. Department of Education, "Overview: The Federal Role in Education," http://www2.ed.gov/about/overview/fed/role.html.
3. Camille L. Ryan, and Julie Siebens, "Educational Attainment in the United States: 2012," U.S. Census Bureau, February 2012.
4. Alliance for Excellent Education, "Fact Sheet: High School Dropouts in America," September 2010.
5. Robert Kominski, "We the Americans: Our Education," U.S. Census Bureau, September 1993.
6. Julie Siebens and Camille L. Ryan, "Field of Bachelor's Degree in the U.S.: 2009," U.S. Census Bureau, February 2012.

CHAPTER 10

Speaking the Languages

Driven largely by a wave of Hispanic immigration over the last three decades, bilingualism has become a hot-button political and social issue. Almost every year, lawmakers have introduced a constitutional amendment to make English the nation's official language; almost every year, the effort has died. The issue of bilingualism has cropped up at state levels, where legislatures have passed tough laws to discourage illegal immigration, and local levels, where the cost of bilingual education for children from Latin America and Asia has posed budget problems for school districts across the country.

Bilingualism was an issue from the nation's inception. John Adams suggested enshrining English as the nation's official language, but the idea was rejected as being "incompatible with the spirit of freedom." The lack of concern about other languages was widely shared. When the first settlers from England arrived in Jamestown, at least 15 languages with more than 200 variants were spoken in North America. By 1664, at least 18 non-Native languages were spoken on Manhattan Island.[1] Advertisements for runaway slaves in the 1700s praised their multilingual abilities.

The issue of non-English language speakers rose to the fore again in the 1880s, when large numbers of Chinese immigrants joined earlier Italian, German, and Irish refugees. Suspicion about immigrants was fueled by the Spanish-American War in 1898, World War I in 1914–1918, and World War II in 1939–1945. In 1920, a Nebraska school teacher was charged with a crime for reading a Bible story in German to a 10-year-old child.[2] The change from an agriculture-based economy to manufacturing also placed a higher priority on speaking English, or at least a common tongue.

Speaking the Language

English is in little danger of being replaced by Spanish or Chinese. Even so, a knowledge of common languages spoken at home is critical for businesses, especially those needing to reach diverse customers in specific communities. One of every five Americans now speaks a language other than English at home, with the largest share—one of every eight—speaking Spanish at home as shown in Table 10.1.

TABLE 10.1   Detailed Languages Spoken at Home by English-speaking Ability for the Population 5 Years and Older: 2007

Characteristic	Number of speakers	Percentage of speakers of a non-English language	English-speaking ability			
			Very well	Well	Not well	Not at all
Population 5 years and older	280,950,438	(X)	(X)	(X)	(X)	(X)
Spoke only English at home	225,505,953	(X)	(X)	(X)	(X)	(X)
Spoke a language other than English at home	55,444,485	100	55.9	19.8	16.3	8.1
Spanish or Spanish Creole	34,547,077	62.3	52.6	18.3	18.4	10.7
Other Indo-European languages	10,320,730	18.6	67.2	19.6	10.4	2.8
French	1,355,805	2.5	78.2	14.5	6.8	0.4
French Creole	629,019	1.1	56.7	24.3	14.8	4.3
Italian	798,801	1.4	71.8	17.2	9.6	1.4
Portuguese	687,126	1.2	56.6	22	14.9	6.4
German	1,104,354	2	82.8	12.6	4.4	0.3
Yiddish	158,991	0.3	70.3	18.3	9.5	1.9
Other West Germanic languages	270,178	0.5	76.2	19.7	3.4	0.7
Scandinavian languages	134,925	0.2	86.4	11.3	2.2	0.1
Greek	329,825	0.6	73	16.5	9.6	1
Russian	851,174	1.5	49.8	25.2	18.2	6.7
Polish	638,059	1.2	56.8	24	15.2	4.1
Serbo-Croatian	276,550	0.5	58.4	24.4	14.3	2.9
Other Slavic languages	312,109	0.6	61.6	23	12.5	2.9
Armenian	221,865	0.4	55.1	21.7	14.9	8.2

(Continued)

Characteristic	Number of speakers	Percentage of speakers of a non-English language	English-speaking ability			
			Very well	Well	Not well	Not at all
Persian	349,686	0.6	61.7	22.6	12.4	3.3
Gujarati	287,367	0.5	64.1	21.5	10.6	3.9
Hindi	532,911	1	79.6	15.3	4	1.1
Urdu	344,942	0.6	70.1	19.1	8.3	2.4
Other Indic languages	616,147	1.1	61.4	24.4	10.2	4
Other Indo-European languages	420,896	0.8	62.5	22.9	11.5	3.2
Asian and Pacific Island languages	8,325,886	15	51.4	26.2	17	5.4
Chinese	2,464,572	4.5	44.4	25.7	19.6	10.3
Japanese	458,717	0.8	53.8	29.1	15.7	1.4
Korean	1,062,337	1.9	41.8	29.3	24.2	4.7
Mon-Khmer, Cambodian	185,056	0.3	46.3	25.6	21.4	6.7
Hmong	181,069	0.3	52.9	24.1	15.5	7.4
Thai	144,405	0.3	48.4	34.8	14.7	2.1
Laotian	149,045	0.3	51.1	23.5	19.9	5.4
Vietnamese	1,207,004	2.2	39.3	29	25.2	6.5
Other Asian languages	634,608	1.1	70.1	20.2	7.5	2.2
Tagalog	1,480,429	2.7	69	23.8	6.5	0.6
Other Pacific Island languages	358,644	0.7	63.1	26	10	0.8
Other languages	2,250,792	4.1	70.1	19.7	8.1	2.1
Navajo	170,717	0.3	75.3	14.4	7.3	2.9
Other Native American languages	200,560	0.4	86.4	10	3.2	0.4
Hungarian	91,297	0.2	71.6	20	7.3	1
Arabic	767,319	1.4	66.2	22.1	9.7	2
Hebrew	213,576	0.4	81.6	14.7	3.1	0.5
African languages	699,518	1.3	66.2	22.6	8.8	2.3
All other languages	107,805	0.2	62.3	19	11.6	7

For information on confidentiality protection, sampling error, nonsampling error, and definitions, see www.census.gov/acs/www/.
Source: U.S. Census Bureau link, http://www.census.gov/prod/2010pubs/acs-12.pdf, page 7.

The primary linguistic question for the American Community Survey asks respondents about the languages spoken at home for the population over 5 years old. The Census Bureau tracks roughly 380 separate languages:

Jamaican Creole	Serbian	Telugu	Carolinian
Krio	Slovene	Kannada	Chamorro
Hawaiian Pidgin	Lithuanian	Malayalam	Gilbertese
Pidgin	Lettish	Tamil	Kusaiean
Gullah	Armenian	Kurukh	Marshallese
Saramacca	Persian	Munda	Mokilese
German	Pashto	Burushaski	Mortlockese
Pennsylvania Dutch	Kurdish	Chinese	Nauruan
Yiddish	Balochi	Hakka	Palau
Dutch	Tadzhik	Kan, Hsiang	Ponapean
Afrikaans	Ossete	Cantonese	Trukese
Frisian	India N.E.C.	Mandarin	Ulithean
Luxembourgian	Hindi	Fuchow	Woleai-Ulithi
Swedish	Bengali	Formosan	Yapese
Danish	Panjabi	Wu	Melanesian
Norwegian	Marathi	Tibetan	Polynesian
Icelandic	Gujarathi	Burmese	Samoan
Faroese	Bihari	Karen	Tongan
Italian	Rajasthani	Kachin	Niuean
French	Oriya	Thai	Tokelauan
Provencal	Urdu	Mien	Fijian
Patois	Assamese	Hmong	Marquesan
French Creole	Kashmiri	Japanese	Rarotongan
Cajun	Nepali	Korean	Maori
Spanish	Sindhi	Laotian	Nukuoro
Catalonian	Pakistan N.E.C.	Mon-Khmer Cambodian	Hawaiian
Ladino	Sinhalese	Paleo-Siberian	Arabic
Pachuco	Romany	Vietnamese	Hebrew
Portuguese	Finnish	Muong	Syriac
Papia Mentae	Estonian	Buginese	Amharic
Romanian	Lapp	Moluccan	Berber
Rhaeto-Romanic	Hungarian	Indonesian	Chadic
Welsh	Other Uralic Lang.	Achinese	Cushite
Breton	Chuvash	Balinese	Sudanic
Irish Gaelic	Karakalpak	Cham	Nilotic
Scottish Gaelic	Kazakh	Javanese	Nilo-Hamitic
Greek	Kirghiz	Madurese	Nubian
Albanian	Karachay	Malagasy	Saharan
Russian	Uighur	Malay	Nilo-Saharan
Bielorussian	Azerbaijani	Minangkabau	Khoisan
Ukrainian	Turkish	Sundanese	Swahili
Czech	Turkmen	Tagalog	Bantu
Kashubian	Yakut	Bisayan	Mande
Lusatian	Mongolian	Sebuano	Fulani
Polish	Tungus	Pangasinan	Gur

Slovak	Caucasian	Ilocano	Kru, Ibo, Yoruba
Bulgarian	Basque	Bikol	Efik
Macedonian	Dravidian	Pampangan	Mbum (and Related)
Serbocroatian	Brahui	Gorontalo	African
Croatian	Gondi	Micronesian	Aleut
Pacific Gulf Yupik	Kuchin	Tonkawa	Serrano
Eskimo	Upper Kuskokwim	Yuchi	Tubatulabal
Inupik	Tanaina	Crow	Pima
St. Lawrence Island Yupik	Tanana	Hidatsa	Yaqui
Yupik	Tanacross	Mandan	Aztecan
Algonquian	Upper Tanana	Dakota	Sonoran N.E.C.
Arapaho	Tutchone	Chiwere	Picuris
Atsina	Chasta Costa	Winnebago	Tiwa
Blackfoot	Hupa	Kansa	Sandia
Cheyenne	Other Athapascan-Eyak	Omaha	Tewa
Cree	Apache	Osage	Towa
Delaware	Kiowa	Ponca	Zuni
Fox	Navaho	Quapaw	Chinook Jargon
Kickapoo	Eyak	Alabama	American Indian
Menomini	Tlingit	Choctaw	Misumalpan
French Cree	Mountain Maidu	Mikasuki	Mayan Languages
Miami	Northwest Maidu	Hichita	Tarascan
Micmac	Southern Maidu	Koasati	Mapuche
Ojibwa	Coast Miwok	Muskogee	Oto-Manguen
Ottawa	Plains Miwok	Cheremacha	Quechua
Passamaquoddy	Sierra Miwok	Yuki	Aymara
Penobscot	Nomlaki	Wappo	Arawakian
Abnaki	Patwin	Keres	Chibchan
Potawatomi	Wintun	Iroquois	Tupi-Guarani
Shawnee	Foothill North Yokuts	Mohawk	Jicarilla
Wiyot	Tachi	Oneida	Chiricahua
Yurok	Santiam	Onondaga	San Carlos
Kutenai	Siuslaw	Cayuga	Kiowa-Apache
Makah	Klamath	Seneca	Kalispel
Kwakiutl	Nez Perce	Tuscarora	Spokane
Nootka	Sahaptian	Wyandot	Han
Lower Chehalis	Upper Chinook	Cherokee	Ingalit
Upper Chehalis	Tsimshian	Arikara	Koyukon
Clallam	Achumawi	Caddo	Walapai
Coeur d'Alene	Atsugewi	Pawnee	Yavapai
Columbia	Karok	Wichita	Chumash
Cowlitz	Pomo	Comanche	Cahuilla
Salish	Shastan	Mono	Cupeno
Nootsack	Washo	Paiute	Luiseno
Okanogan	Upriver Yuman	Northern Paiute	Athapascan
Puget Sound Salish	Cocomaricopa	Southern Paiute	Ahtena
Quinault	Mohave	Chemehuevi	Upland Yuman
Tillamook	Yuma	Kawaiisu	Havasupai
Twana	Diegueno	Ute	Panamint
Haida	Delta River Yuman	Shoshoni	Hopi

Realistically, very few businesses would need to know how many of their customers speak Nomlaki at home. The Census Bureau collapses most questions into four categories: Spanish, Indo-European, Asian and Pacific Islander, and other languages. The broadest language question asks people if they speak English "very well" or "not very well." Finally, the Census Bureau breaks broad linguistic capability into three major age groups: 5- to 17-year-olds, 18- to 64-year-olds, and people over 65 years old.

Another broad measure breaks down home language by four more measures, including age; citizenship status (native population, foreign-born naturalized citizens, and foreign-born noncitizens); poverty status; and educational attainment, by high school dropout, high school graduate, some college, and college graduate. The ACS also includes language spoken—English only; Spanish, very well or not very well; and other language, very well or not very well—by mode of commuting, including driving a car alone, carpooling, public transportation, walking, other means of transportation, or working at home.

Although the ACS predominantly focuses on "speaks English very well" and "speaks English less than very well," the survey has also tables that include more detailed levels of English-speaking ability. The Census Bureau breaks out the three major age groups (5 to 17, 18 to 64, and older than 65) for Spanish-, Indo-European-, Asian-, and other-language-speaking Americans. The levels of English-speaking ability are broken down into "well," "very well," "not well," and "not at all."

If 380 languages are too many, the three major breakdowns may not be enough for some extremely diverse places. The Los Angeles school district has identified more than 90 specific languages spoken at home by its students.[3] The ACS doesn't go quite that far, but it does make English-speaking skills—speak English very well, or less than very well—for 39 separate languages.

Speak only English	Serbo-Croatian	Hmong
Spanish or Spanish Creole	Other Slavic languages	Thai
French (incl. Patois, Cajun)	Armenian	Laotian
French Creole	Persian	Vietnamese
Italian	Gujarati	Other Asian languages
Portuguese or Portuguese Creole	Hindi	Tagalog

German	Urdu	Other Pacific Island languages
Yiddish	Other Indic languages	Navajo
Other West Germanic languages	Other Indo-European languages	Other Native North American languages
Scandinavian languages	Chinese	Hungarian
Greek	Japanese	Arabic
Russian	Korean	Hebrew
Polish	Mon-Khmer, Cambodian	African languages

Another language issue addressed by the American Community Survey is the concept of linguistic isolation (see Figure 10.1). A linguistically isolated household is defined as a household where no person over 14 years old speaks a language other than English or doesn't speak English very well.[4] Obviously, this information is valuable for businesses trying to reach customers, because most economic decisions within a household are made by people older than 14.

FIGURE 10.1 Percentage of Linguistically Isolated Spanish-Language Households, United States

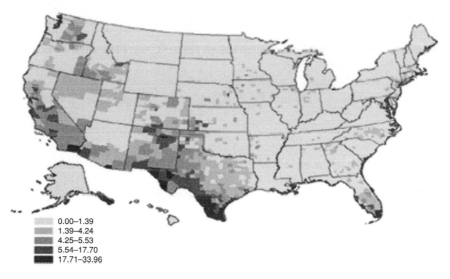

0.00–1.39
1.39–4.24
4.25–5.53
5.54–17.70
17.71–33.96

Source: U.S. Census 2000, page 32.

Conclusion

As the United States becomes less reliant on English as a common language, it's increasingly important to understand which languages are being spoken, and where they're being spoken. Because one in five Americans speak a language other than English at home, the Census Bureau tracks nearly 400 languages spoken by the population.

It's not likely that a significant number of analysts would need to know more than the broad types of languages spoken at home, so the ACS data is presented in broad categories to cover Spanish-, Indo-European-, Asian- and Native-based languages. Within those categories, the Census Bureau provides languages spoken by different age groups, including children, adults, and the elderly. ACS data also provides information about the number of people within different geographic areas who speak English "very well," "well," or "not at all."

The Census Bureau measures linguistic isolation, an obscure but important gauge of assimilation. A linguistically isolated household is defined as one where either no one over the age of 14 speaks English very well, or at all.

Notes

1. Brenda Betts, "Bilingualism in the United States: A Historical Perspective," California State University Stanislaus, Department of Teacher Education, February 14, 2004.
2. *Meyer v. Nebraska*, 262 U.S. 390 (1923).
3. Los Angeles Tourism & Convention Board, "Did You Know?" http://discover losangeles.com/guides/fun-facts/did-you-know.html.
4. Paul Siegel, Elizabeth Martin, and Rosalind Bruno, "Language Use and Linguistic Isolation: Historical Data and Methodological Issues," U.S. Census Bureau, February 12, 2001.

CHAPTER 11

Working with Occupations

In less than a decade, the Census Bureau will begin its second century of collecting data about the work life of Americans. The 1820 census asked only for the number of people in a household who worked in agriculture, commerce, or manufacturing. The American Community Survey has a bit more detail, basing its data on 840 detailed occupations. Like other federal statistical agencies, the Census Bureau uses the Standard Occupational Classification (SOC) system, which collapses those occupations into 461 more narrow jobs, 97 minor groups, and 23 major groups.[1]

The workforce data is important for businesses in at least three major ways. The data can help businesses track emerging businesses and occupations. Twenty years ago, there wasn't an information industry. By 2010, it employed 3.3 million Americans, more than the entire agriculture, forestry, and fishing industries. The industry and occupation data also track pay for occupations, allowing businesses to gauge the employment market and offer fair-market salaries to workers. Finally, the workforce information can be used to research issues that may be interesting to businesses, such as concentrations of certain types of workers in different geographic areas.

One of the largest shortcomings with the ACS workforce data is that it's often overshadowed by the Current Population Survey (CPS), a joint venture sponsored by the Census Bureau and the Bureau of Labor Statistics. The CPS is a monthly survey of roughly 60,000 households, with results released within weeks of the actual survey; the ACS data, which is collected from approximately 250,000 households every month, is released nine months after the end of the previous year. This makes getting occupational data from the BLS and ACS a bit of a trade-off speed against depth, with the BLS monthly surveys being much more timely and the ACS being much more geographically specific.[2]

The two surveys also ask questions differently, leading to occasionally different results. In 2009, the percentage of employed people was 4.5 percent higher in Alabama for the ACS than for the CPS, and 3.2 percent lower in Washington. The largest reasons for the difference are the way the questions are asked and how they're asked. The CPS, for example, asks 16 questions to determine labor force status, whereas the ACS asks only seven. The ACS also relies heavily on mailed questionnaires. The CPS uses trained telephone operators.[3]

Understanding Types of Jobs

The primary ACS question dealing with occupation asks about the type of organization. The types of organization are broken down into eight categories:

1. Private for profit
2. Private not-for-profit
3. Local government
4. State government
5. Federal government
6. Self-employed, incorporated company
7. Self-employed, unincorporated company
8. Working without pay, family business or farm

The ACS also asks the name of the employer or organization. This is done primarily for quality-control purposes; you can't use census data to find out how many people work for ExxonMobil in a given tract, for example, although it is possible to figure out how many people might work in the energy sector.

People are also asked to define the type of activity at their place of work. The question offers examples such as "hospital, newspaper publishing, mail-order house, auto engine manufacturing, bank." The results are standardized for the classification system. The ACS then follows up with a request for a description of the activity:

• Manufacturing
• Wholesale trade
• Retail trade
• Other (agriculture, construction, service, government, other)

Finally, the Census Bureau asks for the specific title and type of work done by the person answering the survey, including examples like "registered nurse, personnel manager, supervisor of order department, secretary, accountant." The occupations are then placed into appropriate occupational classification categories. The 2010 classification includes 840 detailed occupations that are part of 461 broader job occupations. The 461 occupations are broken into 97 minor groups and 23 major groups.

Analyzing occupations over time can be difficult. Between 2000 and 2010, for example, 453 of the 840 detailed occupations had their definitions changed. Twenty-one occupations had a title change, and seven had code changes. The Census Bureau said 392 of the definition changes involved minor editorial revisions.[4] People analyzing data should be extremely cautious and aware of potential changes from year to year to avoid misinterpreting results.

Analyzing Specific Occupations

The occupational changes can cause difficulties for users, but they also can be a mirror on changes in the workforce. During the first decade of the new century, for example, the Census Bureau added about two dozen new occupations:

- Fundraisers
- Information security analysts
- Web developers
- Computer network architects
- Computer network support specialists
- Community health workers
- Special education teachers, preschool
- Special education teachers, all others
- Exercise physiologists
- Nurse anesthetists
- Nurse midwives
- Magnetic resonance imaging technologists
- Ophthalmic medical technicians
- Hearing aid specialists
- Genetic counselors
- Orderlies
- Phlebotomists

- Transportation security screeners
- Morticians, undertakers, and funeral directors
- Financial clerks, all other
- Solar photovoltaic installers
- Wind turbine service technicians
- Food processing workers, all other

The detailed occupational information can be useful, although the highly detailed data such as that shown in Table 11.1 is only available at national levels.

Most occupational data that's available from the ACS on a lower geographical level covers fairly broad categories, such as those shown in Table 11.2.

TABLE 11.1 Detailed Occupation by Median Earnings in the Past 12 Months by full-time, year-round civilian employed female population 16 years and older

	United States	
	Estimate	Margin of Error
Total:	36,121	+/−67
Chief executives	89,842	+/−1,505
General and operations managers	57,343	+/−606
Legislators	50,879	+/−2,055
Advertising and promotions managers	54,057	+/−1,328
Marketing and sales managers	60,755	+/−477
Public relations and fundraising managers	61,831	+/−1,374
Administrative services managers	53,844	+/−1,072
Computer and information systems managers	83,616	+/−1,163
Financial managers	54,152	+/−340
Compensation and benefits managers	59,757	+/−2,003
Human resources managers	61,332	+/−533
Training and development managers	65,587	+/−1,641
Industrial production managers	60,851	+/−1,226
Purchasing managers	59,942	+/−907

Source: U.S. Census Bureau, 2006–2010 American Community Survey.

TABLE 11.2 Occupation by Median Earnings in the Past 12 Months for the Civilian Employed Population 16 Years and Over

Occupation	Median Earnings
Estimate; Total:	$ 32,353
Management, business, science, and arts occupations:	$ 51,277
Management, business, science, and arts occupations: - Management, business, and financial occupations:	$ 57,326
Management, business, science, and arts occupations: - Management, business, and financial occupations: - Management occupations	$ 61,516
Management, business, science, and arts occupations: - Management, business, and financial occupations: - Business and financial operations occupations	$ 51,741
Management, business, science, and arts occupations: - Computer, engineering, and science occupations:	$ 65,727
Management, business, science, and arts occupations: - Computer, engineering, and science occupations: - Computer and mathematical occupations	$ 68,074
Management, business, science, and arts occupations: - Computer, engineering, and science occupations: - Architecture and engineering occupations	$ 67,639
Management, business, science, and arts occupations: - Computer, engineering, and science occupations: - Life, physical, and social science occupations	$ 52,656
Management, business, science, and arts occupations: - Education, legal, community service, arts, and media occupations:	$ 39,272
Management, business, science, and arts occupations: - Education, legal, community service, arts, and media occupations: - Community and social service occupations	$ 36,263
Management, business, science, and arts occupations: - Education, legal, community service, arts, and media occupations: - Legal occupations	$ 69,974
Management, business, science, and arts occupations: - Education, legal, community service, arts, and media occupations: - Education, training, and library occupations	$ 37,862
Management, business, science, and arts occupations: - Education, legal, community service, arts, and media occupations: - Arts, design, entertainment, sports, and media occupations	$ 35,531
Management, business, science, and arts occupations: - Healthcare practitioners and technical occupations:	$ 50,699
Management, business, science, and arts occupations: - Healthcare practitioners and technical occupations: - Health diagnosing and treating practitioners and other technical occupations	$ 60,540

(Continued)

TABLE 11.2 (*Continued*)

Occupation	Median Earnings
Management, business, science, and arts occupations: - Healthcare practitioners and technical occupations: - Health technologists and technicians	$ 34,052
Service occupations:	$ 17,052
Service occupations: - Healthcare support occupations	$ 21,301
Service occupations: - Protective service occupations:	$ 40,387
Service occupations: - Protective service occupations: - Fire fighting and prevention, and other protective service workers including supervisors	$ 29,008
Service occupations: - Protective service occupations: - Law enforcement workers including supervisors	$ 51,947
Service occupations: - Food preparation and serving related occupations	$ 12,336
Service occupations: - Building and grounds cleaning and maintenance occupations	$ 17,633
Service occupations: - Personal care and service occupations	$ 14,593
Sales and office occupations:	$ 27,407
Sales and office occupations: - Sales and related occupations	$ 27,071
Sales and office occupations: - Office and administrative support occupations	$ 27,582
Natural resources, construction, and maintenance occupations:	$ 32,929
Natural resources, construction, and maintenance occupations: - Farming, fishing, and forestry occupations	$ 17,506
Natural resources, construction, and maintenance occupations: - Construction and extraction occupations	$ 31,711
Natural resources, construction, and maintenance occupations: - Installation, maintenance, and repair occupations	$ 39,697
Production, transportation, and material moving occupations:	$ 29,006
Production, transportation, and material moving occupations: - Production occupations	$ 30,450
Production, transportation, and material moving occupations: - Transportation occupations	$ 32,237
Production, transportation, and material moving occupations: - Material moving occupations	$ 21,576

Source: U.S. Census Bureau, 2006–2010 American Community Survey.

As a general rule, the universe of people included in the occupational categories will consist only of those older than 16 years old. The questions also generally cover full-time employees, and are frequently broken down by gender.

Analyzing Military Service

While the ACS occupational data track active-duty military personnel, the survey also collects a variety of information about the one in seven Americans who are veterans. The subject is of more than historical interest for the government; taxpayers are expected to spend roughly $140 billion on veterans' benefits during the 2013 budget year, and the number is not expected to drop with the eventual withdrawal of U.S. troops from long-running wars in Afghanistan and Iraq.[5] The ACS asks if respondents are currently on active duty; have been on active duty in the last year; have ever been on active duty; have only enlisted in the National Guard or reserves; or have never served in the military.

The Census Bureau asks people to define their era of military service:

- September 2001 or later
- August 1990 to August 2001 (including Persian Gulf War)
- September 1980 to July 1990
- May 1975 to August 1980
- Vietnam era (August 1964 to April 1975)
- March 1961 to July 1964
- February 1955 to February 1961
- Korean War (July 1950 to January 1955)
- January 1947 to June 1950
- World War II (December 1941 to December 1946)
- November 1941 or earlier

The question allows the military and Veterans Administration to follow the progress of veterans across a wide variety of social, economic, and cultural issues. Table 11.3, for example, shows the results of a Census Bureau study presented to a 2010 Population Association of America conference, demonstrating that more female veterans who enlisted after September 2001 were engaged in traditionally male occupations in 2008, including security guards, retail sales, customer supervision, and management.[6]

The ACS also asks veterans if they have a service-connected disability rating determined by the Veterans Administration. The ratings range from

TABLE 11.3   Selected Detailed Occupations Classified by Percent Women

1990		2008	
Early AVF Veterans	Nonveterans	Post 9/11 Veterans	Nonveterans
Secretary	Secretary	*Customer service rep*	Cashier
Registered nurse	Cashier	Cashier	Waitress
Nursing aide	Waitress	Waitress	Secretary
Cashier	Elementary school teacher	Secretary	Elementary school teacher
Manager, all other	Bookkeeper	Nursing aide	*Retail salesperson*
Waitress	Registered nurse	Registered nurse	Nursing aide
General office clerk	*Manager, all other*	**Security guard**	*Customer service rep*
Bookkeeper	Nursing aide	*Retail salesperson*	Registered nurse
Sales supervisor	*Sales supervisor*	*Manager, all other*	Child care worker
Typist	General office clerk	*First line supervisor*	*First line supervisor*

Source: U.S. Census Bureau.
Boldface: Male-dominated (0–29% women)
Italics: Mixed (30–69% women)
Underlined: Female-dominated (70–100% women)

a zero, where a mental condition has been diagnosed but it is not formal enough to affect the veteran's ability to hold a job, to 100, where the disability is considered to be total. The question, which was added to the ACS in 2008, allows responses of zero; 10 to 20 percent; 30 to 40 percent; 50 to 60 percent; and 70 percent or more.

Geographic mobility is a related occupational issue addressed by the ACS. The Census Bureau has five major measures of mobility: Same residence within the last year; different residence, moved from same county within past year; different residence, moved from different county within past year; different residence, moved from different state within past year; and different residence, moved from abroad. An example of available data is shown in Figure 11.1.

The Census Bureau also runs a special tabulation that provides estimates for the number of people moving from one geographic area to another, usually down to the county level.[7] This allows businesses in Maricopa County, Arizona, for example, to determine how many people have moved to the area from Orleans Parish, Louisiana, or New York County, New York. Given the regional preferences for new arrivals, this can be extremely useful data.

FIGURE 11.1 Percent Born in State of Residence by State: 2010

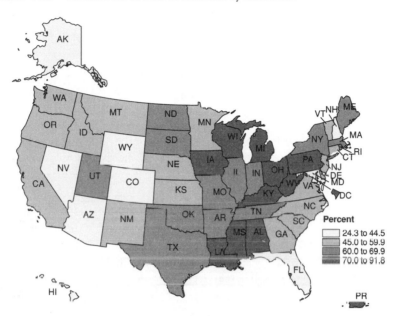

Source: U.S. Census Bureau, 2010 American Community Survey, 2010 Puerto Rico Community Survey.

An influx of people from New York might encourage new businesses such as pizza parlors, home security systems, or more taxis. More people from Orleans Parish might be cause for groceries to carry crawfish or sporting goods stores to stock up on freshwater fishing tackle.

A number of economic characteristics can also be inferred from the county-to-county migration data. An increase in the number of people arriving from Fairfax County, Virginia, one of the nation's wealthiest counties, might mean more business opportunities than an increase in the number of people coming from Shannon County, South Dakota, one of the nation's poorest counties. An increase in residents from a county with a high percentage of homeowners might be a benefit to the construction industry; more people from an area where multiple vehicle ownership is common likely signifies good news for auto parts or repair stores.

A high level of migration out of a county doesn't necessarily indicate an economic slowdown. An exodus from one county to adjacent counties can be a sign of suburbanization, with people retaining jobs in the inner city but purchasing houses in adjacent areas. It should also be noted that mobility correlates highly to the larger economic picture. During the 2007–2009 recession, the worst economic downturn since the Great Depression, mobility dropped to record lows because of the collapse of the housing and credit markets.[8]

Conclusion

The Census Bureau has tracked occupational data for nearly 200 years. Most occupational data is used to track emerging work fields, clusters of workers, or pay among given jobs.

Emerging work fields are among the most useful bits of data in the American Community Survey. New fields are added on an as-needed basis; over the past decade, jobs such as computer network architect and wind turbine service technician have been added to the mix. On the plus side, the U.S. workforce is constantly in flux. For example, few people four decades ago saw the information technology sector as a future major source of jobs. On the downside, it's difficult to compare many jobs over any lengthy period of time.

The ACS provides a wide array of salary data, broken down by sex and occupation. Salary data is useful for employers seeking to attract qualified candidates; workers attempting to judge competitive salaries in different parts of the country; and government officials who enforce equal employment laws.

Data about veterans has become a more integral part of census data over the last decade. The ACS provides eras of service, ranging from World War II to the post–September 11 military. It also asks about service-related disabilities. This question helps the U.S. Department of Veterans Affairs determine where services are best provided.

Notes

1. U.S. Bureau of Labor Statistics, "2010 SOC User Guide," February 2010.
2. Wayne Vroman, "Comparing Labor Market Indicators from the CPS and ACS," Urban Institute for the U.S. Department of Labor, November 2003.
3. Shail Butani, Charles Alexander, and James Esposito, "Using the American Community Survey to Enhance the Current Population Survey: Opportunities and Issues," U.S. Bureau of Labor Statistics and U.S. Census Bureau.
4. BLS, "2010 SOC User Guide."

5. U.S. Department of Veterans Affairs, "Annual Budget Submission, FY 2013," February 13, 2012.

6. Kelly Ann Holder, "Post-9/11 Women Voters," U.S. Census Bureau, presented at annual meeting, Population Association of America, April 15–17, 2010.

7. Ping Ren, "Lifetime Mobility in the United States: 2010," U.S. Census Bureau, November 2011.

8. Ibid.

CHAPTER 12

Analyzing Transportation Trends

Since the first permanent settlers arrived in Jamestown, Virginia, the story of America has been about movement. Americans tamed the East Coast, settled the Midwest, and invaded the West. The French writer Alexis de Tocqueville marveled at the Americans' habit of moving frequently, so unlike their European cousins who were rooted to the same province (if not farm or village) for generations.[1] Karl Marx worried that the American habit of moving would prevent the nation from forming a class of self aware workers.[2] Charles E. Wilson, former defense secretary and chief executive of General Motors Corporation, is best remembered for declaring that "what was good for the country was good for General Motors and vice versa."[3]

Over the past century, that mobility has been fueled by the automobile. We are heading into our second century of a love affair with cars that shows few signs of abating. Even $4 per gallon gasoline, climate change linked to hydrocarbon emissions, incessant traffic, and ever-increasing vehicle license, registration, insurance, and inspection fees haven't made a dent in the national need for households to have one (or more) cars. According to the federal Bureau of Transportation Statistics, there were at least 250.3 million cars in the United States, more than one for every adult in the nation.

The Census Bureau asks the questions about the number of cars on behalf of transportation, social services, and energy agencies. State transportation agencies and more than 350 city and county planning agencies use the data to estimate current vehicle travel figures, create projections of future traffic, and plan infrastructure improvements. The U.S. Department of Energy uses the data to estimate fuel consumption and plan a variety of initiatives, including alternative fuels programs. Social services agencies use the figures

123

to gauge services for the elderly and disabled, as well as establish emergency transportation services in places where few households have vehicles.[4]

Establishing Vehicle Use

Options for respondents include no, one, two, three, four, five, six, or more automobiles, vans, and trucks for home use that are less than one ton in weight. The most common answer is two cars, owned by 58 million Americans over 16 years old, according to the 2010 American Community Survey. Table 12.1 shows the concentration of workers who have cars available, by gender.

The ACS does not include questions about the type of vehicles used. The Census Bureau's Vehicle Inventory and Use Survey, which launched in 1967, was the most authoritative source about U.S. automobile ownership until it was discontinued in 2002.[5] Instead, because vehicle use is associated most heavily with commuting, the Census Bureau provides a wide range of data about the way American workers get to work. This is useful information for government transportation planners and virtually every business in the nation, ranging from mom-and-pop stores that cater to commuters to multinational banks that receive workers' paychecks. In other words, it's not just the real estate business that's fixated on location, location, location.

Transportation, energy, and social services agencies aren't the only parts of government that want the data. The Bureau of Economic Analysis, a part of the U.S. Commerce Department that calculates the gross domestic product, uses commuting patterns to develop place-of-residence earnings from place-of-work reports, or where people actually earn their money, as opposed to where they live. The BEA also uses the data to calculate personal earnings so the federal government can properly allocate tax dollars.[6]

Commuting data also are used by police and fire departments to plan emergency services in high-density work areas; by businesses and equal opportunity agencies to identify discriminatory hiring patterns among minorities within geographically defined labor markets; and by financial institutions to define lending areas and estimate the effects of bank mergers and acquisitions.

Determining Commuting Patterns

The first commuting question asks the specific location of the workplace, down to the street address. This data, of course, isn't released to the public; it's used to establish whether the worker commutes between cities, from one

TABLE 12.1 Sex of Workers by Vehicles Available

Vehicles available	United States
Total	137,864,111
No vehicle available	5,960,956
1 vehicle available	29,092,964
2 vehicles available	58,543,956
3 vehicles available	28,699,499
4 vehicles available	10,940,299
5 or more vehicles available	4,626,437
Male:	73,227,387
Male: No vehicle available	3,059,239
Male: 1 vehicle available	13,726,633
Male: 2 vehicles available	32,093,422
Male: 3 vehicles available	15,702,273
Male: 4 vehicles available	6,026,386
Male: 5 or more vehicles available	2,619,434
Female:	64,636,724
Female: No vehicle available	2,901,717
Female: 1 vehicle available	15,366,331
Female: 2 vehicles available	26,450,534
Female: 3 vehicles available	12,997,226
Female: 4 vehicles available	4,913,913
Female: 5 or more vehicles available	2,007,003

Source: U.S. Census Bureau, American Community Survey, 2006–2010.

county to another, or across state lines. This is useful for governments allocating transportation funds across political boundaries. It's also good information for businesses that want to determine the source of their customers.

The Census Bureau asks about the type of transportation used in the commute:

- Car, truck, or van
- Bus or trolley bus

- Trolley or streetcar
- Subway or elevated
- Railroad
- Ferry boat
- Taxicab
- Motorcycle
- Bicycle
- Walked
- Worked at home
- Other

The most common response by far is car, truck, or van. The Census Bureau also wants to know how many people rode in the car to work. For government transportation planners, this is helpful in determining where commuters might benefit from additional high-occupancy vehicle lanes or where extra traffic lanes could be located or even where sidewalks and bicycle trails should be placed. In New York City, for example, a study of pedestrian accidents found they cost an annual $4.3 billion; the city took action by installing more than 1,500 new pedestrian countdown traffic signals and studied traffic patterns to re-engineer 60 miles of city streets for greater safety.[7]

Not all ACS transportation data involves life-or-death issues. The survey's results are frequently hailed by bicyclists in the Pacific Northwest; Corvallis, Oregon, with 150 days of rain every year, had the highest percentage of people who bicycled to work in 2009, with 9.3 percent of its working population enjoying a pedal-powered commute. Ithaca, New York, had the highest percentage of walking commuters at 15.1 percent of the population. Corvallis was second for walkers. The New York metro area was the undisputed king of public transportation, with nearly one in three workers taking a subway, train, bus, or other transit option to work.[8] Of course, not all people commuted; Figure 12.1 shows the percentage who worked at home in 2010.

The Census Bureau asks the time that people left to go to work, and the number of minutes it took for them to get to work. As with other transportation data, this information helps planners schedule buses and trains; plan hours of operation for high-occupancy vehicle lanes; and develop routes for mass transit. The data are also extremely useful for businesses, especially retailers who need to plan their hours and staffing around commuter patterns. Among civilian workers, for example, Figure 12.2 shows that nearly one-third of all construction workers tend to leave between 6:00 A.M. and 7:00 A.M., which may explain the early hours for hardware stores.

FIGURE 12.1 Percent Working at Home

2006-2010 American community Survey 5-Year Estimates

Thematic Map of Percent; COMMUTING TO WORK - Worked at home
Geography by: State

Supporting documentation on code lists, subject definitions, data accuracy, and statistical testing can be found on the American Community Survey website in the Data and Documentation section.

Sample size and data quality measures (including coverage rates, allocation rates, and response rates) can be found on the American Community survey website in the Methodology section.

Although the American Community Survey (ACS) produces population demographic and housing unit estimates, for 2010, the 2010 Census provides the official counts of the population and housing units for the nation, states, counties, cities and towns. For 2006 to 2009, the Population Estimates Program provides intercensal estimates of the population for the nation, states, and counties.

Legend:

Data Classes

- 2.2–2.5
- 2.9–3.5
- 3.7–4.5
- 4.6–5.5
- 5.7–6.8

Boundaries

- State
- '10 County

Features

- Major Road
- Street
- Stream/Waterbody

Items in grey text are not visible at this zoom level

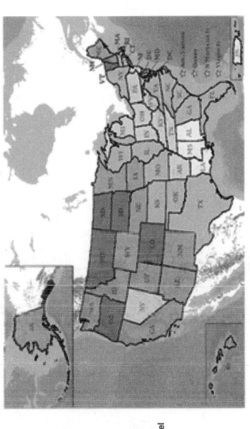

Source: U.S. Census Bureau, American Community Survey, 2006–2010.

127

FIGURE 12.2   Time of Departure by Occupation: 2009

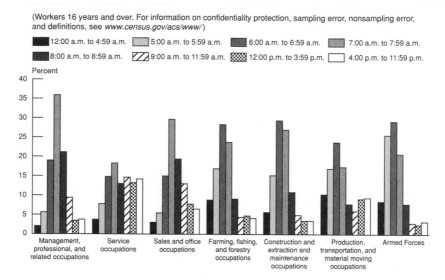

Source: U.S. Census Bureau, American Community Survey, 2009.

In planning transportation networks, researchers and analysts frequently use a geography designed specifically for travel, known as traffic analysis zones, or TAZs, shown in Figure 12.3. These are generally spatial geographies containing approximately 3,000 people, although the size can be as small as a city block or as large as a suburb. In 2007, the Transportation Research Board, part of the National Research Council, noted the importance of American Community Survey data for federal, state, and local planning agencies. Though the TAZ geographies are most commonly used by planning agencies, those agencies interact with a wide variety of businesses, ranging from homebuilders to small companies seeking land-use permits.[9]

Gauging the Importance of Commuting Patterns

Commuting times don't affect just hours and staffing. Travel time in most places is increasing, as shown in Figure 12.4. Some businesses base company offices on traffic patterns, such as the collection of energy companies who have moved headquarters west of downtown Houston, where more affluent workers live. Nearly one in five Houston workers needs more than 40 minutes to get to work in the morning, and the relocations have increased employee productivity and happiness.

FIGURE 12.3 Hierarchy of Census Geographic Entities

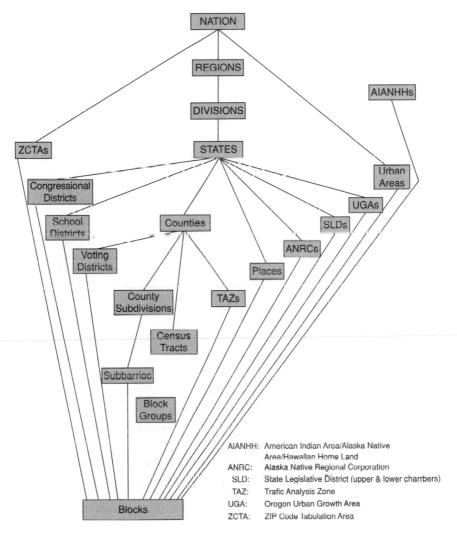

AIANHH: American Indian Area/Alaska Native
         Area/Hawaiian Home Land
ANRC: Alaska Native Regional Corporation
SLD: State Legislative District (upper & lower charrbers)
TAZ: Trafic Analysis Zone
UGA: Oregon Urban Growth Area
ZCTA: ZIP Code Tabulation Area

Source: Transportation Resource Board of the National Academies, "National Cooperative Highway Research Program Report 588: A Guidebook for Using American Community Survey Data for Transportation Planning," 2007, http://onlinepubs.trb.org/onlinepubs/nchrp/nchrp_ rpt_588.pdf.

FIGURE 12.4   Average Travel Time for Workers: 1980–2009

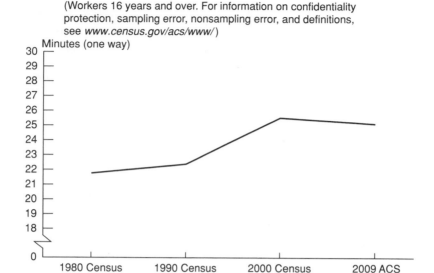

(Workers 16 years and over. For information on confidentiality
protection, sampling error, nonsampling error, and definitions,
see *www.census.gov/acs/www/*)

Sources: U.S. Census Bureau, Decennial Census 1980, 1990, 2000; U.S. Census Bureau, American Community Survey, 2009.

In the future, it's likely that commuting will be a larger factor in household location, as gas prices rise. Already, in parts of the country, some inner cities that have been losing significant numbers of families are being repopulated by young couples who are more concerned about the time and costs associated with longer commutes. This may be a temporary trend, because young people have delayed getting married and having children because of concerns about the economy. Even so, gasoline prices and commuting times aren't likely to decline over the long term.

There's also a growing body of evidence showing that long commutes can hamper worker productivity and happiness. Researchers at Umea University in Sweden found that a 45-minute commute increases the risk of a divorce by 40 percent.[10] A 2005 California study found a strong correlation between vehicle miles of travel and obesity.[11] A 2009 Brown University study reported that each minute spent commuting cut 0.0257 minutes from exercising, 0.0387 minutes from cooking, and 0.2205 minutes from sleeping.[12] A fourth study coauthored by a Princeton University Nobel laureate took a slightly less complex analysis, polling 900 Texas women for their favorite and least-favorite activities. Sex, after-work socializing, and relaxing took the top three spots. The evening commute, workday, and morning commute were at the bottom.[13]

Conclusion

The American society is a mobile society, with more than one car for every adult in the nation. The American Community Survey asks questions about transportation on behalf of the U.S. Transportation and Energy departments, as well as all 50 state transportation agencies and approximately 350 local entities.

The ACS doesn't ask for specific information about the types of vehicles that are used, although it does request the number of vehicles available to each household. More importantly, the survey asks a series of questions about commuting patterns that are crucial for planning agencies, such as the time of day that people leave for work, the length of their commute, and the usual method of commuting, ranging from no commute (working at home) to car, truck, or van used by one person.

Whereas most people think of their commutes in terms of standard geographies, such as traveling from Hoboken, New Jersey, to New York, New York, planning agencies often use a geography known as a traffic analysis zone (TAZ) that is composed of blocks located wholly within counties. Although a TAZ may seem like an obscure geography to the public, it's a useful concept for businesses ranging from homebuilders to environmental advocacy organizations, or any company whose business is affected by transportation planning.

Notes

1. Alexis de Tocqueville, *Democracy in America*, (New York: Adlard and Saunders, 1838).
2. Joseph Ferrie, "The End of American Exceptionalism: Mobility in the U.S. since 1850," National Bureau of Economic Research, Working Paper 11324, May 2005.
3. Staff, "Armed Forces: Engine Charlie," *Time*, October 6, 1961.
4. U.S. Census Bureau, "American Community Survey, Population: Questions on Place of Work and Journey to Work," http://www.census.gov/acs/www/Downloads/QbyQfact/PJ_work.pdf.
5. U.S. Census Bureau, "Vehicle Inventory Use Survey—Discontinued," http://www.census.gov/svsd/www/vius/products.html.

6. Association of Public Data Users, "American Community Survey, Uses and Users," Draft, May 30, 2012.

7. New York City Department of Transportation, "The New York City Pedestrian Safety Study & Action Plan," August 2010.

8. Brian McKenzie, and Melanie Rapino, "Commuting in the United States: 2009," U.S. Census Bureau, September 2011.

9. Transportation Research Board of the National Academies, "NCHRP Report 588: A Guidebook for Using American Community Survey Data for Transportation Planning," 2007.

10. Rebecca Martin, "Long Commutes 'Bad for Marriage': Swedish Study," *The Local*, May 24, 2011.

11. Javier Lopez-Zetina, Howard Lee, and Robert Friis, "The Link Between Obesity and The Built Environment. Evidence from an Ecological Analysis of Obesity and Vehicle Miles of Travel in California," *Health and Place* 12, no. 4 (December 2006).

12. Thomas James Christian, "Opportunity Costs Surrounding Exercise and Dietary Behaviors: Quantifying Trade-Offs Between Commuting Time and Health-Related Activities," Georgia State University Department of Economics, Working Paper, October 21, 2009.

13. Daniel Kahneman and Alan B. Krueger, "Developments in the Measurement of Subjective Well-Being," *Journal of Economic Perspectives* 20, no. 1 (Winter 2006).

CHAPTER 13

Assessing Income

The annual population estimates are the top line of the American Community Survey. Those numbers get the most attention and tell us more about our city, county, state, and nation on an ongoing basis than any other data point that's reported. And to be sure, businesses care deeply about population trends. A shrinking market isn't much of a long-term market. Population data tell businesses where to locate, expand, or cut back, and the annual survey is the best source of that information.

Income data is a close second, in terms of importance to businesses. The ACS covers the waterfront, reporting median household income, per-capita income, and family income, as well as the number of households living in poverty and receiving disability income, Social Security income, self-employment income, public assistance income, and Supplemental Nutritional Assistance Program (SNAP, or food stamp) benefits.

Put mildly, this information is solid gold for businesses. The most relevant and simple indicator of economic well-being is the median household income figure. It's an easy concept, meaning that half of all households earn more and half earn less. It's far superior to an average income calculation, which can be skewed by outliers. For example, say two bricklayers are drinking in a bar. One earns $40,000 annually and the other earns $60,000 annually. Bill Gates, whose annual Microsoft salary is around $1 million, walks into the bar: The average annual income has just gone from $50,000 to $367,000. The median, meanwhile, is $60,000, which is a much more accurate reflection of the income distribution in the bar.

Understanding Income Variability

One of the few downsides to making business decisions involves geographic variability, particularly with income levels shown in Figure 13.1. A median household income of $75,000 may sound like enough to support a reasonably comfortable middle-class lifestyle in Nebraska. It's unlikely that the same median household income will travel as far in New York or the District of Columbia. Other issues include the prevalence of multigenerational households or multiple roommates, who can skew results to the high or low end, especially in small geographic areas, such as census tracts.

A growing number of households consist of people living alone. The percentage, slightly more than a quarter of all U.S. households, has almost quadrupled since 1940. The vast majority still consists of families or roommates living together, and they represent the real value of median household income. As a general rule, households with more than one person don't operate in a financial vacuum. For example, husbands and wives with a combined

FIGURE 13.1 Median Household Income in the Past 12 Months by State and Puerto Rico: 2010 (in 2010 inflation-adjusted dollars)

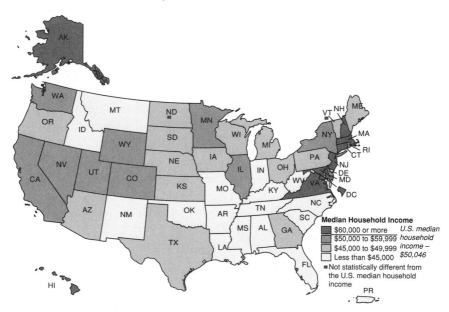

Source: U.S. Census Bureau, 2010 American Community Survey, 2010 Puerto Rico Community Survey.

income of $100,000 generally represent a much more economically viable unit than two separate single-person households earning $50,000.

Median household income isn't the only measure of economic health. Family household income is useful in determining the financial well-being of households that don't consist of single people or roommates. Median family income will usually be higher than household income because more families consist of two working spouses.

The only major person-based income figure is one of the least useful financial statistics provided by the American Community Survey. It's simply the aggregate income divided by population. This number tends to dramatically understate the economic health of a geographic area. The shortcomings of per-capita income are magnified in areas with many children. Utah, for example, ranks very high in median household income but the high number of children makes it rank extremely low for per-capita income.

Having household, family, or per-capita income figures tells most of the story; not all. Wealth in the United States is heavily concentrated in an investor class that doesn't rely on annual wages or salaries to meet living expenses. The ACS displays separate figures for income from wages and salaries; self-employment income, which is usually defined as net income after business expenses; and income from investments, rentals, and dividends. It's possible to use aggregate amounts of these types of income to extrapolate a mean number for different geographies, although the Census Bureau generally provides only the number of households receiving such income rather than the median figures. Care must be taken to ensure that outliers don't skew mean figures when calculating income figures.

Measuring Poverty

The Census Bureau doesn't just measure who has money; it also provides data about people who don't have money. A wide range of poverty figures, such as those shown in Table 13.1, are provided based on annual adjustments to the federal poverty level. The most common measure of poverty is provided for a family of four; in 2011, the figure was $22,350 (Separate poverty thresholds are used for Alaska and Hawaii, because the costs of living in noncontiguous states are so much higher than in the continental United States). The poverty level for a single individual was $10,890 in 2011.[1] Poverty numbers are important to a wide variety of businesses. Although it's true that poor people don't spend as much as high-income households, there are a lot of economic opportunities for providing goods and services to poor people—and there are a lot of poor

TABLE 13.1　Percentage of People in Poverty in the Past 12 Months for Large Metropolitan Areas with Lowest and Highest Poverty Rate: 2010

Ten metro areas with lowest poverty rates	Estimated percentage in poverty	Ten metro areas with highest poverty rates	Estimated percentage in poverty
Washington-Arlington-Alexandria, DC-VA-MD-WV Metro Area	8.4	McAllen-Edinburg-Mission, TX Metro Area	33.4
Honolulu, HI Metro Area	9.1	Fresno, CA Metro Area	26.8
Poughkeepsie-Newburgh-Middletown, NY Metro Area	9.4	El Paso, TX Metro Area	24.3
Bridgeport-Stamford-Norwalk, CT Metro Area	9.4	Bakersfield-Delano, CA Metro Area	21.2
Des Moines-West Des Moines, IA Metro Area	9.9	Augusta-Richmond County, GA-SC Metro Area	19.9
Hartford-West Hartford-East Hartford, CT Metro Area	10.1	Modesto, CA Metro Area	19.9
Ogden-Clearfield, UT Metro Area	10.2	Stockton, CA Metro Area	19.2
Portland-South Portland-Biddeford, ME Metro Area	10.3	Memphis, TN-MS-AR Metro Area	19.1
Boston-Cambridge-Quincy, MA-NH Metro Area	10.3	Durham-Chapel Hill, NC Metro Area	18.9
Lancaster, PA Metro Area	10.5	Greensboro-High Point, NC Metro Area	18.1

Source: U.S. Census Bureau, 2010 American Community Survey.

people, numbering more than 46 million in 2011. The government spends nearly $90 billion on its Supplemental Nutrition Assistance Program (SNAP, formerly known as food stamps) to provide food for poor people, as well as $16 billion for free and reduced school meal programs, and another $7 billion on the Women, Infants and Children (WIC) supplemental food program.[2] The American Community Survey provides poverty numbers by age, sex, and race, paying particular attention to children and seniors.

The government recognizes the dilemma inherent in trying to measure poverty. Not all people who are poor need government help, and a large number of people who aren't poor need some type of government assistance. Studies have shown as many as half of all U.S. households receive some type of federal aid, ranging from the traditional welfare program known as

Temporary Assistance for Needy Families (TANF) to federally subsidized flood insurance for the owners of multimillion-dollar beachfront mansions. The poverty figures also are broken out by the number of households that earn less than 50 percent of the poverty rate; 125 percent; 150 percent; 185 percent; and 200 percent of the poverty rate. The percentage of poverty rates is particularly useful for governments providing help under Medicaid, the joint state-federal health insurance program for the poor and disabled; many states receive more federal matching funds as they increase the percentage at which people become eligible to participate in the program.

The primary shortcoming of measuring poverty, of course, is that there's no one-size-fits-all definition. Any household with four people is going to have a difficult time making ends meet on less than $23,000 annually. That household, however, is going to have a much more difficult time in New York City than in rural Mississippi. Poverty also fluctuates. Few people who fall into poverty can escape, although the "American Dream" is based on people being able to increase their earning power, regardless of their present financial circumstances. Finally, most measures of poverty don't consider supplemental financial assistance received by poor households, such as food stamps, disability income, or the earned income tax credit, which costs taxpayers more than $50 billion annually.[3]

The Census Bureau has developed a Supplemental Poverty Measure (SPM) that attempts to address the disparity in costs between different regions, with key calculations shown in Table 13.2. The measure, released in late 2011, showed that adding benefits such as SNAP, housing subsidies,

TABLE 13.2 Resource Estimates

SPM resources — Money income from all sources	
Plus:	Minus:
Supplemental Nutritional Assistance (SNAP)	Taxes (plus credits such as the Earned Income Tax Credit [EITC])
National School Lunch Program	Expenses related to work
Supplementary Nutrition Program for Women, Infants, and Children (WIC)	Child care expenses
Housing subsidies	Medical out-of-pocket expenses (MOOP)
Low-Income Home Energy Assistance (LIHEAP)	Child support paid

Source: U.S. Census Bureau, Current Population Reports.

FIGURE 13.2   Poverty Rates Using Two Measures for Total Population and by Age Group: 2010

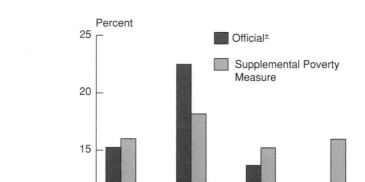

±Includes unrelated individuals under the age of 15.

Source: Current Population Survey, 2011 Annual Social and Economic Supplement.

and energy assistance actually increased the poverty rate after expenses for child care, health, and taxes were subtracted from income. The number of poor people rose from the 46.6 million shown in the American Community Survey to 49.1 million.[4]

The increase in poverty isn't uniform under the supplemental measure, as displayed in Figure 13.2. A decrease in the child poverty rate is more than offset by the increase in adult poverty, particularly among the population over 65 years old. The supplemental measure also decreases poverty among blacks, renters, people living in rural areas, people in the Midwest and South, and people covered by public health insurance.

The Census Bureau hasn't yet indicated when or if it will add supplemental poverty measures to the ACS; it would require significant retooling of the reporting, because the supplemental rate is calculated from the monthly Current Population Survey, rather than the annual American Community

Survey. Because of the relatively small size of the monthly CPS, it's very hard to obtain numbers with any degree of geographic granularity. Even so, the supplemental measure should be checked in an analysis to ensure the accuracy and comparability of ACS statistics, particularly at a national level.

The largest single source of federal income comes from Social Security, the largest government program in the world. The retirement, survivors', and disability insurance program cost $782.7 billion during the 2011 budget year; one in four U.S. households received some type of Social Security benefit, according to the Census Bureau.[5] The ACS breaks down Social Security income into two distinct categories: one showing total Social Security income and the other displaying Supplemental Security income (SSI), which is designed to help the aged, blind, and disabled. The survey includes mean Social Security and SSI figures for most geographies, which is useful in determining places where a large percentage of people live on fixed incomes.

Other government income is included, such as the number of households receiving public assistance from programs such as Temporary Assistance for Needy Families (TANF) and households that receive benefits from the Supplemental Nutrition Assistance Program (SNAP), formerly known as food stamps. In the latter two cases, the number of households receiving benefits is displayed; the value of the benefits is not. The value will vary considerably, depending largely upon the size of the household and its location.

Assessing Income Distribution

The Census Bureau also keeps tabs on income distribution, with a sample of calculations shown in Table 13.3. It's possible to determine which places have the largest percentage of people earning more (or less) than $10,000, $50,000, $100,000, and so on. The American Community Survey provides data on the Gini coefficient for geographic levels, giving users a single number ranging from zero to one that measures the disparity between rich households and poor households.

One of the more esoteric measures of poverty that's tracked by government also yields one of the more surprising results. The American Community Survey tracks what's known as the aggregate income deficit, or the amount that it would take to lift all unrelated individuals out of poverty. The 2011 ACS shows that an investment of $76.9 billion would eliminate poverty among all families if provided in proper increments to bring different households to the federal poverty level, about $23,000 annually for a family of four. That's only slightly more than 2 percent of the federal budget.

TABLE 13.3 Selected Measures of Household Income Dispersion: 1967–2010

Measure of income dispersion	2010	2000
MEASURE		
Household income at selected percentiles		
10th percentile limit	11,904	13,398
20th percentile limit	20,000	22,689
50th (median)	49,445	53,164
80th percentile limit	100,065	103,525
90th percentile limit	138,923	141,805
95th percentile limit	180,810	183,865
Household income ratios of selected percentiles		
90th/10th	11.67	10.58
95th/20th	9.04	8.10
95th/50th	3.66	3.46
80th/50th	2.02	1.95
80th/20th	5.00	4.56
20th/50th	0.4	0.43
Mean household income of quintiles		
Lowest quintile	11,034	12,860
Second quintile	28,636	32,110
Third quintile	49,309	53,472
Fourth quintile	79,040	83,124
Highest quintile	169,633	180,129
Shares of household income of quintiles		
Lowest quintile	3.3	3.6
Second quintile	8.5	8.9
Third quintile	14.6	14.8
Fourth quintile	23.4	23.0
Highest quintile	50.2	49.8

(*Continued*)

Measure of income dispersion	2010	2000
Summary measures		
Gini index of income inequality	0.469	0.462
Mean logarithmic deviation of income	0.572	0.49
Theil	0.399	0.404
Atkinson:		
e = 0.25	0.097	0.096
e = 0.50	0.191	0.185
e = 0.75	0.292	0.275
STANDARD ERROR		
Household income at selected percentiles		
10th percentile limit	81	91
20th percentile limit	110	129
50th (median)	209	167
80th percentile limit	306	304
90th percentile limit	565	614
95th percentile limit	898	1,179
Household income ratios of selected percentiles		
90th/10th	0.093	0.085
95th/20th	0.067	0.07
95th/50th	0.023	0.026
80th/50th	0.01	0.009
80th/20th	0.032	0.029
20th/50th	0.003	0.003
Mean household income of quintiles		
Lowest quintile	41	46
Second quintile	37	41
Third quintile	48	51
Fourth quintile	76	77
Highest quintile	782	1,051

(*Continued*)

TABLE 13.3 (*Continued*)

Measure of income dispersion	2010	2000
Shares of household income of quintiles		
Lowest quintile	0.02	0.03
Second quintile	0.06	0.06
Third quintile	0.1	0.1
Fourth quintile	0.15	0.16
Highest quintile	0.33	0.35
Summary measures		
Gini index of income inequality	0.0027	0.003
Mean logarithmic deviation of income	0.0067	0.0049
Theil	0.0001	0.0002
Atkinson:		
e = 0.25	0.0011	0.0013
e = 0.50	0.0018	0.0021
e = 0.75	0.0024	0.0026

Income in 2010 CPI-U-RS adjusted dollars. For further explanation of income inequality measures, see Current Population Reports, Series P60-204, "The Changing Shape of the Nation's Income Distribution: 1947–1998." Standard errors presented in this table were calculated using general variance formula parameters and may differ from the standard errors in text tables that were calculated using replicate weights. For information on confidentiality protection, sampling error, nonsampling error, and definitions, see www.census.gov/apsd/techdoc/cps/cpsmar11.pdf.
Source: U.S. Census Bureau, Income, Poverty and Health Insurance in the United States: 2010.

The Gini coefficient is a little known but relevant bit of data provided by the Census Bureau. The coefficient, developed by Italian social scientist Federico Gini in the early twentieth century, is simply an index measuring the gap between rich and poor. A Gini of zero means that all income is distributed evenly; a Gini of 1 means one household has all the money. Given the size of the U.S. economy, the Gini moves slowly, although it's been steadily increasing since the 1980s.[6]

At first blush, the U.S. Gini of .469 might be thought to indicate a relatively equal distribution of income. It's far less than the .707 Gini for Namibia, according to the Central Intelligence Agency (and the fact that the CIA tracks income inequality for 140 countries ought to tell you that it's a reasonable predictor of a society's stability). Even so, the United States has more income inequality than Guyana or Iran. And in parts of the United States, the gap between rich and poor far exceeds Third-World levels. The Bridgeport, Connecticut metro area, for example, had a 2010 Gini of .537, higher than Thailand, Mexico, or Zimbabwe.[7]

Though the concept of the Gini is easily understood, the coefficient suffers from two major limitations. The first issue involves the relative complexity of the formula. It's easier to figure out the percentages of households that earn more than $100,000 or less than $10,000 than to figure out the Gini for a given area:

$$G = 2/\upsilon n^2 \sum_{i-1}^{n} i X_i \frac{n+1}{n}$$

In the preceding formula, the Census Bureau calculates the Gini where υ is the weighted population mean, n is the weighted number of observations, X_i is the weighted income of household I, and the household income is weighted by its rank in the income distribution. The second, and far more difficult issue, involves the problems inherent in trying to deconstruct the Gini for different subgroups. A Gini can easily be calculated for a total population, but it's extremely difficult to calculate the coefficient for an individual racial or ethnic group within a given area unless extremely detailed data is available to describe all the characteristics of the particular group.[8]

Conclusion

Knowing about money—who has it and who doesn't—is crucial to business and a major benefit of the American Community Survey. The Census Bureau collects a range of income and poverty data that provide broad measures of economic health.

The primary income measure for an area is the median household income, which represents the midpoint of income—the level at which one-half of all households have more annual income and one-half have less. Salaries and wages make up the largest share of income in the United States; the Census Bureau also provides income figures for sources ranging from investments and dividends to traditional cash assistance, or welfare, payments. The survey also provides the number of people who live in poverty, generally an annual income level set for households of different sizes.

Because the United States has traditionally prided itself on being an egalitarian society, the Census Bureau tracks a variety of indicators that display income inequality throughout the country. While a significant amount of attention is paid to disparities represented by the 1 percent of people who represent the wealthiest Americans, the ACS also provides more traditional measures of income distribution, such as the Gini coefficient.

Notes

1. *Federal Register* 76, no. 13, January 20, 2011, 3637–3638.
2. "Summary of Receipts, Outlays, and Surplus or Deficits, 1789–2017," Historical Tables, Executive Office of the President, Office of Management and Budget, http://www.whitehouse.gov/omb/budget/Historicals/, 21.
3. EITC Statistics, Internal Revenue Service, 2011: http://www.eitc.irs.gov/central/ eitcstats/.
4. Kathleen Short, "The Research Supplemental Poverty Measure: 2010," U.S. Census Bureau, P60-241, November 2011.
5. American Community Survey 2006–2010, U.S. Census Bureau, Table B19055.
6. Carmen DeNavas-Walt, Bernadette Proctor, and Jessica Smith, "Income, Poverty and Health Insurance in the United States: 2010," U.S. Census Bureau Current Population Reports, P60-239, September 2011.
7. "Field Listing: Distribution of Family Income–Gini Index," The World Factbook, Central Intelligence Agency, https://www.cia.gov/library/publications/the-world-factbook/fields/print_2172.html.
8. Frank Cowell and Carlo Fiorio, "Inequality Decompositions," Gini Discussion Paper 4, The GINI Project, December 2010.

CHAPTER 14

Analyzing Health Data

The U.S. health care system is a disappointment, with costs rising even though key indicators lag behind other developed and developing economies. In a study ranking health care among industrialized countries, the Commonwealth Fund has consistently ranked the United States seventh, out of seven nations. Health care now accounts for $1 of every $7 in goods and services produced in the United States, even while 49.9 million Americans don't have access to regular health care through insurance.[1] The American Community Survey tracks a variety of information related to the nation's health care system, ranging from directly related issues such as the number of households without health insurance or people with disabilities to less direct concepts, like the number of people over 85 years old or households in poverty.

The most direct health-related question asked in the ACS is whether people have health insurance. Insurance is more than a simple barometer of health, although countless studies have shown that people with insurance are far more likely to enjoy good health than people without insurance, which is important for employers in all industries. Because of the expenses, fewer people are able to obtain health insurance from their employers; the percentage of Americans insured through their workplace has fallen consistently over the last decade, and only 64 percent of people had private health insurance in 2010.[2]

The health insurance question is a relatively new one to the ACS; it was asked for the first time in 2008, meaning the figures aren't yet available for geographic areas with fewer than 20,000 people. Like income and poverty figures, census health insurance data is duplicated, usually right about the time that the American Community Survey figures are released. The figures aren't exactly duplicates; the ACS asks the question about whether or not people have health insurance differently from the Current Population Survey. The primary difference between the annual ACS and the monthly CPS question involves the length of time that people didn't have health insurance. The CPS asks if people were uninsured for the preceding year; the ACS asks people if they were uninsured at a specific point in time over the preceding year. In 2009, the difference in questions led to a wide margin between the two surveys. The CPS estimated there were 50 million uninsured Americans, whereas the ACS put the figure at 45.3 million, according to the Robert Wood Johnson Foundation.[3]

Understanding Types of Health Insurance

The Census Bureau asks for the type of health insurance. Options include employer-provided insurance; privately purchased insurance; Medicare; Medicaid or any state-sponsored program that provides insurance for the poor or disabled; Tricare, the military health insurance plan; the Veterans Administration; Indian Health Service insurance; or any other type of health insurance.

From there, the ACS provides more information, including health insurance by age brackets (younger than 6 years old, 6 to 17 years old, 18 to 24 years old, 25 to 34 years old, 35 to 44 years old, 45 to 54 years old, 55 to 64 years old, 65 to 74 years old, and over 75 years old) and by race. The census provides data by health insurance type for selected age groups (under 18 years, 18 to 34 years old, 35 to 64 years old, and over 65 years old), as shown in Figure 14.1. It also gives figures by sex and work experience, showing the number of men and women with health insurance who worked part time, full time, or not at all during the previous year. Health insurance data is also provided by age and educational attainment, showing types of coverage by age and last level of education completed.

Parsing Disability Data

The American Community Survey also tracks the number of disabled people, which can be useful information for companies that want or need to hire disabled workers in metropolitan areas, as shown in Figure 14.2. More than 36 million Americans had some type of disability in 2010, ranging from complete to fractional. Six types of disability are tracked: Hearing, vision, cognitive, ambulatory, self-care, and independent living. Hearing disabilities include people who are either deaf or have serious hearing problems. Vision disabilities cover people who are blind or whose poor vision hampers daily activities. Cognitive disabilities include people who have difficulty with

FIGURE 14.1 Health Insurance Coverage of Insured Children by Type: 2008 and 2009

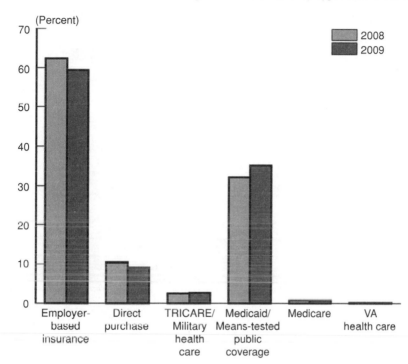

Sources: U.S. Census Bureau, American Community Surveys, 2008 and 2009.

concentration, memory, or making decisions. Ambulatory disabilities can be defined by a range, covering people who can't walk to those who have difficulty climbing stairs. Self-care disabilities encompass people who have difficulty bathing or dressing, and independent living disabilities, which cover people older than 15 years old, include people who have problems performing basic daily tasks.

Obviously, many of these disabilities are subjective judgments. Any parent of a teen-ager, for example, could argue that their child has independent living, self-care, and cognitive disabilities (and possibly hearing or vision problems, as well). The Census Bureau has acknowledged the lack of a "gold standard" for accurately measuring disability and recommends that the figures be compared with other surveys, such as the Survey for Income and Program Participation, which found more than 50 million Americans with disabilities in 2005.[4]

Another major issue with disability statistics deals with comparability. Before 2008, the Census Bureau had different categories for disabilities.

FIGURE 14.2   Disability Rate for Children in Metropolitan Statistical Areas: 2010

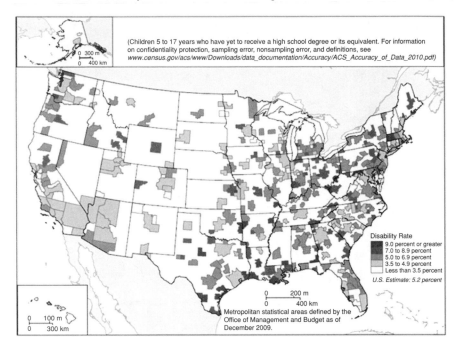

Source: U.S. Census Bureau, 2010 American Community Survey.

Sensory disabilities included people who were both blind or deaf; the Census Bureau also included physical, mental, going-outside-the-home, and employment disabilities. The differences in questions will become less important as the ACS goes forward, although they're real and significant.

Some of the more useful disability figures provided in the ACS include the number of disabilities by gender; and the number of disabled people by work experience, employment status, level of poverty, veteran status, and median earnings.

Understanding Nutrition Data

Data showing the number of households that receive Supplemental Nutrition Assistance Program (SNAP) benefits, formerly known as food stamps, also have been introduced in recent years in the American Community Survey. In March 2012, the USDA reported that more than one in seven Americans needed federal help putting food on the table.[5] These data, such as the figures

FIGURE 14.3 Percentage Receiving Food Stamps/SNAP for Households by State and Puerto Rico: 2010

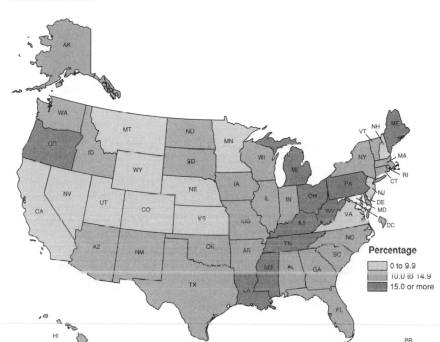

Sources. U.S. Census Bureau, 2010 American Community Survey, 2010 Puerto Rico Community Survey.

shown in Figure 14.3, are useful for virtually every food-related business in the nation, ranging from small farmers' markets deciding whether to participate in the SNAP program to industrial agriculture conglomerates needing to determine how much pasta should be produced over the next year. The USDA spends approximately $72 billion annually on the SNAP program; a fair share of that money goes to some of the nation's largest companies, with Wal-Mart receiving nearly a half-billion dollars in the state of Oklahoma alone.[6]

The link between health and nutrition has ramifications for businesses. Nutrition, of course, is a cornerstone of good health. Healthier employees reduce employer costs in terms of health insurance costs and productivity. Indeed, the U.S. Army launched a decades long effort to improve nutrition after World War I, when it realized that troops weren't as effective without proper meals, and a number of federal programs, including the Women,

Infants and Children (WIC) and free school lunch programs were created as much for economic efficiency as altruism.[7]

Although there has been little done in the way of longitudinal studies on the long-term effects of food stamp participation, a growing body of evidence suggests that people living in poor neighborhoods often reside in "food deserts," or places where fresh, unprocessed food is difficult to find.[8] Approximately half of food stamp retailers are convenience stores or drug stores that don't focus on groceries.

Overlooking an Obvious Health Data Point

An obvious but often overlooked demographic related to health care is the concentration of the elderly, shown in Figure 14.4. The Agency for Healthcare Research and Quality, the research arm of the U.S. Department of Health and Human Services, reported in 2006 that people older than 65 constituted about 13 percent of the U.S. population but consumed 36 percent of all U.S. personal health care expenses.[9] The average health costs for an elderly person were $11,089 in 2002, compared to $3,352 annually for an American between the ages of 19 and 64.[10]

FIGURE 14.4   Percentage Aged 65 and Over of Total State Population: 2006–2008

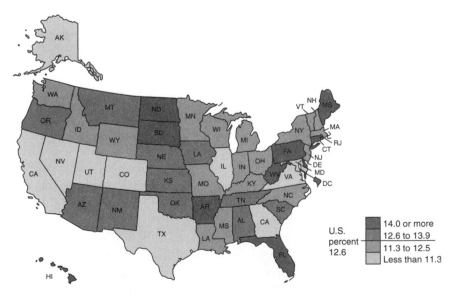

Source: U.S. Census Bureau, American Community Survey, 2006–2008.
Note: Data based on sample. For information on confidentiality protection, sampling error, nonsampling error, and definitions, see www.census.gov/acs/www.

Health care costs aren't expected to go down any time soon, especially as the Baby Boom generation born between 1946 and 1964 ages. The first Baby Boomers turned 65 in 2011 and are expected to threaten the solvency of Medicare, the federal health insurance program for the elderly, if costs aren't brought down. The percentage of senior citizens is expected to rise from the current 13 percent to more than 20 percent by 2050, as shown in Figure 14.5.[11] This may represent an enormous potential market for some

FIGURE 14.5 Percent Aged 65 and Over by Race and Hispanic Origin for the United States: 2010, 2030, and 2050

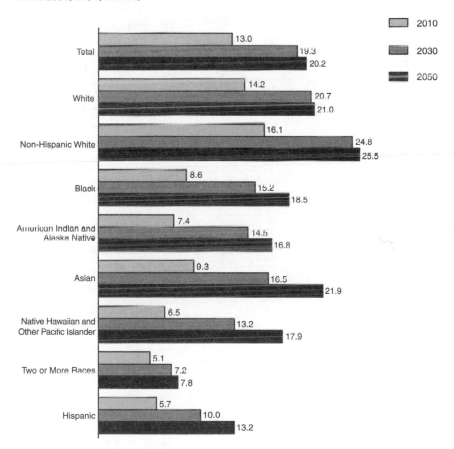

Source: U.S. Census Bureau, 2008.

Note: Unless other wize specified, data refer to the population who reported a race alone. Populations for each race group include both Hispanics and non-Hispanics, unless otherwise specified. Hispanics may be of any race.

businesses; burgeoning health care costs may also represent a significant risk for those same companies.

Conclusion

Nearly one of every six Americans doesn't have health insurance, and the cost of coverage is increasing far faster than most people's incomes. The United States lags badly behind other developed countries in its ability to provide quality, affordable health care to all citizens. The American Community Survey tracks several key indicators of health; it began gathering health insurance data with the 2008 survey.

Although insurance is the most high-profile health topic covered by the annual survey, the Census Bureau also collects data on other topics that are closely related to the subject, such as disabilities. The disability statistics are somewhat hampered by their changing definitions. The ACS also asks about nutrition assistance from the U.S. Department of Agriculture's Supplemental Nutrition Assistance Program (SNAP), formerly known as food stamps. There's a strong correlation between good nutrition and health. In early 2012, nearly one in seven Americans needed federal help putting food on the table.

An often overlooked health indicator is the age of the population. The elderly account for a disproportionate share of health care expenses. Government planners, researchers, and businesses can use basic ACS demographic estimates to find concentrations of young elderly, elderly, and very elderly people at all geographic levels to provide appropriate goods and services.

Notes

1. Carmen DeNavas-Walt, Bernadette Proctor, and Jessica Smith, "Income, Poverty, and Health Insurance Coverage in the United States: 2010," U.S. Census Bureau, September 2011.
2. Ibid.
3. "Comparing Federal Government Surveys That Count the Uninsured," Robert Wood Johnson Foundation/ University of Minnesota State Health Access Data Assistance Center, September 2010.
4. Matthew Brault, "Americans with Disabilities: 2005," U.S. Census Bureau, Current Population Reports, P70-117, December 2008.
5. Program Information Report (Keydata), U.S. Summary, U.S. Department of Agriculture Food and Nutrition Service, March 2012.

6. Michele Simon, "Food Stamps: Follow the Money," Eat Drink Politics, June 2012.
7. Mary Kay Crepinsek and Nancy Burstein, "Maternal Employment and Children's Nutrition, Volume II: Other Nutrition-Related Outcomes," U.S. Department of Agriculture Economic Research Service, June 2004.
8. "USDA Releases Online Tool for Locating Food Deserts," USDA Release 0191-11, May 2, 2011.
9. "The High Concentration of U.S. Health Care Expenditures," Agency for Healthcare Research and Quality, Research in Action Issue 19, June 2006.
10. Ibid.
11. "U.S. Population Projections," U.S. Census Bureau 2008: http://www.census.gov/population/www/projections/summarytables.html.

PART III

Resources

APPENDIX A

Using American FactFinder

Fortunately for users of census data, flat files aren't the only way that the data is presented. The Census Bureau has created American FactFinder, an online tool designed for reasonably quick lookups of data released between 2000 and 2010. It has its limitations, but it's the quickest tool available for doing very simple queries.

Simple Population Count

Let's start by determining the 2010 population of Goliad, a town in south Texas. We go to American FactFinder at http://factfinder2.census.gov (an earlier version of FactFinder at http://factfinder.census.gov was discontinued in fall 2011):

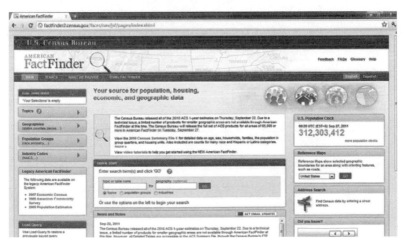

First, we want to select the dataset that's easiest to use. We can click on the blue "Topics" box on the left and expand our "Dataset" options:

We'll select "2010 Redistricting Data SF," because it has the fewest variables and will likely be the easiest to use. Once we click on it, the description should appear in the "Your Selections" box in the upper left corner of the screen:

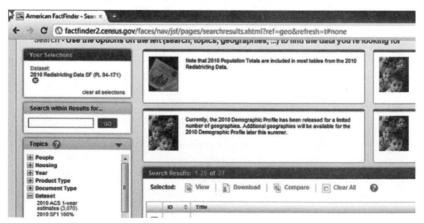

Next, we'll select the geography. In the upper left corner of the page, click on the blue bar labeled "Geographies." A separate, somewhat transparent screen should appear:

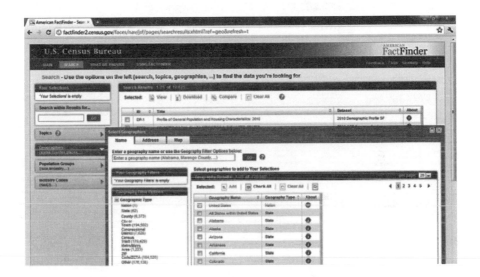

We'll enter "Goliad" into the box labeled "Enter a geography name or use the Geography Filter Options below."

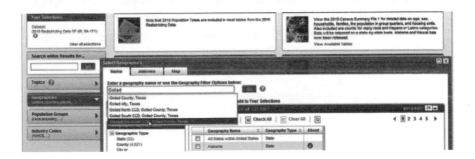

We'll select "Goliad city, Texas," and click on the "Go" button next to the box because it seems to be the closest thing to what we want. It's possible to choose more than one geography. Our results show more options:

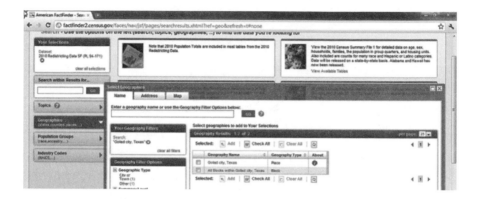

We'll select the first option for the place of Goliad city, Texas. We check the box and click on the hyperlink; the result should appear in the upper left corner of your screen:

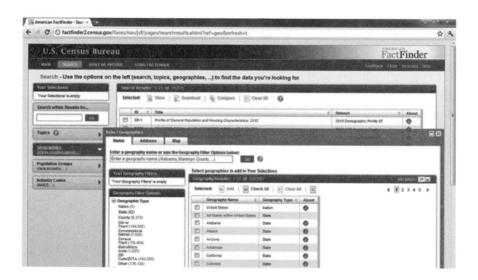

We need to close the geography selection box before doing anything. Move your cursor to the "x" in the upper right corner of the geography selection box and click on it to close.

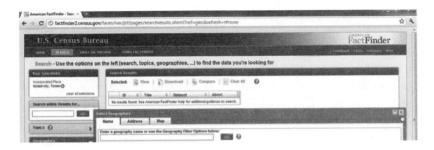

This will leave us with a limited number of options from the 2010 census PL94-171 file. Because the P1 Table, labeled "Race," is the first in a series, we'll check the box and click on the hyperlink.

Once we do that, our results should appear:

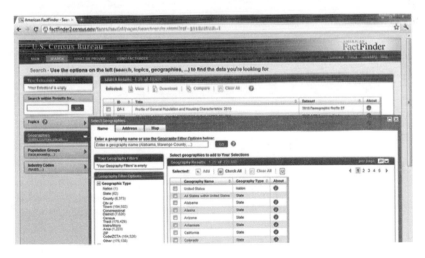

We can see Goliad had 1,908 residents in 2010.

Simple Income Lookup

You're interested in expanding your business to North Carolina. You'd like to be in an urban area that's close to major roads. You probably don't want to locate a business in an economically depressed area, so you'll want to do some research on median household incomes. There are two things to remember about median household income: First, it's the median, which means half the incomes are greater and half are less than those in the area. Secondly, it's the household, which means it's one or more people. The combined incomes of a working husband and wife would count as a single household income.

Browse to American FactFinder and select the "Datasets" menu:

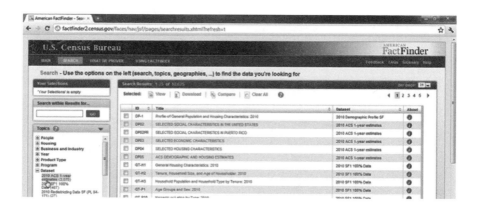

We'll want the 2010 ACS 1-year estimates, because they're the newest data available (although, as more data are available, we'll be able to use ACS 3-year or even 5-year estimates for more accuracy). Next, we'll click on the blue "Geography" button to open the geography selection box:

We're going to want Metro/Micro areas. We'll click on that link. Next, we'll click on the filter "Within State."

We'll select "North Carolina," noting that it has 30 metropolitan or micropolitan areas. A metropolitan area usually has more than 50,000 people; a micropolitan area has 10,000 or more. The metro or micro areas must include more than one place tied to others by commuting patterns.

When we select North Carolina, we get our first page of results. By default, American FactFinder shows only 25 pages per screen. You can change that by clicking on the "per page" pulldown menu in the upper right corner. We'll change it to 50 so we don't have to click through multiple screens to add the metro and micro areas:

When our results are returned, we'll select "Check All," then "Add" from the top of the list. Close the geography selection box. Our selection menu in the upper left corner of the screen should look like this:

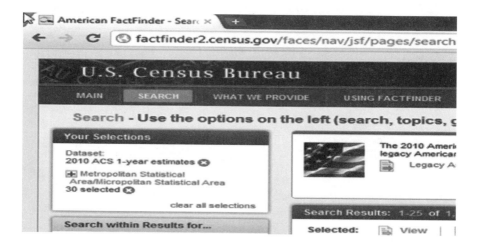

Now, we'll use the "Search within Results for . . ." box below the selection box to find tables about median household income. When we type "median household income" into the box, we'll see our options:

We want Table B19013, "Median household income in the past 12 months (in 2010 inflation-adjusted dollars)" We'll check it and click the hyperlink to get our results:

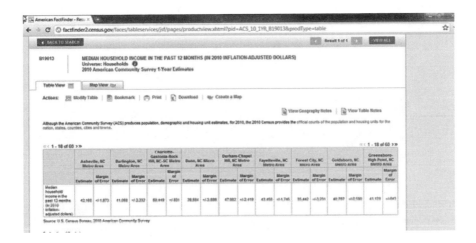

There are two ways to analyze the data. You can download the data by clicking on the "Download" link. This approach has its pros and cons. The upside is, you can import the table into a spreadsheet, and with a bit of work, rank all 30 metro/micro areas by median household income. The downside is that it takes a bit of work. To download the file, click on the blue "Download" hyperlink near the top of the results:

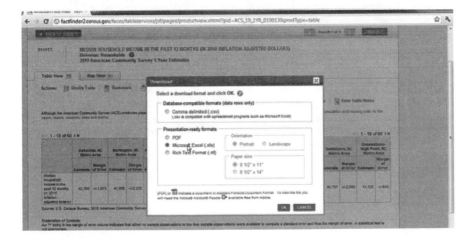

We'll select a "Database-compatible format" by clicking on the top radio button. When we click "OK," we'll get another dialogue box showing the file is downloading:

When we click on the "Download" button, we can see another dialogue box displaying the name of the zipped *.csv file:

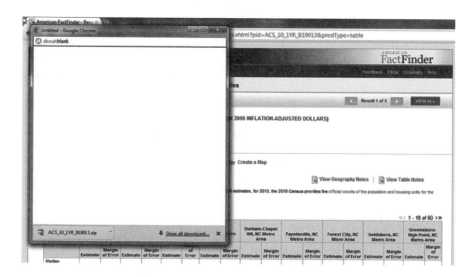

We unzip the file. One of the advantages of saving the file as a database-compatible *.csv over an Excel file is that the *.csv file will typically display the data in columnar form, rather than row form. The file should look like this:

With a few deletions and a simple sort, we can see that the Raleigh-Cary or Virginia Beach-Norfolk-Newport News areas are probably the best places to expand a business:

A database format can be made more useful with spatial analysis. What if you didn't know where the Raleigh or Virginia Beach metropolitan areas were located? FactFinder lets you compare areas on a map, as well. Go back to your results and look for the tab at the top that says "Map View."

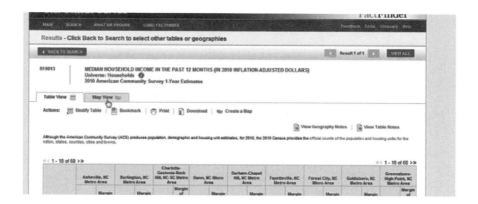

When you click on "Map View," you'll be asked to select a value field for your map:

Click on a row of the table with values you'd like displayed on a map. In this case, we're limited because we've only asked for median household income. When we click on the number for the Ashville metro area, we'll get a dialogue box asking us to confirm our selections:

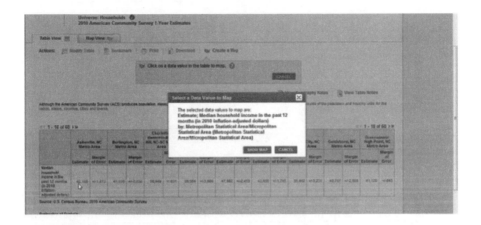

We'll click on the "Show Map" button for a nicely rendered view of the metro areas, color-coded by median household income:

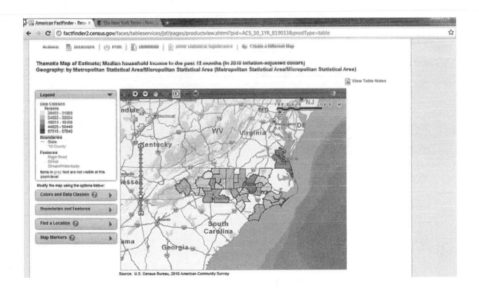

For information about the area, click on one of the shaded areas while the "Information" button, located here directly above the city of Columbus, Ohio, is highlighted.

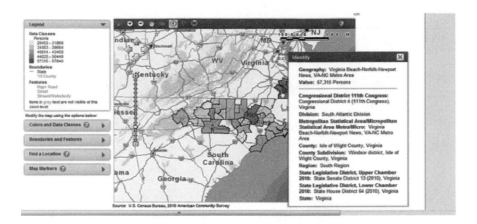

You can also download the map into a number of formats, including *.pdf, *.jpg, and *.shp files with associated data, for creating more custom maps using software programs like ArcView or ArcGIS.

APPENDIX B

Using Raw Data Files

The Census Bureau's American FactFinder is useful for a wide range of queries. When it comes to comparing geographic characteristics, it's often best to use raw data files that can be parsed and manipulated to come up with the best results.

There are a few caveats about using raw data files. It helps to have a solid understanding of relational databases, because all census data files include two components: one geographic file that identifies the area being analyzed, and at least one variable file that contains the data required.

Software is an important factor. The Census Bureau provides shell tables for Microsoft Access and scripts for SAS; these files can be easily altered to obtain the desired variables at different geographical levels. The Census Bureau also offers assistance with links to tools for other database programs, including FoxPro, Oracle, and SPSS.

Relational database programs are important because of the structure of raw census data. Because of the size of files, they're broken into multiple tables; the 2006–2010 American Community Survey, for example, consists of one geographical file, 118 variable files containing estimates, and 118 files displaying the margins of error for each estimate.

An FTP program to download bulk data is also useful and will save users from having to download dozens of individual files.

Census Tables

The primary source of decennial census data is the bureau's FTP site at ftp://ftp.census.gov. The site includes data for the 1980, 1990, 2000, and 2010 censuses.

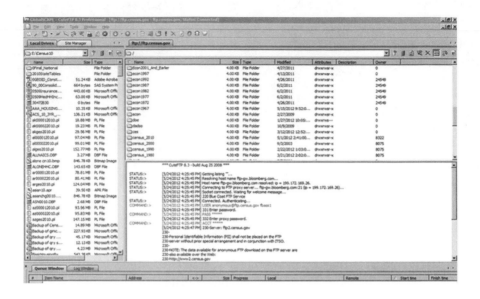

As an example, let's say we want to rank median household income for each state from the 2000 census. We'll start in the census_2000 folder. We know from reading this book that we can retrieve county-level decennial income figures from the Summary File 3 dataset (and after 2009, from the American Community Survey). We'll navigate to the Summary File 3 folder on the FTP site.

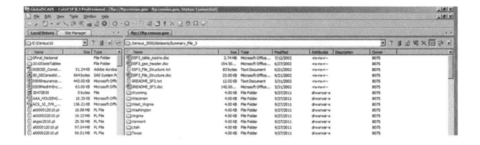

At this point, it's best to open the table matrix file and figure out where median household income figures are listed. We can see from the matrix that median household income is found in Table P53, which is part of segment six, and is nine characters long.

```
$75,000 to $99,999                                    P052013   06 9
$100,000 to $124,999                                  P052014   06 9
$125,000 to $149,999                                  P052015   06 9
$150,000 to $199,999                                  P052016   06 9
$200,000 or more                                      P052017   06 9

P53.    MEDIAN HOUSEHOLD INCOME IN 1999 (DOLLARS) [1]
        Universe:  Households
        Median household income in 1999              P053001   06 9

P54.    AGGREGATE HOUSEHOLD INCOME IN 1999 (DOLLARS) [3]
        Universe:  Households
```

We can open up one of the state folders—let's try Wyoming—and find segment six.

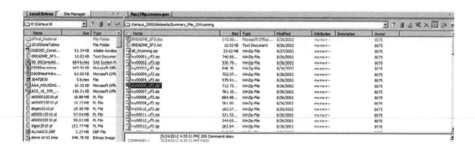

We'll need the matching geography file, as well.

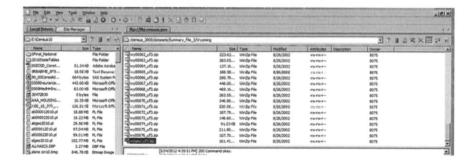

The two files can be downloaded and extracted to create basic text files. The census offers a web site full of good information on using the raw files at http://www.census.gov/support/cen2000_sf3ASCII.html.

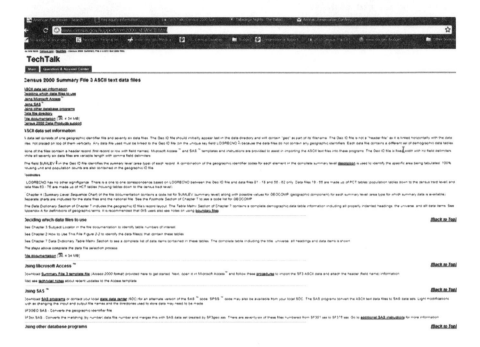

If we use SAS, two files should be downloaded: SF306.sas, which is the sixth segment that we need for the median household income numbers, and sf3geo.sas, which contains the geographical descriptions. The files may be opened in SAS and altered with a few minor changes, such as the locations of the library name and input file; the name of the SAS dataset; and the title.

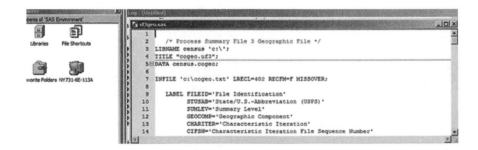

The two files can simply be stacked on top of each other and combined with a simple MERGE statement that looks something like this:

```
DATA CENSUS.MEDHHINC00_WY;
MERGE CENSUS.WYGEO
   CENSUS.WYSF306;
BY LOGRECNO;
RUN:
```

Finally, the data can be subset with a KEEP statement to include only the required variables and geographical levels. The SUMLEV, or summary level, variable in the geography file controls the geography. Common summary levels include:

```
040 -- State
050 -- County
060 -- Town
160 -- Place
500 -- Congressional District
```

The only variable from the data file that we'd be terribly interested in keeping would be P053001. So our final script for Wyoming median household income by county might look something like this:

```
DATA CENSUS.MEDHHINC_WY00 (KEEP=STUSAB
                          SUMLEV
                          GEOCOMP
                          STATE
                          COUNTY
                          NAME
                          POP100
                          P053001);
SET CENSUS.MEDHHINC00_WY;
WHERE SUMLEV='050':
RUN;
```

For comparing counties in more than one state, it's easy enough to modify the same script with a macro that loops through multiple geography and variable files to yield a result:

```
%MACRO DOSTATE(ST);
DATA CENSUS.MEDHHINC_&st.00 (KEEP=STUSAB
                          SUMLEV
                          GEOCOMP
                          STATE
                          COUNTY
                          NAME
                          POP100
                          P053001);
```

```
SET CENSUS.MEDHHINC00_&st;
WHERE SUMLEV='050':
RUN;
%DOSTATE(AK);
%DOSTATE(AL);
%DOSTATE(AR);
%DOSTATE(AZ);
%DOSTATE(CA);

. . .

%DOSTATE(VT);
%DOSTATE(WA);
%DOSTATE(WI);
%DOSTATE(WV);
%DOSTATE(WY);
```

For a full reference to each field, download the Summary File 3 Technical Documentation at http://www.census.gov/prod/cen2000/doc/sf3.pdf. Similar documentation is available for the PL94-171 (redistricting) and Summary File 1 datasets.

American Community Survey Tables

Developing tables for the American Community Survey is similar to working with decennial census data. Unlike the decennial census, though, the ACS documentation is scattered over several files in an FTP site. As an example, we'll replicate the median household income data that we examined from the 2000 census. We start at the FTP site, using five-year ACS figures.

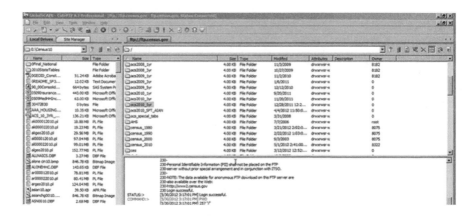

We'll drill down to the "summaryfile" subfolder and find a file labeled "Sequence Number and Table Number Lookup." Open it, and search for the phrase "Median Household Income."

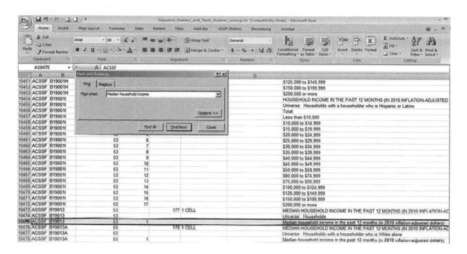

We can tell from the spreadsheet that we want the first (and only) data element in Table B19013, segment 53. There are 118 tables, or segments, in the 2006–2010 ACS sample. Next, we'll go to the "User Tools" folder and download the SAS scripts that the Census Bureau has made available.

When we unzip the folder, we'll look for the 53rd segment for Alaska. We can modify the segment with a macro later to include the entire United States.

We'll also need a geographic identifier file, which we can pull from the "SF All Macro" file, also in the "User Tools" folder.

```
SF_All_Macro.sas                                                                                    _□×
 1   DM "clear log";
 2   /*Libname stubs location of SequenceNumberTableNumberLookup dataset geographic*/
 3   LIBNAME stubs '/tab4/sumfile/prod/2006thru2010/docs';
 4   LIBNAME sas '/prt03/kck/sumfile/code_kc/';
 5   ********************************************************************************;
 6
 7 ⊟ %macro AnyGeo(geography);
 8   /*  All ACS geographic Summary File headers have the same following layout
 9       See Technical documentation for more information on geographic header files
10       and additional ACS Geography information                                    */
11   data work.&geography;
12             /*Location on geographic header file saved to from;                    */
13     INFILE "/tab4/sumfile/prod/2006thru2010/geo/&geography..txt" MISSOVER TRUNCOVER LRECL=500;
14
15     LABEL FILEID  ='File Identification'        STUSAB   ='State Postal Abbreviation'
16           SUMLEVEL='Summary Level'              COMPONENT='geographic Component'
17           LOGRECNO='Logical Record Number'      US       ='US'
18           REGION  ='Region'                     DIVISION ='Division'
19           STATECE ='State (Census Code)'        STATE    ='State (FIPS Code)'
20           COUNTY  ='County'                     COUSUB   ='County Subdivision (FIPS)'
21           PLACE   ='Place (FIPS Code)'          TRACT    ='Census Tract'
22           BLKGRP  ='Block Group'                CONCIT   ='Consolidated City'
23           CSA     ='Combined Statistical Area'  METDIV   ='Metropolitan Division'
24           UA      ='Urban Area'                 UACP     ='Urban Area Central Place'
25           VTD     ='Voting District'            ZCTA3    ='ZIP Code Tabulation Area (3-digit)'
26           SUBMCD  ='Subbarrio (FIPS)'           SDELM    ='School District (Elementary)'
27           SDSEC   ='School District (Secondary)' SDUNI   ='School District (Unified)'
28           UR      ='Urban/Rural'                PCI      ='Principal City Indicator'
29           TAZ     ='Traffic Analysis Zone'      UGA      ='Urban Growth Area'
30           GEOID   ='geographic Identifier'      NAME     ='Area Name'
31           AIANHH  ='American Indian Area/Alaska Native Area/Hawaiian Home Land (Census)'
32           AIANHHFP='American Indian Area/Alaska Native Area/Hawaiian Home Land (FIPS)'
33           AIHHTLI ='American Indian Trust Land/Hawaiian Home Land Indicator'
34           AITSCE  ='American Indian Tribal Subdivision (Census)'
35           AITS    ='American Indian Tribal Subdivision (FIPS)'
36           ANRC    ='Alaska Native Regional Corporation (FIPS)'
37           CBSA    ='Metropolitan and Micropolitan Statistical Area'
38           MACC    ='Metropolitan Area Central City'
39           MEMI    ='Metropolitan/Micropolitan Indicator Flag'
40           NECTA   ='New England City and Town Combined Statistical Area'
41           CNECTA  ='New England City and Town Area'
42           NECTADIV='New England City and Town Area Division'
43           CDCURR  ='Current Congressional District'
44           SLDU    ='State Legislative District Upper'
```

Next, we download our tables for each state. We can use one of three methods:

1. We can download all tables in two very large files.
2. We can download all tables by state, either in a file that includes tracts and block groups, or a file that includes all geographies except tracts or block groups.
3. We can download all tables by state, selecting individual segment files.

For the purposes of this example, we'll download the giant files, which include all data variables, plus the geography files. We'll run the geography script and the SAS script for segment 53, and then use the following script to merge the two:

```
libname acs10 'e:\acs10';
run;
%macro domacro(st);
data acs10.&st.geo10;
/*Location on geographic header file saved to from*/
infile "e:\acs10\g20105&st..txt" missover truncover lrecl=
500;
LABEL FILEID  ='File Identification'
STUSAB   ='State Postal Abbreviation'
SUMLEVEL='Summary Level'
COMPONENT='geographic Component'
LOGRECNO='Logical Record Number'
US       ='US'
REGION  -'Region'
DIVISION ='Division'
STATECE -'State (Census Code)'
STATE    ='State (FIPS Code)'
COUNTY  ='County'
COUSUB   ='County Subdivision (FIPS)'
PLACE   -'Place (FIPS Code)'
TRACT    ='Census Tract'
BLKGRP  ='Block Group'
CONCIT   ='Consolidated City'
CSA     ='Combined Statistical Area'
METDIV  ='Metropolitan Division'
UA       ='Urban Area'
UACP    ='Urban Area Central Place'
VTD     ='Voting District'
ZCTA3  ='ZIP Code Tabulation Area (3-digit)'
SUBMCD  -'Subbarrio (FIPS)'
SDELM  ='School District (Elementary)'
SDSEC   ='School District (Secondary)'
SDUNI  ='School District (Unified)'
UR       ='Urban/Rural'
PCI      ='Principal City Indicator'
TAZ      ='Traffic Analysis Zone'
UGA     ='Urban Growth Area'
GEOID   ='geographic Identifier'
NAME    ='Area Name'
AIANHH  ='American Indian Area/Alaska Native Area/Hawaiian
Home Land (Census)'
AIANHHFP='American Indian Area/Alaska Native Area/Hawaiian
Home Land (FIPS)'
```

```
AIHHTLI ='American Indian Trust Land/Hawaiian Home Land
Indicator'
AITSCE  ='American Indian Tribal Subdivision (Census)'
AITS    ='American Indian Tribal Subdivision (FIPS)'
ANRC    ='Alaska Native Regional Corporation (FIPS)'
CBSA    ='Metropolitan and Micropolitan Statistical Area'
MACC    ='Metropolitan Area Central City'
MEMI    ='Metropolitan/Micropolitan Indicator Flag'
NECTA   ='New England City and Town Combined Statistical
Area'
CNECTA  ='New England City and Town Area'
NECTADIV='New England City and Town Area Division'
CDCURR  ='Current Congressional District'
SLDU    ='State Legislative District Upper'
SLDL    ='State Legislative District Lower'
ZCTA5   ='ZIP Code Tabulation Area (5-digit)'
PUMA5   ='Public Use Microdata Area - 5% File'
PUMA1   ='Public Use Microdata Area - 1% File'      ;
  INPUT
FILEID      $ 1-6
STUSAB      $ 7-8
SUMLEVEL    $ 9-11
COMPONENT   $ 12-13
LOGRECNO    $ 14-20
US          $ 21-21
REGION      $ 22-22
DIVISION    $ 23-23
STATECE     $ 24-25
STATE       $ 26-27
COUNTY      $ 28-30
COUSUB      $ 31-35
PLACE       $ 36-40
TRACT       $ 41-46
BLKGRP      $ 47-47
CONCIT      $ 48-52
AIANHH      $ 53-56
AIANHHFP    $ 57-61
AIHHTLI     $ 62-62
AITSCE      $ 63-65
AITS        $ 66-70
ANRC        $ 71-75
CBSA        $ 76-80
CSA         $ 81-83
METDIV      $ 84-88
MACC        $ 89-89
MEMI        $ 90-90
NECTA       $91-95
```

```
CNECTA      $ 96-98
NECTADIV    $ 99-103
UA          $ 104-108
UACP        $ 109-113
CDCURR      $ 114-115
SLDU        $ 116-118
SLDL        $ 119-121
VTD         $ 122-127
ZCTA3       $ 128-130
ZCTA5       $ 131-135
SUBMCD      $ 136-140
SDELM       $ 141-145
SDSEC       $ 146-150
SDUNI       $ 151-155
UR          $ 156-156
PCI         $ 157-157
TAZ         $ 158-163
UGA         $ 164-168
PUMA5       $ 169-173
PUMA1       $ 174-178
GEOID       $ 179-218
NAME        $ 219-418 ;
run;
DATA acs10.&st.53a;
LENGTH FILEID    $6
 FILETYPE $6
  STUSAB    $2
  CHARITER $3
  SEQUENCE $4
  LOGRECNO $7;

INFILE "e:\acs10\e20105&st.0053000.txt" DSD TRUNCOVER
DELIMITER =',' LRECL=3000;
  LABEL FILEID  ='File Identification'
    FILETYPE='File Type'
  STUSAB  ='State/U.S.-Abbreviation (USPS)'
  CHARITER='Character Iteration'
  SEQUENCE='Sequence Number'
  LOGRECNO='Logical Record Number'
/*HOUSEHOLD INCOME IN THE PAST 12 MONTHS (IN 2009
INFLATION-ADJUSTED DOLLARS) */
/*Universe:  Households */
B19001e1='Total:'
B19001e2='Less than $10,000'
B19001e3='$10,000 to $14,999'
B19001e4='$15,000 to $19,999'
B19001e5='$20,000 to $24,999'
```

```
B19001e6='$25,000 to $29,999'
B19001e7='$30,000 to $34,999'
B19001e8='$35,000 to $39,999'
B19001e9='$40,000 to $44,999'
B19001e10='$45,000 to $49,999'
B19001e11='$50,000 to $59,999'
B19001e12='$60,000 to $74,999'
B19001e13='$75,000 to $99,999'
B19001e14='$100,000 to $124,999'
B19001e15='$125,000 to $149,999'
B19001e16='$150,000 to $199,999'
B19001e17='$200,000 or more'
/*HOUSEHOLD INCOME IN THE PAST 12 MONTHS (IN 2009
INFLATION-ADJUSTED DOLLARS) (WHITE ALONE HOUSEHOLDER) */
/*Universe:  Households with a householder who is White
alone */
B19001Ae1='Total:'
B19001Ae2='Less than $10,000'
B19001Ae3='$10,000 to $14,999'
B19001Ae4='$15,000 to $19,999'
B19001Ae5='$20,000 to $24,999'
B19001Ae6='$25,000 to $29,999'
B19001Ae7='$30,000 to $34,999'
B19001Ae8='$35,000 to $39,999'
B19001Ae9='$40,000 to $44,999'
B19001Ae10='$45,000 to $49,999'
B19001Ae11='$50,000 to $59,999'
B19001Ae12='$60,000 to $74,999'
B19001Ae13='$75,000 to $99,999'
B19001Ae14='$100,000 to $124,999'
B19001Ae15='$125,000 to $149,999'
B19001Ae16='$150,000 to $199,999'
B19001Ae17='$200,000 or more'
/*HOUSEHOLD INCOME IN THE PAST 12 MONTHS (IN 2009
INFLATION-ADJUSTED DOLLARS) (BLACK OR AFRICAN AMERICAN
ALONE HOUSEHOLDER) */
/*Universe:  Households with a householder who is Black or
African American alone */
B19001Be1='Total:'
B19001Be2='Less than $10,000'
B19001Be3='$10,000 to $14,999'
B19001Be4='$15,000 to $19,999'
B19001Be5='$20,000 to $24,999'
B19001Be6='$25,000 to $29,999'
B19001Be7='$30,000 to $34,999'
B19001Be8='$35,000 to $39,999'
B19001Be9='$40,000 to $44,999'
```

```
B19001Be10='$45,000 to $49,999'
B19001Be11='$50,000 to $59,999'
B19001Be12='$60,000 to $74,999'
B19001Be13='$75,000 to $99,999'
B19001Be14='$100,000 to $124,999'
B19001Be15='$125,000 to $149,999'
B19001Be16='$150,000 to $199,999'
B19001Be17='$200,000 or more'
/*HOUSEHOLD INCOME IN THE PAST 12 MONTHS (IN 2009
INFLATION-ADJUSTED DOLLARS) (AMERICAN INDIAN AND ALASKA
NATIVE ALONE HOUSEHOLDER) */
/*Universe:  Households with a householder who is
American Indian and Alaska Native alone */
B19001Ce1='Total:'
B19001Ce2='Less than $10,000'
B19001Ce3='$10,000 to $14,999'
B19001Ce4='$15,000 to $19,999'
B19001Ce5='$20,000 to $24,999'
B19001Ce6='$25,000 to $29,999'
B19001Ce7='$30,000 to $34,999'
B19001Ce8='$35,000 to $39,999'
B19001Ce9='$40,000 to $44,999'
B19001Ce10='$45,000 to $49,999'
B19001Ce11='$50,000 to $59,999'
B19001Ce12='$60,000 to $74,999'
B19001Ce13='$75,000 to $99,999'
B19001Ce14='$100,000 to $124,999'
B19001Ce15='$125,000 to $149,999'
B19001Ce16='$150,000 to $199,999'
B19001Ce17='$200,000 or more'
/*HOUSEHOLD INCOME IN THE PAST 12 MONTHS (IN 2009
INFLATION-ADJUSTED DOLLARS) (ASIAN ALONE HOUSEHOLDER) */
/*Universe:  Households with a householder who is Asian
alone */
B19001De1='Total:'
B19001De2='Less than $10,000'
B19001De3='$10,000 to $14,999'
B19001De4='$15,000 to $19,999'
B19001De5='$20,000 to $24,999'
B19001De6='$25,000 to $29,999'
B19001De7='$30,000 to $34,999'
B19001De8='$35,000 to $39,999'
B19001De9='$40,000 to $44,999'
B19001De10='$45,000 to $49,999'
B19001De11='$50,000 to $59,999'
B19001De12='$60,000 to $74,999'
B19001De13='$75,000 to $99,999'
```

```
B19001De14='$100,000 to $124,999'
B19001De15='$125,000 to $149,999'
B19001De16='$150,000 to $199,999'
B19001De17='$200,000 or more'
/*HOUSEHOLD INCOME IN THE PAST 12 MONTHS (IN 2009
INFLATION-ADJUSTED DOLLARS) (NATIVE HAWAIIAN AND OTHER
PACIFIC ISLANDER ALONE HOUSEHOLDER) */
/*Universe:  Households with a householder who is Native
Hawaiian and Other Pacific Islander alone */
B19001Ee1='Total:'
B19001Ee2='Less than $10,000'
B19001Ee3='$10,000 to $14,999'
B19001Ee4='$15,000 to $19,999'
B19001Ee5='$20,000 to $24,999'
B19001Ee6='$25,000 to $29,999'
B19001Ee7='$30,000 to $34,999'
B19001Ee8='$35,000 to $39,999'
B19001Ee9='$40,000 to $44,999'
B19001Ee10='$45,000 to $49,999'
B19001Ee11='$50,000 to $59,999'
B19001Ee12='$60,000 to $74,999'
B19001Ee13='$75,000 to $99,999'
B19001Ee14='$100,000 to $124,999'
B19001Ee15='$125,000 to $149,999'
B19001Ee16='$150,000 to $199,999'
B19001Ee17='$200,000 or more'
/*HOUSEHOLD INCOME IN THE PAST 12 MONTHS (IN 2009
INFLATION-ADJUSTED DOLLARS) (SOME OTHER RACE ALONE
HOUSEHOLDER) */
/*Universe:  Households with a householder who is Some
other race alone */
B19001Fe1='Total:'
B19001Fe2='Less than $10,000'
B19001Fe3='$10,000 to $14,999'
B19001Fe4='$15,000 to $19,999'
B19001Fe5='$20,000 to $24,999'
B19001Fe6='$25,000 to $29,999'
B19001Fe7='$30,000 to $34,999'
B19001Fe8='$35,000 to $39,999'
B19001Fe9='$40,000 to $44,999'
B19001Fe10='$45,000 to $49,999'
B19001Fe11='$50,000 to $59,999'
B19001Fe12='$60,000 to $74,999'
B19001Fe13='$75,000 to $99,999'
B19001Fe14='$100,000 to $124,999'
B19001Fe15='$125,000 to $149,999'
```

```
B19001Fe16='$150,000 to $199,999'
B19001Fe17='$200,000 or more'
/*HOUSEHOLD INCOME IN THE PAST 12 MONTHS (IN 2009
INFLATION-ADJUSTED DOLLARS) (TWO OR MORE RACES
HOUSEHOLDER) */
/*Universe:  Households with a householder who is Two or
more races */
B19001Ge1='Total:'
B19001Ge2='Less than $10,000'
B19001Ge3='$10,000 to $14,999'
B19001Ge4='$15,000 to $19,999'
B19001Ge5='$20,000 to $24,999'
B19001Ge6='$25,000 to $29,999'
B19001Ge7='$30,000 to $34,999'
B19001Ge8='$35,000 to $39,999'
B19001Ge9='$40,000 to $44,999'
B19001Ge10='$45,000 to $49,999'
B19001Ge11='$50,000 to $59,999'
B19001Ge12='$60,000 to $74,999'
B19001Ge13='$75,000 to $99,999'
B19001Ge14='$100,000 to $124,999'
B19001Ge15='$125,000 to $149,999'
B19001Ge16='$150,000 to $199,999'
B19001Ge17='$200,000 or more'
/*HOUSEHOLD INCOME IN THE PAST 12 MONTHS (IN 2009
INFLATION-ADJUSTED DOLLARS) (WHITE ALONE, NOT HISPANIC OR
LATINO HOUSEHOLDER) */
/*Universe:  Households with a householder who is White
alone, not Hispanic or Latino */
B19001He1='Total:'
B19001He2='Less than $10,000'
B19001He3='$10,000 to $14,999'
B19001He4='$15,000 to $19,999'
D19001He5='$20,000 to $24,999'
B19001He6='$25,000 to $29,999'
B19001He7='$30,000 to $34,999'
B19001He8='$35,000 to $39,999'
B19001He9='$40,000 to $44,999'
B19001He10='$45,000 to $49,999'
B19001He11='$50,000 to $59,999'
B19001He12='$60,000 to $74,999'
B19001He13='$75,000 to $99,999'
B19001He14='$100,000 to $124,999'
B19001He15='$125,000 to $149,999'
B19001He16='$150,000 to $199,999'
B19001He17='$200,000 or more'
```

```
/*HOUSEHOLD INCOME IN THE PAST 12 MONTHS (IN 2009
INFLATION-ADJUSTED DOLLARS) (HISPANIC OR LATINO
HOUSEHOLDER) */
/*Universe:  Households with a householder who is Hispanic
or Latino */
B19001Ie1='Total:'
B19001Ie2='Less than $10,000'
B19001Ie3='$10,000 to $14,999'
B19001Ie4='$15,000 to $19,999'
B19001Ie5='$20,000 to $24,999'
B19001Ie6='$25,000 to $29,999'
B19001Ie7='$30,000 to $34,999'
B19001Ie8='$35,000 to $39,999'
B19001Ie9='$40,000 to $44,999'
B19001Ie10='$45,000 to $49,999'
B19001Ie11='$50,000 to $59,999'
B19001Ie12='$60,000 to $74,999'
B19001Ie13='$75,000 to $99,999'
B19001Ie14='$100,000 to $124,999'
B19001Ie15='$125,000 to $149,999'
B19001Ie16='$150,000 to $199,999'
B19001Ie17='$200,000 or more'
/*MEDIAN HOUSEHOLD INCOME IN THE PAST 12 MONTHS (IN 2009
INFLATION-ADJUSTED DOLLARS) */
/*Universe:  Households */
B19013e1='Median household income in the past 12 months
(in 2009 inflation-adjusted dollars)'
/*MEDIAN HOUSEHOLD INCOME IN THE PAST 12 MONTHS (IN 2009
INFLATION-ADJUSTED DOLLARS) (WHITE ALONE HOUSEHOLDER) */
/*Universe:  Households with a householder who is White
alone */
B19013Ae1='Median household income in the past 12 months
(in 2009 inflation-adjusted dollars)'
/*MEDIAN HOUSEHOLD INCOME IN THE PAST 12 MONTHS (IN 2009
INFLATION-ADJUSTED DOLLARS) (BLACK OR AFRICAN AMERICAN
ALONE HOUSEHOLDER) */
/*Universe:  Households with a householder who is Black
or African American alone */
B19013Be1='Median household income in the past 12 months
(in 2009 inflation-adjusted dollars)'
/*MEDIAN HOUSEHOLD INCOME IN THE PAST 12 MONTHS (IN 2009
INFLATION-ADJUSTED DOLLARS) (AMERICAN INDIAN AND ALASKA
NATIVE ALONE HOUSEHOLDER) */
/*Universe:  Households with a householder who is American
Indian and Alaska Native alone */
B19013Ce1='Median household income in the past 12 months
(in 2009 inflation-adjusted dollars)'
```

```
/*MEDIAN HOUSEHOLD INCOME IN THE PAST 12 MONTHS (IN 2009
INFLATION-ADJUSTED DOLLARS) (ASIAN ALONE HOUSEHOLDER) */
/*Universe:  Households with a householder who is
Asian alone */
B19013De1='Median household income in the past 12 months
(in 2009 inflation-adjusted dollars)'
/*MEDIAN HOUSEHOLD INCOME IN THE PAST 12 MONTHS (IN 2009
INFLATION-ADJUSTED DOLLARS) (NATIVE HAWAIIAN AND OTHER
PACIFIC ISLANDER ALONE HOUSEHOLDER) */
/*Universe:  Households with a householder who is Native
Hawaiian and Other Pacific Islander alone */
B19013Ee1='Median household income in the past 12 months
(in 2009 inflation-adjusted dollars)'
/*MEDIAN HOUSEHOLD INCOME IN THE PAST 12 MONTHS (IN 2009
INFLATION-ADJUSTED DOLLARS) (SOME OTHER RACE ALONE
HOUSEHOLDER) */
/*Universe.  Households with a householder who is some
other race alone */
B19013Fe1='Median household income in the past 12 months
(in 2009 inflation-adjusted dollars)'
/*MEDIAN HOUSEHOLD INCOME IN THE PAST 12 MONTHS (IN 2009
INFLATION-ADJUSTED DOLLARS) (TWO OR MORE RACES
HOUSEHOLDER) */
/*Universe:  Households with a householder who is Two or
more races */
B19013Ge1='Median household income in the past 12 months
(in 2009 inflation-adjusted dollars)'
/*MEDIAN HOUSEHOLD INCOME IN THE PAST 12 MONTHS (IN 2009
INFLATION-ADJUSTED DOLLARS) (WHITE ALONE, NOT HISPANIC
OR LATINO HOUSEHOLDER) */
/*Universe:  Households with a householder who is White
alone, not Hispanic or Latino */
B19013He1='Median household income in the past 12 months
(in 2009 inflation-adjusted dollars)'
/*MEDIAN HOUSEHOLD INCOME IN THE PAST 12 MONTHS (IN 2009
INFLATION-ADJUSTED DOLLARS) (HISPANIC OR LATINO
HOUSEHOLDER) */
/*Universe:  Households with a householder who is
Hispanic or Latino */
B19013Ie1='Median household income in the past 12 months
(in 2009 inflation-adjusted dollars)'
/*MEDIAN HOUSEHOLD INCOME IN THE PAST 12 MONTHS (IN 2009
INFLATION-ADJUSTED DOLLARS) BY HOUSEHOLD SIZE */
/*Universe:  Households */
B19019e1='Total:'
B19019e2='1-person households'
B19019e3='2-person households'
```

```
B19019e4='3-person households'
B19019e5='4-person households'
B19019e6='5-person households'
B19019e7='6-person households'
B19019e8='7-or-more-person households'
/*AGGREGATE HOUSEHOLD INCOME IN THE PAST 12 MONTHS (IN 2009
INFLATION-ADJUSTED DOLLARS) */
/*Universe:  Households */
B19025e1='Aggregate household income in the past 12 months
(in 2009 inflation-adjusted dollars)'
/*AGGREGATE HOUSEHOLD INCOME IN THE PAST 12 MONTHS (IN 2009
INFLATION-ADJUSTED DOLLARS) (WHITE ALONE HOUSEHOLDER) */
/*Universe:  Households with a householder who is White
alone */
B19025Ae1='Aggregate household income in the past 12 months
(in 2009 inflation-adjusted dollars)'
/*AGGREGATE HOUSEHOLD INCOME IN THE PAST 12 MONTHS (IN 2009
INFLATION-ADJUSTED DOLLARS) (BLACK OR AFRICAN AMERICAN
ALONE HOUSEHOLDER) */
/*Universe:  Households with a householder who is Black or
African American alone */
B19025Be1='Aggregate household income in the past 12 months
(in 2009 inflation-adjusted dollars)'
/*AGGREGATE HOUSEHOLD INCOME IN THE PAST 12 MONTHS (IN 2009
INFLATION-ADJUSTED DOLLARS) (AMERICAN INDIAN AND ALASKA
NATIVE ALONE HOUSEHOLDER) */
/*Universe:  Households with a householder who is American
Indian and Alaska Native alone */
B19025Ce1='Aggregate household income in the past 12 months
(in 2009 inflation-adjusted dollars)'
/*AGGREGATE HOUSEHOLD INCOME IN THE PAST 12 MONTHS (IN 2009
INFLATION-ADJUSTED DOLLARS) (ASIAN ALONE HOUSEHOLDER) */
/*Universe:  Households with a householder who is Asian
alone */
B19025De1='Aggregate household income in the past 12 months
(in 2009 inflation-adjusted dollars)'
/*AGGREGATE HOUSEHOLD INCOME IN THE PAST 12 MONTHS (IN 2009
INFLATION-ADJUSTED DOLLARS) (NATIVE HAWAIIAN AND OTHER
PACIFIC ISLANDER ALONE HOUSEHOLDER) */
/*Universe:  Households with a householder who is Native
Hawaiian and Other Pacific Islander alone */
B19025Ee1='Aggregate household income in the past 12 months
(in 2009 inflation-adjusted dollars)'
/*AGGREGATE HOUSEHOLD INCOME IN THE PAST 12 MONTHS (IN 2009
INFLATION-ADJUSTED DOLLARS) (SOME OTHER RACE ALONE
HOUSEHOLDER) */
```

```
/*Universe:  Households with a householder who is Some other
race alone */
B19025Fe1='Aggregate household income in the past 12 months
(in 2009 inflation-adjusted dollars)'
/*AGGREGATE HOUSEHOLD INCOME IN THE PAST 12 MONTHS (IN 2009
INFLATION-ADJUSTED DOLLARS) (TWO OR MORE RACES
HOUSEHOLDER) */
/*Universe:  Households with a householder who is Two or
more races */
B19025Ge1='Aggregate household income in the past 12 months
(in 2009 inflation-adjusted dollars)'
/*AGGREGATE HOUSEHOLD INCOME IN THE PAST 12 MONTHS (IN 2009
INFLATION-ADJUSTED DOLLARS) (WHITE ALONE, NOT HISPANIC
OR LATINO HOUSEHOLDER) */
/*Universe:  Households with a householder who is White
alone, not Hispanic or Latino */
B19025He1='Aggregate household income in the past 12 months
(in 2009 inflation-adjusted dollars)'
/*AGGREGATE HOUSEHOLD INCOME IN THE PAST 12 MONTHS (IN 2009
INFLATION-ADJUSTED DOLLARS) (HISPANIC OR LATINO
HOUSEHOLDER) */
/*Universe:  Households with a householder who is Hispanic
or Latino */
B19025Ie1='Aggregate household income in the past 12 months
(in 2009 inflation-adjusted dollars)'
;
INPUT
FILEID    $
FILETYPE  $
STUSAB    $
CHARITER  $
SEQUENCE  $
LOGRECNO  $
B19001e1
B19001e2
B19001e3
B19001e4
B19001e5
B19001e6
B19001e7
B19001e8
B19001e9
B19001e10
B19001e11
B19001e12
B19001e13
```

```
B19001e14
B19001e15
B19001e16
B19001e17
B19001Ae1
B19001Ae2
B19001Ae3
B19001Ae4
B19001Ae5
B19001Ae6
B19001Ae7
B19001Ae8
B19001Ae9
B19001Ae10
B19001Ae11
B19001Ae12
B19001Ae13
B19001Ae14
B19001Ae15
B19001Ae16
B19001Ae17
B19001Be1
B19001Be2
B19001Be3
B19001Be4
B19001Be5
B19001Be6
B19001Be7
B19001Be8
B19001Be9
B19001Be10
B19001Be11
B19001Be12
B19001Be13
B19001Be14
B19001Be15
B19001Be16
B19001Be17
B19001Ce1
B19001Ce2
B19001Ce3
B19001Ce4
B19001Ce5
B19001Ce6
B19001Ce7
B19001Ce8
B19001Ce9
```

```
B19001Ce10
B19001Ce11
B19001Ce12
B19001Ce13
B19001Ce14
B19001Ce15
B19001Ce16
B19001Ce17
B19001De1
B19001De2
B19001De3
B19001De4
B19001De5
B19001De6
B19001De7
B19001De8
B19001De9
B19001De10
B19001De11
B19001De12
B19001De13
B19001De14
B19001De15
B19001De16
B19001De17
B19001Ee1
B19001Ee2
B19001Ee3
B19001Ee4
B19001Ee5
B19001Ee6
B19001Ee7
B19001Ee8
B19001Ee9
B19001Ee10
B19001Ee11
B19001Ee12
B19001Ee13
B19001Ee14
B19001Ee15
B19001Ee16
B19001Ee17
B19001Fe1
B19001Fe2
B19001Fe3
B19001Fe4
B19001Fe5
```

```
B19001Fe6
B19001Fe7
B19001Fe8
B19001Fe9
B19001Fe10
B19001Fe11
B19001Fe12
B19001Fe13
B19001Fe14
B19001Fe15
B19001Fe16
B19001Fe17
B19001Ge1
B19001Ge2
B19001Ge3
B19001Ge4
B19001Ge5
B19001Ge6
B19001Ge7
B19001Ge8
B19001Ge9
B19001Ge10
B19001Ge11
B19001Ge12
B19001Ge13
B19001Ge14
B19001Ge15
B19001Ge16
B19001Ge17
B19001He1
B19001He2
B19001He3
B19001He4
B19001He5
B19001He6
B19001He7
B19001He8
B19001He9
B19001He10
B19001He11
B19001He12
B19001He13
B19001He14
B19001He15
B19001He16
B19001He17
```

```
B19001Ie1
B19001Ie2
B19001Ie3
B19001Ie4
B19001Ie5
B19001Ie6
B19001Ie7
B19001Ie8
B19001Ie9
B19001Ie10
B19001Ie11
B19001Ie12
B19001Ie13
B19001Ie14
B19001Ie15
B19001Ie16
B19001Te17
B19013e1
B19013Ae1
B19013Be1
B19013Ce1
B19013De1
B19013Ee1
B19013Fe1
B19013Ge1
B19013He1
B19013Ie1
B19019e1
B19019e2
B19019e3
B19019e4
B19019e5
B19019e6
B19019e7
B19019e8
B19025e1
B19025Ae1
B19025Be1
B19025Ce1
B19025De1
B19025Ee1
B19025Fe1
B19025Ge1
B19025He1
B19025Ie1;
RUN;
```

```
data acs10.&st.medhhinc10a;
merge acs10.&st.geo10
     acs10.&st.53a;
by logrecno;
run;
data acs10.&st.medhhinc10 (keep=stusab
                            state
                            county
                           place
                            cousub
                            name
                            b19013e1);
length state $2.
       county $3.
 place $5.
 cousub $5.
 name $36.
 stusab $2.
 b19013e1 8.0;
set acs10.&st.medhhinc10a;
where sumlevel in ('040','050','060','160') and
component='00';
stusab=UPCASE(stusab);
run;
proc delete data=acs10.&st.medhhinc10a;
run;
proc delete data=acs10.&st.geo10;
run;
proc delete data=acs10.&st.53a;
run;
proc delete data=acs10.&st.medhhinc10;
run;
%mend;
%domacro(AL);
%domacro(AK);
%domacro(AZ);
%domacro(AR);
%domacro(CA);
%domacro(CO);
%domacro(CT);
%domacro(DE);
%domacro(DC);
%domacro(FL);
%domacro(GA);
%domacro(HI);
%domacro(ID);
%domacro(IL);
```

```
%domacro(IN);
%domacro(IA);
%domacro(KS);
%domacro(KY);
%domacro(LA);
%domacro(ME);
%domacro(MD);
%domacro(MA);
%domacro(MI);
%domacro(MN);
%domacro(MS);
%domacro(MO);
%domacro(MT);
%domacro(NE);
%domacro(NV);
%domacro(NH);
%domacro(NJ);
%domacro(NM);
%domacro(NY);
%domacro(NC);
%domacro(ND);
%domacro(OH);
%domacro(OK);
%domacro(OR);
%domacro(PA);
%domacro(RI);
%domacro(SC);
%domacro(SD);
%domacro(TN);
%domacro(TX);
%domacro(UT);
%domacro(VT);
%domacro(VA);
%domacro(WA);
%domacro(WV);
%domacro(WI);
%domacro(WY);
data acs10.usmedhhinc10;
set acs10.ALmedhhinc10
acs10.AKmedhhinc10
acs10.AZmedhhinc10
acs10.ARmedhhinc10
acs10.CAmedhhinc10
acs10.COmedhhinc10
acs10.CTmedhhinc10
acs10.DEmedhhinc10
acs10.DCmedhhinc10
```

```
acs10.FLmedhhinc10
acs10.GAmedhhinc10
acs10.HImedhhinc10
acs10.IDmedhhinc10
acs10.ILmedhhinc10
acs10.INmedhhinc10
acs10.IAmedhhinc10
acs10.KSmedhhinc10
acs10.KYmedhhinc10
acs10.LAmedhhinc10
acs10.MEmedhhinc10
acs10.MDmedhhinc10
acs10.MAmedhhinc10
acs10.MImedhhinc10
acs10.MNmedhhinc10
acs10.MSmedhhinc10
acs10.MOmedhhinc10
acs10.MTmedhhinc10
acs10.NEmedhhinc10
acs10.NVmedhhinc10
acs10.NHmedhhinc10
acs10.NJmedhhinc10
acs10.NMmedhhinc10
acs10.NYmedhhinc10
acs10.NCmedhhinc10
acs10.NDmedhhinc10
acs10.OHmedhhinc10
acs10.OKmedhhinc10
acs10.ORmedhhinc10
acs10.PAmedhhinc10
acs10.RImedhhinc10
acs10.SCmedhhinc10
acs10.SDmedhhinc10
acs10.TNmedhhinc10
acs10.TXmedhhinc10
acs10.UTmedhhinc10
acs10.VTmedhhinc10
acs10.VAmedhhinc10
acs10.WAmedhhinc10
acs10.WVmedhhinc10
acs10.WImedhhinc10
acs10.WYmedhhinc10;
run;
```

APPENDIX C

Glossary of Census Terms

The 2010 census data products provide, except where specifically noted, counts of the resident population of the United States. The U.S. resident population includes everyone whose usual place of residence was in the 50 states and the District of Columbia at the time of the 2010 census.

In the design of summary file tables, the Census Bureau strives for consistency in terminology and cell label structure to facilitate processing, review, and usability. Data users see the same patterns repeated in various cross-tabulated tables. Unfortunately, at times, the use of a pattern creates illogical results, such as the display of data for the population 65 years and over in juvenile correctional facilities.

All definitions below are derived directly from Census Bureau technical documentation.

Population Characteristics

Age

The data on age were derived from answers to a two-part question (i.e., age and date of birth). The age classification for a person in census tabulations is the age of the person in completed years as of April 1, 2010, the census reference date. Both age and date of birth responses are used in combination to determine the most accurate age for the person as of the census reference date. Inconsistently reported and missing values are assigned or allocated based on the values of other variables for that person, from other people in the household or from people in other households (i.e., hot-deck imputation).

Age data are tabulated in age groupings and single years of age. Data on age also are used to classify other characteristics in census tabulations.

Median Age—This measure divides the age distribution into two equal parts: one-half of the cases falling below the median value and one-half above the value. Median age is computed on the basis of a single-year-of-age distribution using a linear interpolation method.

Alaska Native Tribe

See "Race."

American Indian Tribe

See "Race."

Hispanic or Latino Origin

The data on the Hispanic or Latino population were derived from answers to a question that was asked of all people. The terms "Hispanic," "Latino," and "Spanish" are used interchangeably. Some respondents identify with all three terms, whereas others may identify with only one of these three specific terms. People who identify with the terms "Hispanic," "Latino," or "Spanish" are those who classify themselves in one of the specific Hispanic, Latino, or Spanish categories listed on the questionnaire ("Mexican," "Puerto Rican," or "Cuban") as well as those who indicate that they are "another Hispanic, Latino, or Spanish origin." People who do not identify with one of the specific origins listed on the questionnaire but indicate that they are "another Hispanic, Latino, or Spanish origin" are those whose origins are from Spain, the Spanish-speaking countries of Central or South America, or the Dominican Republic. Up to two write-in responses to the "another Hispanic, Latino, or Spanish origin" category are coded.

Origin can be viewed as the heritage, nationality group, lineage, or country of birth of the person or the person's parents or ancestors before their arrival in the United States. People who identify their origin as Hispanic, Latino, or Spanish may be any race.

Some tabulations are shown by the origin of the householder. In all cases where the origin of households, families, or occupied housing units is classified as Hispanic, Latino, or Spanish, the origin of the householder is used. (See the discussion of householder under "Household Type and Relationship.")

Household Type and Relationship

Household

A household includes all the people who occupy a housing unit. (People not living in households are classified as living in group quarters.) A housing unit is a house, an apartment, a mobile home, a group of rooms, or a single room that is occupied (or if vacant, is intended for occupancy) as separate living quarters. Separate living quarters are those in which the occupants live separately from any other people in the building and which have direct access from the outside of the building or through a common hall. The occupants may be a single family, one person living alone, two or more families living together, or any other group of related or unrelated people who share living arrangements. In the 2010 census data products, the count of households or householders equals the count of occupied housing units.

Average Household Size—Average household size is a measure obtained by dividing the number of people in households by the number of households. In cases where people in households are cross-classified by race or Hispanic origin, people in the household are classified by the race or Hispanic origin of the householder rather than the race or Hispanic origin of each individual. Average household size is rounded to the nearest hundredth.

Relationship to Householder

Householder—The data on relationship to householder were derived from answers to Question 2, which was asked of all people in housing units. One person in each household is designated as the householder. In most cases, this is the person, or one of the people, in whose name the home is owned, being bought, or rented, and who is listed on line one of the questionnaire. If there is no such person in the household, any adult household member 15 years old and over could be designated as the householder.

Households are classified by type according to the sex of the householder and the presence of relatives. Two types of householders are distinguished: a family householder and a nonfamily householder. A family householder is a householder living with one or more individuals related to him or her by birth, marriage, or adoption. The householder and all people in the household related to him or her are family members. A nonfamily householder is a householder living alone or with nonrelatives only.

Spouse—The "spouse" category includes a person identified as the husband or wife of the householder and who is of the opposite sex. For most of the tables, unless otherwise specified, it does not include same-sex spouses even if a marriage was performed in a state issuing marriage certificates for same-sex couples.

Child—The "child" category includes a son or daughter by birth, a stepchild, or adopted child of the householder, regardless of the child's age or marital status. The category excludes sons-in-law, daughters-in-law, and foster children.

> **Biological Son or Daughter**—The son or daughter of the householder by birth.
>
> **Adopted Son or Daughter**—The son or daughter of the householder by legal adoption. If a stepson, stepdaughter, or foster child has been legally adopted by the householder, the child is then classified as an adopted child.
>
> **Stepson or Stepdaughter**—The son or daughter of the householder through marriage but not by birth, excluding sons-in-law and daughters-in-law. If a stepson or stepdaughter of the householder has been legally adopted by the householder, the child is then classified as an adopted child.
>
> **Own Children**—A child under 18 years who is a son or daughter by birth, a stepchild, or an adopted child of the householder is included in the "own children" category.
>
> **Related Children**—Any child under 18 years old who is related to the householder by birth, marriage, or adoption is included in the "related children" category. Children, by definition, exclude persons under 18 years who maintain households or are spouses or unmarried partners of householders.
>
> **Other Relatives**—In tabulations, the category "other relatives" includes any household member related to the householder by birth, marriage, or adoption but not included specifically in another relationship category. In certain detailed tabulations, the following categories may be shown:
>
>> **Grandchild**—The grandson or granddaughter of the householder.
>>
>> **Brother/Sister**—The brother or sister of the householder, including stepbrothers, stepsisters, and brothers and sisters by adoption. Brothers-in-law and sisters-in-law are included in the "Other Relative" category on the questionnaire.
>>
>> **Parent**—The father or mother of the householder, including a stepparent or adoptive parent. Fathers-in-law and mothers-in-law are included in the "Parent-in-law" category on the questionnaire.

Parent-in-Law—The mother-in-law or father-in-law of the householder.

Son-in-Law or Daughter-in-Law—The spouse of the child of the householder.

Other Relatives—Anyone not listed in a reported category above who is related to the householder by birth, marriage, or adoption (brother-in-law, grandparent, nephew, aunt, cousin, and so forth).

Nonrelatives—This category includes any household member not related to the householder by birth, marriage, or adoption. The following categories may be presented in more detailed tabulations:

Roomer or Boarder—A roomer or boarder is a person who lives in a room in the household of the householder. Some sort of cash or noncash payment (e.g., chores) is usually made for their living accommodations.

Housemate or Roommate—A housemate or roommate is a person aged 15 years and over who is not related to the householder and who shares living quarters primarily in order to share expenses.

Unmarried Partner—An unmarried partner is a person aged 15 years and over who is not related to the householder, who shares living quarters, and who has a close personal relationship with the householder. Responses of "same-sex spouse" are edited into this category.

Other Nonrelatives—Anyone who is not related by birth, marriage, or adoption to the householder and who is not described by the categories given above. Unrelated foster children or unrelated foster adults are included in this category, "Other Nonrelatives." A foster child who has been adopted by the householder is classified as an adopted child. When relationship is not reported for an individual, it is allocated according to the responses for age and sex for that person while maintaining consistency with responses for other individuals in the household. (For more information on allocation, see "2010 Census: Operational Overview and Accuracy of the Data.")

Families

Family Type—A family consists of a householder and one or more other people living in the same household who are related to the householder by birth, marriage, or adoption. All people in a household who are related to the householder are regarded as members of his or her family. A family household may contain people not related to the householder, but those people are not included as part of the householder's family in tabulations. Thus, the number of family households is equal to the number of families, but family households may include more members than do families. A household can contain only one family for purposes of tabulations. Not all households contain families because a household may be comprised of a group of unrelated people or of one person living alone—these are called "nonfamily households." Same-sex unmarried partner households are included in the "family households" category only if there is at least one additional person related to the householder by birth or adoption.

Families are classified by type as either a "husband-wife family" or "other family" according to the sex of the householder and the presence of relatives. The data on family type are based on answers to questions on sex and relationship.

Husband-Wife Family—A family in which the householder and his or her spouse of the opposite sex are enumerated as members of the same household.

Other Family:

Male householder, no wife present—A family with a male householder and no wife of householder present.

Female householder, no husband present—A family with a female householder and no husband of householder present.

Average Family Size—Average family size is a measure obtained by dividing the number of people in families by the total number of families (or family householders). In cases where the measures "people in family" or "people per family" are cross-tabulated by race or Hispanic origin, the race or Hispanic origin refers to the householder rather than the race or Hispanic origin of each individual. Nonrelatives of the householder living in family households are not counted as part of the family. They are included in the count of average household size. Average family size is rounded to the nearest hundredth.

Multigenerational Household

A multigenerational household is one that contains three or more parent-child generations; for example, the householder, child of householder (either biological, stepchild, or adopted child), and grandchildren of householder. A householder with a parent or parent-in-law of the householder and a child of the householder may also be a multigenerational household.

Unmarried-Partner Household

An unmarried-partner household is a household other than a husband-wife household that includes a householder and an unmarried partner. An unmarried partner can be of the same sex or of the opposite sex as the householder. An unmarried partner in an unmarried-partner household is an adult who is unrelated to the householder but shares living quarters and has a close personal relationship with the householder. An unmarried-partner household also may be a family household or a nonfamily household, depending on the presence or absence of another person in the household who is related to the householder. There may be only one unmarried partner per household, and an unmarried partner may not be included in a husband-wife household, as the householder cannot have both a spouse and an unmarried partner. Same-sex married-couple households are edited into this category.

Race

The data on race were derived from answers to the question on race that was asked of all people. The U.S. Census Bureau collects race data in accordance with guidelines provided by the U.S. Office of Management and Budget (OMB), and these data are based on self-identification. The racial categories included in the census questionnaire generally reflect a social definition of race recognized in this country and not an attempt to define race biologically, anthropologically, or genetically. In addition, it is recognized that the categories of the race item include racial and national origin or sociocultural groups. People may choose to report more than one race to indicate their racial mixture, such as "American Indian" and "white." People who identify their origin as Hispanic, Latino, or Spanish may be any race.

Definitions from OMB guide the Census Bureau in classifying written responses to the race question:

> **White**—A person having origins in any of the original peoples of Europe, the Middle East, or North Africa. It includes people who indicate their race as "white" or report entries such as Irish, German, Italian, Lebanese, Arab, Moroccan, or Caucasian.
>
> **Black or African American**—A person having origins in any of the black racial groups of Africa. It includes people who indicate their race as

"Black, African Am., or Negro" or report entries such as African American, Kenyan, Nigerian, or Haitian.

American Indian or Alaska Native—A person having origins in any of the original peoples of North and South America (including Central America) and who maintains tribal affiliation or community attachment. This category includes people who indicate their race as "American Indian or Alaska Native" or report entries such as Navajo, Blackfeet, Inupiat, Yup'ik, or Central American Indian groups or South American Indian groups.

Asian—A person having origins in any of the original peoples of the Far East, Southeast Asia, or the Indian subcontinent, including, for example, Cambodia, China, India, Japan, Korea, Malaysia, Pakistan, the Philippine Islands, Thailand, and Vietnam. It includes people who indicate their race as "Asian Indian," "Chinese," "Filipino," "Korean," "Japanese," "Vietnamese," and "Other Asian" or provide other detailed Asian responses.

Asian Indian—Includes people who indicate their race as "Asian Indian" or report entries such as India or East Indian.

Bangladeshi—Includes people who provide a response such as Bangladeshi or Bangladesh.

Bhutanese—Includes people who provide a response such as Bhutanese or Bhutan.

Burmese—Includes people who provide a response such as Burmese or Burma.

Cambodian—Includes people who provide a response such as Cambodian or Cambodia.

Chinese—Includes people who indicate their race as "Chinese" or report entries such as China or Chinese-American. In some census tabulations, written entries of Taiwanese are included with Chinese, whereas in others they are shown separately.

Filipino—Includes people who indicate their race as "Filipino" or report entries such as Philippines or Filipino American.

Hmong—Includes people who provide a response such as Hmong or Mong.

Indonesian—Includes people who provide a response such as Indonesian or Indonesia.

Japanese—Includes people who indicate their race as "Japanese" or report entries such as Japan or Japanese American.

Korean—Includes people who indicate their race as "Korean" or report entries such as Korea or Korean American.

Laotian—Includes people who provide a response such as Laotian or Laos.

Malaysian—Includes people who provide a response such as Malaysian or Malaysia.

Nepalese—Includes people who provide a response such as Nepalese or Nepal.

Pakistani—Includes people who provide a response such as Pakistani or Pakistan.

Sri Lankan—Includes people who provide a response such as Sri Lankan or Sri Lanka.

Taiwanese—Includes people who provide a response such as Taiwanese or Taiwan.

Thai—Includes people who provide a response such as Thai or Thailand.

Vietnamese—Includes people who indicate their race as "Vietnamese" or report entries such as Vietnam or Vietnamese-American.

Other Asian, specified—Includes people who provide a response of another Asian group, such as Iwo Jiman, Maldivian, Mongolian, Okinawan, or Singaporean.

Other Asian, not specified—Includes respondents who checked the Other Asian response category on the census questionnaire and did not write in a specific group or wrote in a generic term such as "Asian" or "Asiatic."

Native Hawaiian or Other Pacific Islander—A person having origins in any of the original peoples of Hawaii, Guam, Samoa, or other Pacific Islands. It includes people who indicate their race as "Native Hawaiian," "Guamanian or Chamorro," "Samoan," and "Other Pacific Islander" or provide other detailed Pacific Islander responses.

Native Hawaiian—Includes people who indicate their race as "Native Hawaiian" or report entries such as Part Hawaiian or Hawaiian.

Samoan—Includes people who indicate their race as "Samoan" or report entries such as American Samoan or Western Samoan.

Tongan—Includes people who provide a response such as Tongan or Tonga.

Other Polynesian—Includes people who provide a response of another Polynesian group, such as Tahitian, Tokelauan, or wrote in a generic term such as "Polynesian."

Guamanian or Chamorro—Includes people who indicate their race as "Guamanian or Chamorro" or report entries such as Chamorro or Guam.

Marshallese—Includes people who provide a response such as Marshallese or Marshall Islands.

Other Micronesian—Includes people who provide a response of another Micronesian group, such as Carolinian, Chuukese, I-Kiribati, Kosraean, Mariana Islander, Palauan, Pohnpeian, Saipanese, Yapese, or wrote in a generic term such as "Micronesian."

Fijian—Includes people who provide a response such as Fijian or Fiji.

Other Melanesian—Includes people who provide a response of another Melanesian group, such as Guinean, Hebrides Islander, Solomon Islander, or wrote in a generic term such as "Melanesian."

Other Pacific Islander, not specified—Includes respondents who checked the Other Pacific Islander response category on the census questionnaire and did not write in a specific group or wrote in a generic term such as "Pacific Islander."

Some Other Race—Includes all other responses not included in the "White," "Black or African American," "American Indian or Alaska Native," "Asian," and "Native Hawaiian or Other Pacific Islander" race categories described above. Respondents reporting entries such as multiracial, mixed, interracial, or a Hispanic, Latino, or Spanish group (for example, Mexican, Puerto Rican, Cuban, or Spanish) in response to the race question are included in this category.

Two or More Races—People may choose to provide two or more races either by checking two or more race response check boxes, by providing multiple responses, or by some combination of check boxes and other responses. The race response categories shown on the questionnaire are collapsed into the five minimum race groups identified by OMB and the Census Bureau's "Some Other Race" category. For data product purposes, "Two or More Races" refers to combinations of two or more of the following race categories:

1. White
2. Black or African-American
3. American Indian or Alaska Native
4. Asian
5. Native Hawaiian or Other Pacific Islander
6. Some Other Race

There are 57 possible combinations involving the race categories shown above. Thus, according to this approach, a response of "white" and "Asian" was tallied as Two or More Races, whereas a response of "Japanese" and "Chinese" was not because "Japanese" and "Chinese" are both Asian responses.

Sex

Individuals were asked to mark either "male" or "female" to indicate their sex. For most cases in which sex was not reported, the appropriate entry was determined from the person's given (i.e., first) name and household relationship. Otherwise, sex was allocated according to the relationship to the householder and the age of the person. (For more information on allocation, see "2010 Census: Operational Overview and Accuracy of the Data.")

Sex Ratio—The sex ratio represents the balance between the male and female populations. Ratios above 100 indicate a larger male population, and ratios below 100 indicate a larger female population. This measure is derived by dividing the total number of males by the total number of females and then multiplying by 100. It is rounded to the nearest tenth.

Living Quarters

All living quarters are classified as either housing units or group quarters. Living quarters are usually found in structures that are intended for residential use, but they also may be found in structures intended for nonresidential use. Any place where someone lives is considered to be a living quarters, such as an apartment, dormitory, shelter for people experiencing homelessness, barracks, or nursing facility. Even tents, old railroad cars, and boats are considered to be living quarters if someone claims them as his or her residence. Note that structures that do not meet the definition of a living quarters at the time of listing may meet the definition at the time of enumeration. Some types of structures, such as those cited in items 1 and 2 below, are included in address canvassing operations as place holders, with the final decision on their living quarters status made during enumeration. Other types of structures, such as those cited in items 3 and 4 below, are not included in the address canvassing operation.

The following four examples are not considered living quarters:

1. Structures, such as houses and apartments, that resemble living quarters but are being used entirely for nonresidential purposes, such as a store or an

office, or used for the storage of business supplies or inventory, machinery, or agricultural products, are not enumerated.

2. Single units as well as units in multiunit residential structures under construction in which no one is living or staying are not considered living quarters until construction has reached the point where all exterior windows and doors are installed and final usable floors are in place. Units that do not meet these criteria are not enumerated.

3. Structures in which no one is living or staying that are open to the elements—that is, the roof, walls, windows, and/or doors no longer protect the interior from the elements—are not enumerated. Also, vacant structures with a posted sign indicating that they are condemned or they are to be demolished are not enumerated.

4. Boats, recreational vehicles (RVs), tents, caves, and similar types of shelter that no one is using as a usual residence are **not** considered living quarters and are not enumerated.

Group Quarters

Group quarters are places where people live or stay in a group living arrangement, which are owned or managed by an entity or organization providing housing and/or services for the residents. This is not a typical household-type living arrangement. These services may include custodial or medical care as well as other types of assistance, and residency is commonly restricted to those receiving these services. People living in group quarters are usually not related to each other.

Group quarters include such places as college residence halls, residential treatment centers, skilled-nursing facilities, group homes, military barracks, correctional facilities, and workers' dormitories.

Institutional Group Quarters

Institutional group quarters (group quarters type codes 101–106, 201–203, 301, 401–405) are facilities that house those who are primarily ineligible, unable, or unlikely to participate in the labor force while residents.

Correctional Facilities for Adults (codes 101–106)—Correctional facilities for adults include the following types:

Federal detention centers (code 101)—Federal detention centers are stand-alone, generally multilevel, federally operated correctional facilities that provide short-term confinement or custody of adults pending adjudication or sentencing. These facilities may hold pretrial detainees, holdovers, sentenced offenders, and Immigration and Customs Enforcement (ICE) inmates, formerly called Immigration and Naturalization Service (INS) inmates. These facilities include Metropolitan Correctional Centers (MCCs), Metropolitan Detention Centers (MDCs), Federal Detention Centers (FDCs), Bureau of Indian Affairs Detention Centers, ICE Service Processing Centers, and ICE Contract Detention Facilities.

Federal (code 102) and state (code 103) prisons—Federal and state prisons are adult correctional facilities where people convicted of crimes serve their sentences. Common names include prison, penitentiary, correctional institution, federal or state correctional facility, and conservation camp. The prisons are classified by two types of control: (1) federal (operated by or for the Bureau of Prisons of the U.S. Department of Justice) and (2) state. Residents who are forensic patients or criminally insane are classified on the basis of where they resided at the time of enumeration. Patients in hospitals (units, wings, or floors) operated by or for federal or state correctional authorities are counted in the prison population. Other forensic patients will be enumerated in psychiatric hospital units and floors for long-term nonacute patients. This category may include privately operated correctional facilities.

Local jails and other municipal confinement facilities (code 104)—Local jails and other municipal confinement facilities are correctional facilities operated by or for counties, cities, and American Indian and Alaska Native tribal governments. These facilities hold adults detained pending adjudication and/or people committed after adjudication. This category also includes work farms and camps used to hold people awaiting trial or serving time on relatively short sentences. Residents who are forensic patients or criminally insane are classified on the basis of where they resided at the time of enumeration. Patients in hospitals (units, wings, or floors) operated by or for local correctional authorities are counted in the jail population. Other forensic patients will be enumerated in psychiatric hospital units and floors for long-term non-acute care patients. This category may include privately operated correctional facilities.

Correctional residential facilities (code 105)—Correctional residential facilities are community-based facilities operated for correctional purposes. The facility residents may be allowed extensive contact with the community, such as for employment or attending school, but are obligated to occupy the premises at night. Examples of correctional residential facilities are halfway houses, restitution centers, and prerelease, work release, and study centers.

Military disciplinary barracks and jails (code 106)—Military disciplinary barracks and jails are correctional facilities managed by the military to hold those awaiting trial or convicted of crimes.

Juvenile Facilities (codes 201–203)—Juvenile facilities include the following:

Group homes for juveniles (noncorrectional) (code 201)—Group homes for juveniles include community-based group living arrangements for youth in residential settings that are able to accommodate three or more clients of a service provider. The group home provides room and board and services, including behavioral, psychological, or social programs. Generally, clients are not related to the caregiver or to each other. Examples of noncorrectional group homes for juveniles are maternity homes for unwed mothers, orphanages, and homes for abused and neglected children in need of services. Group homes for juveniles do not include residential treatment centers for juveniles or group homes operated by or for correctional authorities.

Residential treatment centers for juveniles (noncorrectional) (code 202)—Residential treatment centers for juveniles include facilities that provide services primarily to youth on-site in a highly structured live-in environment for the treatment of drug/alcohol abuse, mental illness, and emotional/behavioral disorders. These facilities are staffed 24 hours a day. The focus of a residential treatment center is on the treatment program. Residential treatment centers for juveniles do not include facilities operated by or for correctional authorities.

Correctional facilities intended for juveniles (code 203)—Correctional facilities intended for juveniles include specialized facilities that provide strict confinement for their residents and detain juveniles awaiting adjudication, commitment, or placement, and/or those being held for diagnosis or classification. Also included are correctional facilities where residents are permitted contact with the community for purposes such as attending school or holding a job. Examples of correctional facilities intended for juveniles are residential training schools and farms, reception and diagnostic centers, group homes operated by or for correctional authorities, detention centers, and boot camps for juvenile delinquents.

Nursing Facilities/Skilled-Nursing Facilities (code 301)—Nursing facilities/skilled-nursing facilities include facilities licensed to provide medical care with 7-day, 24-hour coverage for people requiring long-term non-acute care. People in these facilities require nursing care, regardless of age. Either of these types of facilities may be referred to as nursing homes.

Other Institutional Facilities (codes 401–405)—Other institutional facilities include the following:

Mental (psychiatric) hospitals and psychiatric units in other hospitals (code 401)—Mental (psychiatric) hospitals and psychiatric units in other hospitals include psychiatric hospitals, units, and floors for long-term non-acute care patients. The primary function of the hospital, unit, or floor is to provide diagnostic and treatment services for long-term nonacute patients who have psychiatric-related illness. All patients are enumerated in this category.

Hospitals with patients who have no usual home elsewhere (code 402)—Hospitals with patients who have no usual home elsewhere include hospitals that have any patients who have no exit or disposition plan, or who are known as "boarder patients" or "boarder babies." All hospitals are eligible for inclusion in this category except psychiatric hospitals, units, wings, or floors operated by federal, state, or local correctional authorities. Patients in hospitals operated by these correctional authorities will be counted in the prison or jail population. Psychiatric units and hospice units in hospitals are also excluded. Only patients with no usual home elsewhere are enumerated in this category.

In-patient hospice facilities (both free-standing and units in hospitals) (code 403)—In-patient hospice facilities (both freestanding and units in hospitals) include facilities that provide palliative, comfort, and supportive care for terminally ill patients and their families. Only patients with no usual home elsewhere are tabulated in this category.

Military treatment facilities with assigned patients (code 404)—Military treatment facilities with assigned patients include military hospitals and medical centers with active duty patients assigned to the facility. Only these patients are enumerated in this category.

Residential schools for people with disabilities (code 405)—Residential schools for people with disabilities include schools that provide the teaching of skills for daily living, education programs, and care for students with disabilities in a live-in environment. Examples of residential schools for people with disabilities are residential schools for the physically or developmentally disabled.

Noninstitutional Group Quarters

Noninstitutional group quarters (group quarters type codes 501, 601, 602, 701, 702, 704, 706, 801, 802, 900, 901, 903, 904) are facilities that house those who are primarily eligible, able, or likely to participate in the labor force while residents.

College/University Student Housing (code 501)—College/University student housing includes residence halls and dormitories, which house college and university students in a group living arrangement. These facilities are owned, leased, or managed either by a college, university, or seminary, or by a private entity or organization. Fraternity and sorority housing recognized by the college or university are included as college student housing. However, students attending the U.S. Naval Academy, U.S. Military Academy (West Point), U.S. Coast Guard Academy, and U.S. Air Force Academy are counted in military group quarters.

Military Quarters (codes 601 and 602)—Military quarters (code 601) are facilities that include military personnel living in barracks (including open barrack transient quarters) and dormitories and military ships (code 602). Patients assigned to Military Treatment Facilities and people being held in military disciplinary barracks and jails are not enumerated in this category. Patients in Military Treatment Facilities with no usual home elsewhere are not enumerated in this category.

Other Noninstitutional Facilities (codes 701, 702, 704, 706, 801, 802, 900, 901, 903, and 904)—Other noninstitutional facilities include the following:

> *Emergency and transitional shelters (with sleeping facilities) for people experiencing homelessness (code 701)*—Emergency and transitional shelters (with sleeping facilities) for people experiencing homelessness are facilities where people experiencing homelessness stay overnight. These include:

- Shelters that operate on a first-come, first-serve basis where people must leave in the morning and have no guaranteed bed for the next night.
- Shelters where people know that they have a bed for a specified period of time (even if they leave the building every day).
- Shelters that provide temporary shelter during extremely cold weather (such as churches). This category does not include shelters that operate only in the event of a natural disaster.

Examples are emergency and transitional shelters; missions; hotels and motels used to shelter people experiencing homelessness; shelters for children who are runaways, neglected, or experiencing homelessness; and similar places known to have people experiencing homelessness.

Soup kitchens, regularly scheduled mobile food vans, and targeted nonsheltered outdoor locations (codes 702, 704, and 706)—This category includes soup kitchens that offer meals organized as food service lines or bag or box lunches for people experiencing homelessness; street locations where mobile food vans regularly stop to provide food to people experiencing homelessness; and targeted nonsheltered outdoor locations where people experiencing homelessness live without paying to stay. This also would include persons staying in preidentified car, recreational vehicle (RV), and tent encampments. Targeted nonsheltered outdoor locations must have a specific location description; for example, "the Brooklyn Bridge at the corner of Bristol Drive," "the 700 block of Taylor Street behind the old warehouse," or the address of the parking lot being utilized.

Group homes intended for adults (code 801)—Group homes intended for adults are community-based group living arrangements in residential settings that are able to accommodate three or more clients of a service provider. The group home provides room and board and services, including behavioral, psychological, or social programs. Generally, clients are not related to the caregiver or to each other. Group homes do not include residential treatment centers or facilities operated by or for correctional authorities.

Residential treatment centers for adults (code 802)—Residential treatment centers for adults provide treatment on-site in a highly structured live-in environment for the treatment of drug/alcohol abuse, mental illness, and emotional/behavioral disorders. They are staffed 24 hours a day. The focus of a residential treatment center is on the treatment program. Residential treatment centers do not include facilities operated by or for correctional authorities.

Maritime/Merchant vessels (code 900)—Maritime/merchant vessels include U.S. owned and operated flag vessels used for commercial or noncombatant government-related purposes at U.S. ports, on the sea, or on the Great Lakes.

Workers' group living quarters and Job Corps centers (code 901)—Workers' group living quarters and Job Corps centers include facilities such as dormitories, bunkhouses, and similar types of group living arrangements for agricultural and nonagricultural workers. This category also includes facilities that provide a full-time, year-round residential program offering a vocational training and employment program that helps young people 16 to 24 years old learn a trade, earn a high school diploma or GED, and get help finding a job. Examples are group living quarters at migratory farm-worker camps, construction workers' camps, Job Corps centers, and vocational training facilities.

Living quarters for victims of natural disasters (code 903)—Living quarters for victims of natural disasters are temporary group living arrangements established as a result of natural disasters.

Religious group quarters and domestic violence shelters (code 904)—Religious group quarters are living quarters owned or operated by religious organizations that are intended to house their members in a group living situation. This category includes such places as convents, monasteries, and abbeys. Living quarters for students living or staying in seminaries are classified as college student housing, not religious group quarters. Domestic violence shelters are community-based homes, shelters, or crisis centers that provide housing for people who have sought shelter from household violence and who may have been physically abused.

Housing Units

A housing unit is a living quarters in which the occupant or occupants live separately from any other individuals in the building and have direct access to their living quarters from outside the building or through a common hall. Housing units are usually houses, apartments, mobile homes, groups of rooms, or single rooms that are occupied as separate living quarters. They are residences for single individuals, groups of individuals, or families who live together. A single individual or a group living in a housing unit is defined to be a household. Additional details about housing for the elderly population and group homes are provided in the section "Housing for the Older Population." For vacant housing units, the criteria of separateness and direct access are applied to the intended occupants whenever possible. Nontraditional living quarters such as boats, RVs, and tents are considered to be housing units **only** if someone is living in them and they are either the occupant's usual residence or the occupant has no usual residence elsewhere. These nontraditional living arrangements are not considered to be housing units if they are vacant.

Housing units are classified as being either occupied or vacant.

Occupied Housing Unit—A housing unit is classified as occupied if it is the usual place of residence of the individual or group of individuals living in it on census day, or if the occupants are only temporarily absent, such as away on vacation, in the hospital for a short stay, or on a business trip, and will be returning.

The occupants may be an individual, a single family, two or more families living together, or any other group of related or unrelated individuals who share living arrangements.

Occupied rooms or suites of rooms in hotels, motels, and similar places are classified as housing units only when occupied by permanent residents; that is, occupied by individuals who consider the hotel their usual place of residence or who have no usual place of residence elsewhere. However, when rooms in hotels and motels are used to provide shelter for people experiencing homelessness, they are not housing units. Rooms used in this way are considered group quarters.

Vacant Housing Unit—A housing unit is classified as vacant if no one is living in it on census day, unless its occupant or occupants are only temporarily absent—such as away on vacation, in the hospital for a short stay, or on a business trip—and will be returning.

Housing units temporarily occupied at the time of enumeration entirely by individuals who have a usual residence elsewhere are classified as vacant. When housing units are vacant, the criteria of separateness and direct access are applied to the intended occupants whenever possible. If that information cannot be obtained, the criteria are applied to the previous occupants.

Boats, RVs, tents, caves, and similar shelter that no one is using as a usual residence are **not** considered living quarters and therefore are not enumerated at all.

Housing Characteristics

Household Size

This question is based on the count of people in occupied housing units. All people occupying the housing unit are counted, including the householder, occupants related to the householder, and lodgers, roomers, boarders, and so forth.

Average Household Size of Occupied Unit—The average household size of an occupied unit is a measure obtained by dividing the number of people living in occupied housing units by the total number of occupied housing units. This measure is rounded to the nearest hundredth.

Average Household Size of Owner-Occupied Unit—The average household size of an owner-occupied unit is a measure obtained by dividing the number of people living in owner-occupied housing units by the total number of owner-occupied housing units. This measure is rounded to the nearest hundredth.

Average Household Size of Renter-Occupied Unit—The average household size of a renter-occupied unit is a measure obtained by dividing the number of people living in renter-occupied housing units by the total number of renter-occupied housing units. This measure is rounded to the nearest hundredth.

Tenure

Tenure was asked at all occupied housing units. All occupied housing units are classified as either owner-occupied or renter-occupied.

Owner-Occupied—A housing unit is owner-occupied if the owner or co-owner lives in the unit even if it is mortgaged or not fully paid for. The owner or co-owner must live in the unit and usually is Person 1 on the questionnaire. The unit is "Owned by you or someone in this household with a mortgage or loan" if it is being purchased with a mortgage or some other debt arrangement, such as a deed of trust, trust deed, contract to purchase, land contract, or purchase agreement. The unit is also considered owned with a mortgage if it is built on leased land and there is a mortgage on the unit.

A housing unit is "Owned by you or someone in this household free and clear (without a mortgage or loan)" if there is no mortgage or other similar debt on the house, apartment, or mobile home, including units built on leased land if the unit is owned outright without a mortgage. Although most tables show total owner-occupied counts, selected tables separately identify the two owner categories.

Renter-Occupied—All occupied housing units which are not owner-occupied, whether they are rented or occupied without payment of rent, are classified as renter-occupied. "Rented" includes units in continuing care, sometimes called life care arrangements. These arrangements usually involve a contract between one or more individuals and a service provider guaranteeing the individual shelter, usually an apartment, and services, such as meals or transportation to shopping or recreation. The "no rent paid" category includes units provided free by friends or relatives or in exchange for services, such as a resident manager, caretaker, minister, or tenant farmer. Housing units on military bases are also classified in the "No rent paid" category.

Vacancy Status

The data on vacancy status were obtained from Enumerator Questionnaire item C. Vacancy status and other characteristics of vacant units were determined by census enumerators obtaining information from landlords, owners, neighbors, rental agents, and others. Vacant units are subdivided according to their housing market classification as follows:

For Rent—These are vacant units offered for rent and vacant units offered either for rent or for sale.

Rented, Not Occupied—These are vacant units rented but not yet occupied, including units where money has been paid or agreed on, but the renter has not yet moved in.

For Sale Only—These are vacant units being offered for sale only, including units in cooperatives and condominium projects if the individual units are offered for sale only. If units are offered either for rent or for sale, they are included in the for rent classification.

Sold, Not Occupied— These are vacant units sold but not yet occupied, including units that have been sold recently, but the new owner has not yet moved in.

For Seasonal, Recreational, or Occasional Use—These are vacant units used or intended for use only in certain seasons or for weekends or other occasional use throughout the year. Seasonal units include those used for summer or winter sports or recreation, such as beach cottages and hunting cabins. Seasonal units also may include quarters for such workers as herders and loggers. Interval ownership units, sometimes called shared-ownership or time-sharing condominiums, also are included here.

For Migrant Workers— These include vacant units intended for occupancy by migratory workers employed in farm work during the crop season. (Work in a cannery, freezer plant, or food-processing plant is not farm work.)

Other Vacant—If a vacant unit does not fall into any of the categories specified above, it is classified as "Other vacant." For example, this category includes units held for occupancy by a caretaker or janitor and units held for personal reasons of the owner.

Homeowner Vacancy Rate—The homeowner vacancy rate is the proportion of the homeowner inventory that is vacant for sale. It is computed by dividing the number of vacant units for sale only by the sum of the owner-occupied units, vacant units that are for sale only, and vacant units that have been sold but not yet occupied, and then multiplying by 100. This measure is rounded to the nearest tenth.

Rental Vacancy Rate—The rental vacancy rate is the proportion of the rental inventory that is vacant for rent. It is computed by dividing the number of vacant units for rent by the sum of the renter-occupied units, vacant units that are for rent, and vacant units that have been rented but not yet occupied, and then multiplying by 100. This measure is rounded to the nearest tenth.

Available Housing Vacancy Rate—The available housing vacancy rate is the proportion of the housing inventory that is vacant for sale only and vacant for rent. It is computed by dividing the sum of vacant for sale only housing units and vacant-for-rent housing units, by the sum of occupied units, vacant for sale only housing units, vacant sold not occupied housing units, vacant for rent housing units, and vacant rented not occupied housing units, and then multiplying by 100. This measure is rounded to the nearest tenth.

Derived Measures

Census data products include various derived measures, such as medians, means, and percentages, as well as certain rates and ratios. Derived measures that round to less than 0.1 are not shown but indicated as zero.

Area Measurement and Density

The 2010 census summary file geographic header record provides the size, in square meters, of geographic entities for which the U.S. Census Bureau tabulates and disseminates data. Land area is shown in Field Name AREALAND (starting position 199) and water area in Field Name AREAWATR (starting position 213). To convert square meters to square kilometers, divide by 1,000,000; to convert square kilometers to square miles, divide by 2.589988; to convert square meters to square miles, divide by 2,589,988.

Population density (average number of people per square mile) is calculated by dividing the number of people in a specified geographic area by its land area in square miles.

Housing unit density (average number of housing units per square mile) is calculated by dividing the number of housing units in a specified geographic area by its land area in square miles.

Average

See "Mean."

Interpolation

Interpolation is frequently used to calculate medians or quartiles and to approximate standard errors from tables based on interval data. Different kinds of interpolation may be used to estimate the value of a function between two known values, depending on the form of the distribution. The most common distributional assumption is that the data are linear, resulting in linear interpolation.

Mean

This measure represents an arithmetic average of a set of values. It is derived by dividing the sum (or aggregate) of a group of numerical items by the total number of items in that group. For example, average family size is obtained by dividing the number of people in families by the total number of families (or family householders). (Additional information on means and aggregates is included in the separate explanations of many of the population and housing subjects.)

Median

This measure represents the middle value (if *n* is odd) or the average of the two middle values (if *n* is even) in an ordered list of *n* data values. The median divides the total frequency distribution into two equal parts: one-half of the cases falling below the median and one-half above the median. Each median is calculated using a standard distribution. The standard distribution for the calculation of median age is:

AGE [116]
    Under 1 year
    1 year
    2 years
    3 years
    4 years
    5 years
    .
    .
    .
    112 years
    113 years
    114 years
    115 years and over

(For more information, see "Interpolation.")

Jam values will be assigned whenever the median falls in an open-ended interval. For example, if the median age value fell in the open-ended category 115 years and over, the value displayed would be 115 + . The presentation of jam values will vary between products and types of media.

For data products displayed in American FactFinder, publications, or in display table format, medians that fall in the uppermost category of an open-ended distribution will be shown with a plus symbol (+) appended, and medians that fall in the lowest category of an open-ended distribution will be shown with a minus symbol (–) appended. For other data products and data files that are downloaded by users (i.e., FTP files), plus and minus signs will not be appended.

Percentage

This measure is calculated by taking the number of items in a group possessing a characteristic of interest and dividing by the total number of items in that group, and then multiplying by 100.

Rate

This is a measure of occurrences in a given period of time divided by the possible number of occurrences during that period. For example, the homeowner vacancy rate is calculated by dividing the number of vacant units for sale only by the sum of owner-occupied units, vacant units that are for sale only, and vacant units that have been sold but not yet occupied, and then multiplying by 100. Rates are sometimes presented as percentages.

Online Resources

U.S. Census Bureau, http://www.census.gov

This is the gateway to the Census Bureau's trove of data. The bureau, an arm of the U.S. Commerce Department, was created in 1902 by President Theodore Roosevelt. The bureau describes itself as the "leading source of quality data about the nation's people and economy."

American FactFinder, http://factfinder2.census.gov

The Census Bureau's primary portal for decennial census and American Community Survey data was launched in 1998. It currently contains data from the 2000 and 2010 decennial censuses, as well as tables from the American Community Survey that date to 2005.

Integrated Public Use Microdata Series, http://ipums.org

The University of Minnesota's Population Center, which administers the website, offers terabytes of free data to users who want to dive deeper into census and ACS data. It describes the IPUMS-USA site: "The Integrated Public Use Microdata Series (IPUMS-USA) consists of more than fifty high-precision samples of the American population drawn from fifteen federal censuses and from the American Community Surveys of 2000–2010. Some of these samples have existed for years, and others were created specifically for this database. These samples, which draw on every surviving census from 1850–2000, and the 2000–2010 ACS samples, collectively constitute our richest source of quantitative information on long-term changes in the American population. However, because different investigators created these samples at different times, they employed a wide variety of record layouts, coding schemes, and documentation. This has complicated efforts to use them to study change over time. The IPUMS assigns uniform codes across all the samples and brings relevant documentation into a coherent form to facilitate analysis of social and economic change."

Brookings Institution, http://www.brookings.edu/about/ programs/metro

The Washington-based think tank offers some of the best analysis of demographic-related issues in the nation. Brookings is the premier source for matching demographic trends with economic analysis.

Pew Social and Demographic Trends, http://www.pewsocialtrends. org/

Operated by the Pew Research Center, this is another Washington-based think tank that specializes in demographic-oriented research and analysis, including ongoing studies dealing with economic recovery, younger Americans, and family relationships.

Population Association of America, http://www. populationassociation.org/

The organization is among the top professional groups for demographic researchers and analysts. One of its main benefits is ongoing lobbying in Washington to emphasize the importance of sound demographic and economic data in policy decisions.

University of Michigan Social Science Data Analysis Network, http://www.ssdan.net/content/censusscope

The SSDAN isn't as thorough as American FactFinder. In many instances, its presentation of data through its CensusScope portal is far more compelling and useful. The university also sponsors a companion website for teaching: **http://teachingwithdata.org**.

University of Missouri Office of Social and Economic Data Analysis (OSEDA), http://www.oseda.missouri.edu/

Although the office is focused on Missouri data, it's become a prime source for demographic researchers across the nation who use its code and definitions in their own work.

University of Michigan Population Studies Center, http://www.psc. isr.umich.edu/

The center, created in 1961, supports a wide variety of demographic research on families, income, health and aging. Its data services division maintains a major collection of population-related publications and supports researchers around the world.

SAS Institute, http://www.sas.com

The world's largest privately held software company is also a tool used commonly by the U.S. Census Bureau; the government even provides SAS scripts that allow researchers to quickly and (almost) painlessly translate gigabytes of flat text files into actionable results.

ESRI, http://www.esri.com

This Redlands, California–based software company provides a wide range of mapping software that allow users to visualize data trends and patterns. It is compatible with the shapefile (*.shp) formats that the Census Bureau provides in the "Geography" section of its website.

APPENDIX E

Mapping Census Data

If a picture can tell a story worth 1,000 words, a map can shed light on millions of numbers. For many analyses, the sheer scope of the task demands some sort of visual orientation. Even someone who's spent their entire career looking at demographic data may fail to see patterns among 3,144 U.S. counties, or even 50 states. The Census Bureau has added a rudimentary mapping capability to American FactFinder that's useful for creating images, although not as flexible as shapefiles imported into commercial mapping software and tied to relational databases.

We'll start with an example using an "S" table on American FactFinder. The S-series of tables generally offers percentage estimates from the American Community Survey. We'll look to see if there are any geographic patterns among all U.S. counties for households with children younger than 18 years old receiving food stamp, or SNAP, benefits. We start by selecting "All Counties within United States" from the Geographies tab, and "2010 ACS 5-year estimates" as our dataset. We'll use the search bar to determine that we want Table S2201, "Food Stamps/SNAP."

When we click on the hyperlink to the table, we see our results in tabular form:

We can see there's a link to "Create a Map" in the top third of the page, about halfway across the columns. First, we need to define the field to be mapped. We click on the "Create a Map" link, and the cells in the table turn blue:

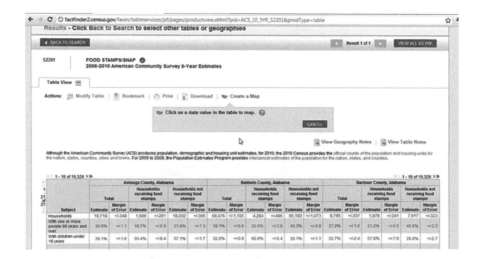

Next, we move the mouse to the estimate number for households receiving food stamps, with children under 18 years old:

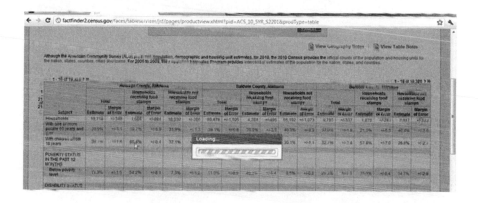

Depending on the complexity of the data and bandwidth, it may take a while for FactFinder to respond.

We'll be asked for confirmation:

The initial result is generally not spectacular. Eventually, the map resolves the county boundaries. This may take some patience, though.

This points out a shortcoming of the American FactFinder mapping tools that are common to all online mapping programs. It's very difficult to get excellent resolution when many geographies are being considered, and the online nature of the tool means the responses will be slow. We can use the zoom function to get a clearer view of a given region:

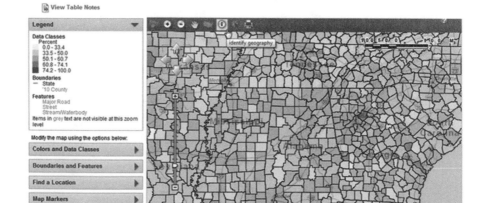

We can use the "Identify Geography" button to get more information about the darkly shaded county in northern Florida that appears to have a high percentage of households with children that receive SNAP benefits:

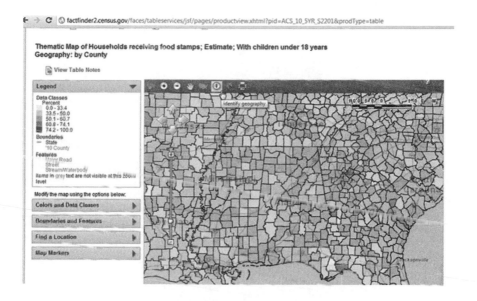

We use the tool to find out that 84.2 percent of Wakulla County, Florida, households receiving food stamps have children younger than 18 years old:

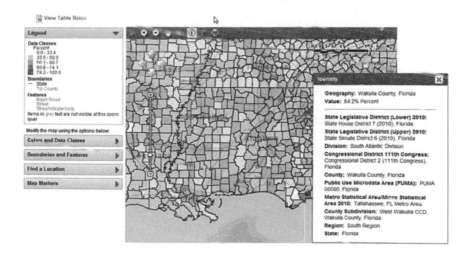

The American FactFinder mapping tool is an impressive technical achievement, although more flexibility can be gained with an understanding of census geographical FIPS codes (found at http://www.census.gov/geo/www/ansi/ansi.html); relational databases; census shapefiles (available for download at http://www.census.gov/geo/www/cob/); and appropriate mapping software, such as ESRI's ArcGIS suite.

APPENDIX F

Comparing Census and American Community Survey Characteristics

The American Community Survey is an outgrowth of the decennial Census. That doesn't mean the data is directly comparable. A list of topics that can often be compared (or never compared) is presented here:

(T)—Differences in tabulation
(Q)—Differences in question wording
(RP)—Differences in reference period
(U)—Differences in universe

Comparable, 2000–2010 Census and ACS

- Ancestry
- Citizenship Status (T)
- Nativity
- Year of Entry
- Place of Birth
- Journey to Work (T)
- Grandparents and Grandchildren
- School Enrollment
- Educational Attainment
- Language
- Poverty (RP)
- Income and Earnings (RP)

- Veteran Status
- Period of Military Service
- Employment Status (Q)
- Hours and Weeks Worked
- Industry (T)
- Occupation (T)
- Class of Worker (T)
- Rooms and Bedrooms (Q)
- Cost of Utilities
- House Heating Fuel
- Kitchen Facilities (Q)
- Monthly Rent
- Mortgage Status
- Occupants/Room (Q)
- Owner Costs (T)
- Plumbing Facilities (Q)
- Tenure
- Units in Structure
- Home Value (Q)
- Vehicles Available
- Group Quarters Population (U)

Comparable Across Decennial Census Only

- Age
- Sex
- Race
- Hispanic or Latino Origin
- Relationship
- Household/Family Type
- Subfamilies
- Vacancy

Characteristics That Should Not Be Compared

- Migration
- Marital Status
- Disability Status
- Plumbing Facilities
- Contract Rent and Gross Rent

- Gross Rent as a Percentage of Income
- Real Estate Taxes
- Telephone Service
- Year Moved In
- Year Structure Built

Characteristics That Cannot Be Compared (No 2000 Census Data)

- Fertility
- Food Stamp/SNAP Receipt
- Marital History
- Field of Degree
- Disability Status
- Service-Connected Disability Status
- Health Insurance Coverage

About the Website

This book is accompanied by a website that provides examples of data available for each section discussed in the book. The website is composed of 14 sections, outlined here:

Decennial population
Decennial relationships
Decennial housing
Decennial origin
ACS housing
ACS education
ACS language
ACS occupation
ACS transportation
ACS income and poverty
ACS health
Technical documentation and links
Census/ACS scripts (SAS)
Glossary of terms

To access the site, go to www.wiley.com/go/censusguide (password: bass123).

About the Author

Frank Bass is a data editor and enterprise reporter for Bloomberg News. He has worked for the Associated Press, *Wall Street Journal, Houston Post,* and *Alabama Journal.* Before coming to Bloomberg, Bass worked for 12 years as the AP's director of computer-assisted reporting and as a national investigative reporter. He is the author of the *Associated Press Guide to Internet Research and Reporting* (2001) and *Health is Everything: Using Data to Report Great Stories on Your Community's Health* (2012).

His work has been honored with awards that include the Gerald Loeb Award, two national Associated Press Managing Editors awards, the Texas Headliners Foundation Reporter of the Year Award, and the 1988 Pulitzer Prize for General News Reporting.

Bass has taught at seminars for professional organizations, including Investigative Reporters and Editors, National Institute for Computer-Assisted Reporting, Freedom of Information Foundation, and the Association of Health Care Journalists. He has lectured at college seminars across the country, including the Massachusetts College of Liberal Arts, Harvard, and Columbia. He has taught advanced reporting skills to journalists in Asia, Australia, and Europe, and has been a Snedden Fellow at the University of Alaska Fairbanks.

When he's not working in New York or Washington, Bass helps operate a small family farm in southern Vermont. He and his wife raise dairy goats, cattle, poultry, bees, Maine Coon cats, and border collies. His hobbies include running, reading, cheese-making, and organic gardening. His family is a member of the Northeast Organic Farmers Association, Rural Vermont, and the Long Trail Club.

Index

Abnaki, 107
Achinese, 106
Achumawi, 107
Afghanistan, 61, 75, 76, 117
Africa, 58
African, languages, 106, 107, 109
Afrikaans, 106
Age, 13
Agency for Healthcare Research and
    Quality, 150
Aggregate income deficit, 139
Agriculture, job activity, 112
Ahtena, 107
Akron, Ohio, 24
Alabama:
    employment, 112
    Paradox, 31
    immigration laws, 59
    language, 107
Alaska Athabascan, origin, 37, 46
Alaska:
    Native tribes, 62
    plumbing facilities, 83
Albanian, 106
Albuquerque, New Mexico, 33
Aleut:
    language, 107
    origin, 37, 46
Alexandria city, Virginia, 22
Algonquian, 107
Alliance for Excellent Education, 92
American Community Survey:
    overview, 11, 14, 18, 71
    drawbacks, 74, 76
    general topics, 73
    geographic scope, 73, 76

implementation, 73
margins of error, 74
median household income, 24, 71
origins, 72
political issues, 74, 76
sample size, 73
stages, 22, 23
voluntary participation, 74
American Housing Survey, 14
American Indian, language, 107
Amharic, 106
Ancestry, 13
Anchorage Municipality, Alaska, 22
Andalusian, 59
Apache:
    language, 107
    origin, 37, 46
Apartments and condominiums, 82
Arabic, 106, 109
Arapaho:
    language, 107
    origin, 46
Arawakian, 107
Argentina:
    dispute with Columbia, Ecuador, 48
    origin, 36, 47, 59
Arikara, 107
Arizona:
    immigration laws, 59
    Navajo Nation, 63
    redistricting, 32, 33
Arkansas, minor civil divisions, 24
Arlington County, Virginia, 19, 22
Armenia, 61
Armenian, 106, 108
Asian groups, 36, 48

Asian Indian, origin, 36, 48, 61
Asiatic, 61
Assamese, 106
Assiniboine Sioux, 46
Asturian, 59
Athapascan, 107
Athens city, Ohio, 24
Athens township, Athens County, Ohio,
    24
Athens township, Harrison County, Ohio,
    24
Athens-Clarke County, Georgia, 25
Atlanta, Georgia, 22
Atlanta-Sandy Springs-Marietta
    metropolitan area, 19
Atsina, 107
Atsugewi, 107
Augusta-Richmond County, Georgia, 25
Austin, Robert L., 9
Aymara, 107
Azerbaijan, 61
Azerbaijani, 106
Aztecan, 107

Baby Boom, 10, 151
Balearic Islanders, 59
Balinese, 106
Balochi, 106
Baltimore, Maryland, 9
Bangladeshi, 36, 48, 61
Bantu, 106
Basque, 107
Bengali, 106
Berber, 106
Bhutanese, 48, 61
Bielorussian, 106
Bihari, 106
Bikol, 107
Bisayan, 106
Blackfeet, origin, 37, 46
Blackfoot, language, 107
Blodgett, John, 74
Bloomberg, Michael, 5
Boats, 50, 82
Bolivian, 36, 47, 59
Boston, Massachusetts, 4, 9, 10
Brahui, 107

Brennan Center, New York Uiversity School
    of Law, 32
Breton, 106
Brewer, Jan, 33
Bridgeport, Connecticut, 143
Brown University, 130
Bryant, Barbara E., 10
Budget, 11, 13
Buginese, 106
Bulgarian, 107
Bureau of Economic Analysis, 124
Bureau of Labor Statistics, 14, 111
Bureau of Transportation Statistics, 123
Burmese:
    language, 106
    origin, 48, 61
Burushaski, 106
Butte-Silver Bow, Montana, 25

Caddo, 107
Cahuilla, 107
Cajun, 106
California:
    population, 19
    redistricting, 32
Californio, origin, 59
Cambodian, 36, 48, 61
Canada, 13
Canadian and French American Indian, 46
Canarian, 59
Cantonese, 106
Carolinian:
    language, 106
    origin, 47
Castillian, 59
Catalonian:
    language, 106
    origin, 59
Caucasian, 107
Cayuga, 107
Census of Governments, 14
Census of Religious Bodies, 13
Census, 1790, 3, 4
Census, 1800, 6
Census, 1820, 5, 6, 111
Census, 1840, 6, 89
Census, 1850, 6, 31

Census, 1860, 6
Census, 1870, 7, 57
Census, 1880, 31
Census, 1890, 7
Census, 1900, 8, 57
Census, 1910, 8, 31
Census, 1920, 8, 31
Census, 1930, 9, 31
Census, 1940, 10, 89
Census, 1950, 9
Census, 1960, 63
Census, 1970, 10, 63
Census, 1980, 10
Census, 1990, 10, 60, 63
Census, 2000, 10, 14, 34, 43, 44, 71, 58, 63
Census, 2010:
  overview, 5, 12, 44
  Asians, 58, 60
  education, 89
  Hispanics, 57, 58
  Pacific Islander, 63
  ZCTAs, 21
Census, 2020, 13
Central American Indian, 46, 47
Central Intelligence Agency, 142
Chadic, 106
Cham, 106
Chamorro, 106
Chasta Costa, 107
Chemchuevi, 107
Cherokee:
  language, 107
  origin, 37, 46
Chetemacha, 107
Cheyenne:
  language, 107
  origin, 37, 46
Chibchan, 107
Chicago, Illinois, 9
Chickasaw, 37, 46
Chilean, 36, 47, 59
Chinese:
  immigration, 103
  language, 106, 109
  origin, 36, 48, 60
Chinook Jargon, 107
Chippewa, 37, 46

Chiricahua, 107
Chiwere, 107
Choctaw:
  language, 107
  origin, 37, 46
Chumash, 107
Chuukese, 47
Chuvash, 106
Clallam, 107
Cleveland, Ohio, 9
Coast Miwok, 107
Cocomaricopa, 107
Coeur D'Alene, 107
College dormitories, 42, 54
Colombia, 48
Colombian, origin, 36, 47, 59
Columbia, language, 107
Columbus, Georgia, 25
Colville, 37, 46
Comanche:
  language, 107
  origin, 37, 46
Commonwealth Fund, 144
Community health workers, 113
Commuting:
  bicycles, 126
  buses or trolley buses, 125
  cars, trucks and vans, 125
  cooking, 130
  data uses, 123, 124, 131
  divorce, 130
  emergency planning, 124
  ferry boats, 126
  modes of commuting, 125
  motorcycles, 126
  obesity, 130
  other, 126
  overview, 124, 125
  railroad, 126
  sex, 130
  sleeping, 130
  socializing, 130
  subways or elevateds, 126
  taxicabs, 126
  time of departure, 126
  trolleys or street cars, 126
  vehicles available, 124

Commuting (*Continued*)
  walking, 126
  working at home, 126
Computer, 7, 9, 10
Computer network architects, 113, 120
Computer network support specialists,
  113
Congressional Research Service, 30
Connecticut, minor civil divisions, 24
Consolidated Federal Funds Report, 14
Construction, job activity, 112
Corvallis, Oregon, 126
Costa Rican, 36, 47
Cowlitz, 107
Cree:
  language, 107
  origin, 37, 47
Creek, 37, 47
Criollo, 59
Croatian, 107
Crow, language, 107
Crow, origin, 37, 47
Cuban, 36, 47, 59
Cupeno, 107
Current Population Survey, 14, 75, 111
Current Population Survey vs. American
  Community Survey, occupations, 111
Cushite, 106
Czech, 106

Dakota, 107
Dallas, Texas, 22, 71
Danish, 106
de Tocqueville, Alexis, 123
Decennial Census, 13, 14
Delaware:
  language, 107
  origin, 37, 47
Delta River Yuman, 107
Density, calculation, 52
Denver, Colorado, 22
Detroit, Michigan, 9, 10
Diegueno, 107
Disability:
  longitudinal comparisons, 147, 148
  measuring and difficulties, 147
  overview, 146, 152

District of Columbia, Washington, D.C.
  metro area, 19
Diversity index, 35
Diversity, overview, 11
Dominican, 36, 47, 59
Dravidian, 107
Dutch, 106

Earned Income Tax Credit, 137
Eastern Tribes, 47
Ecuador, 48
Ecuadorian, origin, 36, 47, 59
Education:
  spending, 13
  as economic proxy, 90
  attainment, 89, 91, 92, 93, 96, 97, 98,
    102
  costs, 89
  degrees, 97, 98, 99
  earnings, 90, 91
  enrollment, 91
  federal funding, 89, 90
  literacy, 89
  median earnings by attainment, 98,
    99
  nativity, 98
  race, 98, 102
  types of school, 92
  veterans, 98, 102
  women, 98, 102
Efik, 107
Eskimo:
  language, 107
  origin, 37, 47, 63
Estonian, 106
Exercise physiologists, 113
ExxonMobil Inc., 112
Eyak, 107

Fairbanks, Alaska, 14
Fairfax city, Virginia, 22
Fairfax County, Virginia, 119
Falls Church city, Virginia, 22
Faroese, 106
Federal Assistance Awards Data, 14
Federal government, job category, 112
Federal Reserve Board, 81

Fijian:
  language, 106
  origin, 47
Filipino, 36, 48, 61
Finance, Insurance and Real Estate (FIRE)
  sector, 79
Financial clerks, all other, 114
Finnish, 106
Flood insurance, 137
Florida, redistricting, 32
Food deserts, 150
Food processing workers, all other, 114
Food stamps. *See also* Supplemental
  Nutritional Assistance Program, 75
Foothill North Yokuts, 107
Formosan, 106
Fox, 107
Fredericksburg, Texas, 19
French, 106, 108
French Cree, 107
French Creole, 106, 108
Frisian, 106
Fuchow, 106
Fulani, 106
Fundraisers, 113

Gallego, 59
Gambling, 62
Gay and lesbian population, 43, 44
Gender, 13
Genetic counselors, 113
Geography:
  blocks, 19, 28
  Census blocks, advantages, 27
  Census blocks, boundary changes, 27, 28
  Census blocks, characteristics, 26
  Census blocks, limitations, 27
  Census tracts, 17, 28
  Census tracts, boundary changes, 25
  Census tracts, characteristcs, 25
  Census tracts, neighborhood equivalent,
    25
  Census tracts, size, 25
  Census-designated places, 17, 24, 25
  cities, 17
  congressional districts, 20, 29
  congressional districts, at-large states, 33

consolidated cities, 17, 25
  core-based statistical areas, 19
  counties, 17, 22
  county subdivisions, 17, 25, 28
  metropolitan areas, 19
  micropolitan areas, 19
  minor civil division, 24
  places, 17, 25, 28
  states, 17, 18, 28
  suburbs, 23
  taxonomy, 17, 18
  zip code tabulation areas (ZCTAs), 21,
    74
  zip codes, 17, 20, 21, 28
Georgia, 11th Congressional District, 12
German:
  immigration, 103
  language, 106, 109
Gerrymandering, 32
Gilbertese, 106
Gini coefficient, 139, 142, 143, 144
Gini, formula, 143
Gondi, 107
Gorontalo, 107
Government contracts, 5, 6, 31
Government grants, 31
Government, job activity, 112
Great Britain, 29, 48
Great Depression, 9
Great Recession, 75
Greek, 106, 109
Group homes, 42
Group quarters, 42
Growth in Census, 7
Guamanian or Chamorro, 47, 63
Guatemalan, 36, 47
Gujarathi, 106, 108
Gullah, 106
Gur, 106
Guyana, 143
Gwinnett County, Georgia, 19

Haida, 107
Hakka, 106
Halfway houses, 42
Hamilton, Alexander, 31
Han, 107

Han Dynasty, 3
Harvard College, 89
Havasupai, 107
Hawaii, redistricting, 32
Hawaiian Pidgin, language, 106
Hawaiian, language, 106
Health insurance:
  ages, 146
  American Community Survey vs.
    Current Population Survey, 145, 146
  educational attainment, 146
  employer-provided, 146
  overview, 75, 145, 152
  privately purchased, 146
  sex, 146
Health, elderly, 150, 152
Hearing aid specialists, 113
Hebrew, 106, 109
Hichita, 107
Hidatsa, 107
Hindi, 106, 108
Hispanic groups, 36
Hispanics, 10, 34, 63, 68, 103
Hispanics, illegal immigrants, 58
Historically underutilized zones, 6
Hmong:
  language, 106, 108
  origin, 36, 48, 61
Home heating fuel, 13, 84
Homeless and domestic violence shelters,
  42
Honduran, 36, 47
Hopi:
  language, 107
  origin, 47
Houma, origin, 37, 47
Households:
  advantages, 42
  age of householder, 45
  average size, 45
  comparison with population, 44
  elderly population, 46
  family household components, 43
  family households, 42
  grandparents, 44
  householders, 42
  married-couple, 44

minor population, 45
nonrelative household components, 43
nonrelative households, 42
number of people, 45
overview, 13
overview, 41
racial groups, 46
relationships, 42
Summary File 2, 46
unmarried partners, 43
Housing data, proxy for economic
  well-being, 86
Housing units:
  acreage, 82, 87
  age, 82, 87
  agriculture, 83
  attached businesses, 83, 87
  full plumbing and kitchen facilities, 83,
    87
  hazard insurance, 85
  incremental values, 84
  median value, 84
  monthly mortgage amounts, 85, 87
  monthly rent, 85
  mortgaged, 84
  number of rooms, 83
  occupied, 50
  overview, 41, 42, 49
  owned free and clear, 84
  percentage of income spent on housing,
    85
  property taxes, 85
  ratio of value to income, 85
  rented, 84
  second mortgages, 85, 87
  telephone service, 83
  unoccupied, 51
  value overstatements, 86, 87
  vehicles owned, 85
Housing variables:
  2008 market collapse, 49, 54, 79, 85,
    120
  changes in data release, 52
  density, 51
  group quarters, 54
  median values, 80
  mortgaged, 52

overview, 13
owner-occupied age categories, 52, 53
seasonal, 51
tenure, 52
Houston, Texas, 24, 128
Hungarian, 106, 109
Hupa, 107

Icelandic, 106
Idaho, redistricting, 32
I-Kiribati, 47
Illinois:
 minor civil division, 24
 redistricting, 33
Ilocano, 107
Immigration laws, 59, 103
Immigration, suspicion, 103
Income:
 and wealth, 135
 disability, 133
 distribution, 139
 family, 133
 family, advantages, 135
 median household, 133
 median household, advantages, 134, 135,
  143
 overview, 133, 143
 per-capita, 133, 135
 public assistance, 133
 Social Security, 133
 Supplemental Nutrition Assistance
  Program, 133
Indian Health Service, 146
Indiana, minor civil divisions, 24
Indianapolis, Indiana, 25
Indo-Chinese, 61
Indonesian:
 language, 106
 origin, 36, 48, 61
Information security analysts, 113
Ingalit, 107
Integrated Postsecondary Education Data
  System (IPEDS), 98
Internet, 10
Internet access, 76, 77
Inupiat, 47, 63
Inupik, 107

Iowa:
 minor civil division, 24
 redistricting, 32
Iran, 143
Iraq, 61, 75, 76, 117
Irish Gaelic, 106
Irish, immigration, 103
Iroquois:
 language, 107
 origin, 37, 47
Italian:
 immigration, 103
 language, 106, 108
Ithaca, New York, 126
Iwo Jiman, 61

Jamaican Creole, 106
Jamestown, Virginia, 57, 103, 123
Japanese:
 language, 106, 109
 origin, 36, 48, 60, 61
Javanese, 106
Jefferson, Thomas, 3, 31
Jicarilla, 107
Job activity, 112
Job titles, 113
Juvenile detention facilities, 42

Kachin, 106
Kalispel, 107
Kan, Hsiang, 106
Kannada, 106
Kansa, 107
Kansas, minor civil divisions, 24
Karachay, 106
Karakalpak, 106
Karen, 106
Karok, 107
Kashmiri, 106
Kashubian, 106
Kawaiisu, 107
Kazakh, 106
Kazakhstan, 61
Kendall County, Illinois, 21
Keres, 107
Khoisan, 106
Kickapoo, 107

Kiowa:
    language, 107
    origin, 37, 47
Kiowa-Apache, 107
Kirghiz, 106
Kish, Leslie, 72
Klamath, 107
Koasati, 107
Korean:
    language, 106, 109
    origin, 36, 48, 61
Kosraean, 47
Koyukon, 107
Krio, 106
Kru, Ibo, Yoruba, 107
Kuchin, 107
Kurdish, 106
Kurukh, 106
Kusaiean, 106
Kutenai, 107
Kwakiutl, 107
Kyrgyzstan, 61

Ladino, 106
Language:
    age groups, 108, 110
    Asian and Pacific Islander category, 108,
        110
    citizenship status, 108
    commuting, 108
    educational attainment, 108
    English ability, 108
    general categories, 108, 110
    Indo-European category, 108, 110
    linguistic isolation, 109, 110
    overview, 8
    poverty status, 108
    Spanish category, 108, 110
    spoken at home, 104
Laotian:
    language, 106, 108
    origin, 36, 48, 61
Lapp, 106
Latin American Natives, 37
Lehman Brothers, 79, 80
Lettish, 106
Life expectancy, 6

Lithuanian, 106
Local government, job category, 112
Long-term hospitals, 42
Louisiana, minor civil divisions, 24
Lower Chehalis, 107
Luiseno, 107
Lumbee, 37, 46
Lusatian, 106
Luxembourgian, 106

Macedonian, 107
Madison, Thomas, 32
Madurese, 106
Magnetic resonance imaging technicians,
    113
Maine:
    minor civil division, 24
    redistricting, 32
Makah, 107
Malagasy, 106
Malay, 106
Malayalam, 106
Malaysian, 36, 48, 61
Maldivian, 61
Mandan, 107
Mandarin, 106
Mande, 106
Manhattan Island, 103
Manufacturing, job activity, 112
Maori, 106
Mapuche, 107
Marathi, 106
Mariana Islander, 47
Marital status, 75
Maritime lodging, 42
Marquesan, 106
Marshallese:
    language, 106
    origin, 47
Marx, Karl, 123
Maryland:
    minor civil division, 24
    Washington, D.C. metro area, 19
Massachusetts, minor civil divisions, 24
Mathis, Colleen, 33
Mayan Languages, 107
Mbum, 107

McIntosh, Shawn, 35
McMansions, 83
Medicaid, 146
Medicare, 146, 151
Melanesian:
  language, 106
  origin, 47
Menominee, origin, 37, 46
Menomini, 107
Mexican:
  1930 Census, 10
  percentage of U.S. residents, 59
  origin, 36, 46–47, 59
Mexico, Gini coefficient, 143
Meyer, Phil, 35
Miami, language, 107
Michigan:
  population loss, 19
  minor civil division, 24
Micmac, 107
Micronesian:
  language, 107
  origin, 47
Microsoft Corp., 133
Mien, 106
Mikasuki, 107
Milford, Connecticut, 25
Military barracks, 42, 54
Minangkabau, 106
Minnesota:
  minor civil division, 7
  population growth, 24
  redistricting, 32
Mississippi, minor civil divisions,
  24
Missouri City, Texas, 24
Missouri, minor civil divisions, 24
Misumalpan, 107
Mobile homes, 50, 82
Mobility, geographic, 118, 119, 120
Mohave, 107
Mohawk, 107
Mokilese, 106
Moluccan, 106
Mongolian:
  language, 106
  origin, 48, 61

Mon-Khmer, Cambodian, language, 106,
  109
Mono, 107
Monroe County, Florida, 14
Montana, representation, 30
Monthly housing costs, 82
Morticians, undertakers and funeral
  directors, 114
Mortlockese, 106
Mosbacher, Robert, 10
Mountain Maidu, 107
Munda, 106
Muong, 106
Muskogee, 107

Namibia, 142
Nashville-Davidson, Tennessee, 25
National Bureau of Economic Research, 80
National Congress of American Indians, 62
National Science Foundation, 98, 99
Native Americans, 8, 34
Native groups, 37
Native Hawaiian, 47, 63
Nauruan, 106
Navajo:
  language, 106, 107109
  Navajo Nation, 63
  origin, 37, 46
Nebraska.
  cost of living, 134
  minor civil division, 24
Nepalese, origin, 4861
Nepali, 106
Nevada, 19, 36
New Hampshire, minor civil divisions, 24
New Jersey, redistricting, 32
New Mexico, Navajo Nation, 63
New York City, New York, 4, 9, 10, 27, 30,
  59, 126, 134
New York County, New York, 118, 119
New York:
  geographic differences, 19
  minor civil divisions, 24
  Native Americans, 63
Newport, Rhode Island, 4
Nez Perce, 107
Nicaraguan, 36, 47

Nilo-Hamitic, 106
Nilo-Saharan, 106
Nilotic, 106
Niuean, 106
Nomlaki, 107, 108
Nootka, 107
Nootsack, 107
North Carolina:
  minor civil division, 24
  representation, 30
North Dakota, minor civil divisions, 24
Northern Paiute, 107
Northwest Maidu, 107
Norwegian, 106
Nubian, 106
Nuevo Mexicano, 59
Nukuoro, 106
Nurse anesthetists, 113
Nurse midwives, 113
Nursing homes, 42, 54

Obama, Barack, 33
Occupations:
  ages, 117
  newly created, 113, 120
  overview, 111, 120
Office of Management and Budget,
  19
Ohio:
  center of population, 7
  minor civil divisions, 24
  population loss, 19
  townships, 24
Ojibwa, 107
Okanogan, 107
Okinawan, 48, 61
Omaha, 107
Oneida, 107
Onondaga, 107
Ophthalmic medical technicians, 113
Orderlies, 113
Oregon, representation, 30
Oriental, 61
Oriya, 106
Orleans Parish, Louisiana, 118, 119
Osage:
  language, 107
  origin, 37, 46

Ossete, 106
Other, job activity, 112
Oto-Manguen, 107
Ottawa:
  language, 107
  origin, 37, 46

Pachuco, 106
Pacific Gulf Yupik, 107
Paiute:
  language, 107
  origin, 37, 46
Pakistani, origin, 36, 48, 61
Palau, language, 106
Palauan, 47
Paleo-Siberian, 106
Pampangan, 107
Panamanian, 36, 47
Panamint, 107
Pangasinan, 106
Panjabi, 106
Papia Mentae, 106
Papua New Guinean, 47
Paraguayan, origin, 36, 47, 59
Pashto, 106
Passamaquoddy, 107
Patois, 106
Patwin, 107
Pawnee, 107
Pennsylvania:
  minor civil divisions, 24
  population loss, 19
Pennsylvania Dutch, 106
Penobscot, 107
Perry, Rick, 33
Persian, 106, 108
Peruvian, 36, 47, 59
Philadelphia, Pennsylvania, 4, 9
Phlebotomists, 113
Pickens County, Georgia, 19
Picuris, 107
Pidgin, 106
Pima:
  language, 107
  origin, 37, 46
PL94-171 (redistricting) file:
  age, 34
  ethnicity, 34

overview, 13, 33, 38, 41
  race, 34
Place of birth, parents, 76
Plains Miwok, 107
Pohnpeian, 47
Polish, 106, 109
Polygamy, 62
Polynesian:
  language, 106
  origin, 47
Pomo, 107
Ponapean, 106
Ponca, 107
Population abroad, 9
Population Association of America, 117
Portuguese, 106, 108
Portuguese or Portuguese Creole, 106
Potawatomi:
  language, 107
  origin, 37, 46
Poverty:
  2011 threshhold, 135
  fluctuations, 137
  opportunities, 135
  overview, 135
  percentages, 137
Princeton University, 130
Prisons, 42, 54
Private for profit, job category, 112
Private not-for-profit, job category, 112
Provencal, 106
Pueblo, 37, 46
Puerto Rican, 36, 47, 59
Puget Sound Salish:
  language, 107
  origin, 37, 46

Quapaw, 107
Quechua, 107
Quinault, 107

Race:
  Arab, 57
  Asian, 60, 63
  black, 57, 58
  Caucasian, 57
  European, 57
  German, 57

Irish, 57
Italian, 57
Lebanese, 57
Middle Eastern, 57
Moroccan, 57
multiracial, 34
multiracial, 57
Native American, 62, 68
Native American reservations, 62
Native American tribal affiliation
  changes, 63
North Africa, 57
other, 59
other vs. Hispanic, 59
overview, 57, 63, 68
Pacific Islander, 60, 63, 64–67
white, 59
white, non-Hispanic, 57
Racial classification, 10, 11
Rajasthani, 106
Rarotongan, 106
Reapportionment:
  alternative methods, 31
  alternative methods, fractional
    representation, 31
  alternative methods, Webster, 31
  civil rights, 12
  current method, 9, 29, 30
Recreational vehicles, 50, 82
Redistricting, overview, 20, 31, 32
Relationships, 13
Retail trade, job activity, 112
Rhaeto-Romanic, 106
Rhode Island, minor civil divisions, 24
Robert Wood Johnson Foundation, 146
Romanian, 106
Romany, 106
Rule of 100, 46
Rush, Bobby, 33
Russian, 106, 109

Sahaptian, 107
Saharan, 106
Saipanese, 47
Salish, 107
Salvadoran, 36, 47
Samoan, 47
Samoan, 106

Sampling, 10
San Carlos, 107
Sandia, 107
Santiam, 107
Saramacca, 106
Scandinavian languages, 106
Scottic Gaelic, 106
Seaton, Edward, 7
Sebuano, 106
Self-employed incorporated company, job
        category, 112
Self-employed unincorporated company,
        job category, 112
Seminole, 37, 46
Seneca, 107
Serbian, 106
Serbo-Croatian, 107, 108
Serrano, 107
Service, job activity, 112
Shannon County, South Dakota, 119
Shastan, 107
Shaw, George Bernard, 48
Shawnee:
    language, 107
    origin, 46
Shoshone, 37, 46
Shoshoni, 106
Sierra Miwok, 107
Sindhi, 106
Singaporean, origin, 48, 61
Single-family home, 82
Sinhalese, 106
Sioux, 37, 46
Siuslaw, 107
Slavery, 6, 7
Slovak, 107
Slovene, 106
Small Business Administration, 6
Social Security, 139
Solar photovoltaic installers, 114
Sonoran, n.e.c., 107
South American Indian, origin, 47, 59
South American, origin, 47
South Dakota, minor civil divisions, 24
Southern Maidu, 107
Southern Paiute, 107
Soviet Union, 61

Spaniard, origin, 36, 47
Spanish Basque, 59
Spanish:
    language, 106, 108
    origin, 36
Spanish-American Indian, origin, 47
Spanish-American War, 103
Spanish-American, origin, 36
Special education teachers, all others, 113
Special education teachers, preschool, 113
Spokane (language), 107
Sri Lankan, 36, 48, 61
St Lawrence Island Yupik, 107
St. Louis, Missouri, 9
Standard Occupational Classification
        (SOC) system, 111
State government, job category, 112
Statistical Abstract of the United States, 14
Sudanic, 106
Summary File 1:
    median age calculations, 36
    overview, 13, 36, 38, 41, 49, 54
    overview, 36
    release schedule, 36
Summary File 2, 37
Summary File 3, 73, 76
Sun Belt, 11
Sundanese, 106
Supplemental Nutritional Assistance
        Program (food stamps), 75, 136, 139,
        148, 152
Supplemental Poverty Meausre, 137, 138,
        139
Survey of Income and Program
        Participation, 147
Swahili, 106
Swedish, 106
Syriac, 106

Tachi, 107
Tadzhik, 106
Tagalog, 106, 108
Tahitian, 47
Taiwanese, 36, 48, 61
Tajikistan, 61
Tamil, 106
Tanacross, 107

Tanaina, 107
Tanana, 107
Tarascan, 107
Tejano, 59
Telephone service, 13
Telugu, 106
Temporary Assistance for Needy Families, 137, 139
Tennessee, minor civil divisions, 24
Tents, 50
Tenure, 81
Tewa, 107
Texas:
    30th Congressional District, 12
    redistricting, 33
Thai:
    language, 106, 108
    origin, 36, 48, 61
Thailand, Gini coefficient, 143
The Woodlands, Texas, 24
Tibetan, 106
Tillamook, 107
Tiwa, 107
Tlingit, language, 107
Tlingit-Haida, origin, 37, 47
Tohono O'odham, 37, 47
Toilets, broken, 14
Tokelauan:
Tokelauan, language, 106
Tokelauan, origin, 47
    language, 106
    origin, 47
Tonkawa, 107
Towa, 107
Traffic Analysis Zones, 128, 131
Transportation Research Board, 128
Transportation security screeners, 114
Tricare, 146
Trukese, 106
Tsimshian:
    language, 107
    origin, 47
Tubatulabal, 107
Tungus, 106
Tupi-Guarani, 107
Turkish, 106
Turkmen, 106

Turkmenistan, 61
Tuscarora, 107
Tutchone, 107
Twana, 107

U.S. Department of Agriculture, 83
U.S. Department of Education, 13
U.S. Department of Energy, 123
U.S. Department of Health and Human Services, 13
U.S. Department of Homeland Security, 59
U.S. Supreme Court, 12, 30, 33
Uighur, 106
Ukrainian, 106
Ulithean, 106
Umeå University, 130
Undercount, 10, 30
Up River Yuman, 107
Upland Yuman, 107
Upper Chehalis, 107
Upper Chinook, 107
Upper Kuskokwim, 107
Upper Tanana, 107
Urdu, 106, 109
Uruguayan, 36, 47, 59
USA Today, 35
Utah, Navajo Nation, 36, 63
Ute:
    language, 107
    origin, 37, 47
Uzbekistan, 61

Valencian, 59
Vans, 50, 82
Vehicle Inventory and Use Survey, 124
Venezuela, 48
Venezuelan, origin, 36, 47, 59
Vermont, minor civil divisions, 24
Veteran:
    era of service, 117, 120
    service-connected disability rating, 75, 117, 120
    status, 76, 117
Veto, presidential, 31
Vietnamese:
    language, 106, 108
    origin, 36, 48, 61

Virginia:
    center of population, 7
    Washington, D.C. metro area, 19
    counties and independent cities, 22
    minor civil divisions, 24
    state-sanctioned racism, 62
Voting Rights Act, 33

Walapai, 107
Wal-Mart Stores Inc., 149
Wappo, 107
Washington-Arlington-Alexandria
    metropolitan area, 19
Washington, D.C., 10, 22, 134
Washington, George, 3, 31
Washington state:
    employment, 112
    redistricting, 32
Washo, 107
Web developers, 113
Welsh, 106
West Virgnia:
    minor civil divisions, 24
    Washington, D.C. metro area, 19
Whello, 61
Wholesale trade, job activity, 112
Wichita, language, 107
Wilson, Charles E., 123
Wind turbine service technicians, 114, 120
Winnebago, 107
Wintun, 107
Wisconsin, minor civil divisions, 24
Wiyot, 107
Woleai-Ulithi, 106

Women, Infants and Children supplemental
    food program, 136, 149, 150
Working without pay, job category, 112
World War I, 103, 149
World War II, 103
Wu, 106
Wyandot, 107
Wyoming:
    population, 19
    representation, 30

Yakama, 37, 47
Yakut, 106
Yakutat City and Borough, Alaska, 22
Yapese:
    language, 106
    origin, 47
Yaqui:
    language, 107
    origin, 37, 47
Yavapai, 107
Yello, 61
Yiddish, 106
Yuchi, 107
Yuki, 107
Yuma, language, 107
Yuman, origin, 37, 47
Yup'ik:
    language, 107
    origin, 47, 63
Yurok, 107

Zimbabwe, Gini coefficient, 143
Zuni, 107